BIRTH OF A NEW J

≈

A Cathartic Memoir

Julie Guardado

Copyright ©2014 by Julie Guardado All rights reserved.

ISBN: 1500315265
ISBN 13: 9781500315269
Library of Congress Control Number: 2014913148 Createspace Independent Publishing Platform North Charleston, South Carolina

For Haydee

"Not everyone will understand your journey.

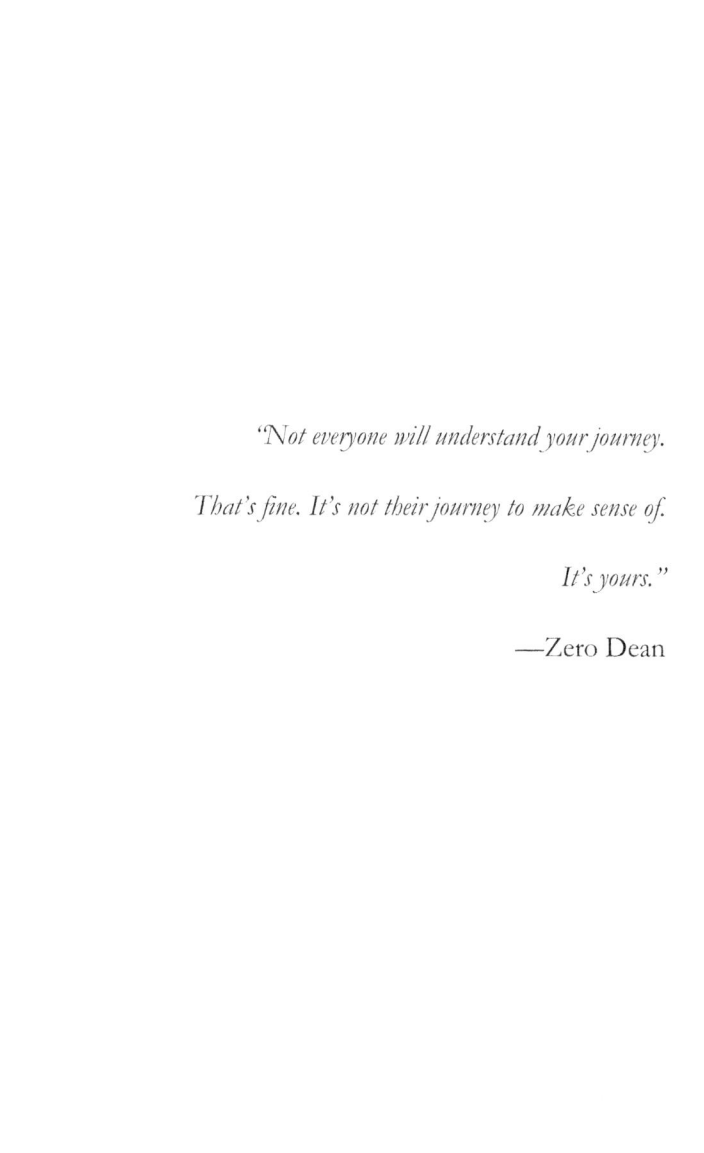

That's fine. It's not their journey to make sense of.

It's yours."

—Zero Dean

JULIE

PROLOGUE

I was born buttocks first, shortly after the hour of the wolf, on a sweltering summer night in July of 1972. It was a Wednesday, and there was a full moon sitting low in the dark, blue-black sky. The delivering doctor wasn't my mother's primary obstetrician, as he was on vacation. I like to imagine that the vacationing doctor went somewhere foreign, like Senegal or Mongolia, and not some place typical and touristy, like Mexico or Hawaii. Why this is important to me, I don't know. Since we're all interconnected, I want everyone passing through my life (even while I was in utero) to reach beyond the ordinary. I like to think that I'm constantly reaching, or at least that I remain curious, to what's beyond the ordinary. Therefore, I want everyone else to be doing the same as well.

    The doctor that did deliver me prodded and pulled me out of the womb, folded in half. It was a tug of war until I dove straight into the world, ass first, in a not-so-perfect pike position. The vacationing doctor either didn't know I was breech or failed to mention it to anyone. It was traumatic for me as I resisted the entire way (so I'm told), and it was even more distressing for my mother. She vowed she'd "never have another child after that ordeal! One of us or both of us could have died! That darn doctor leaving for vacation, overlooking something so critical. Your poor butt was all black and blue from being suctioned out."

Everything about the above-mentioned birth is true except there was no full moon in the sky. The only full moon in the month of July 1972 was on Wednesday, July 26. I was born two weeks prior on July 12. On the night of labor, July 11, there was a new moon—hence, no visible moon in the sky. Not that this detail matters either, but I love the idea of being born on a full-moon night. I think perhaps it was the gravitational pull of the moon that caused me to be born butt first. Seeing as the moon has the power to control the ebb and flow of every tide, it surely has enough strength to pull at my little baby butt. If it had been a full-moon night, I could somehow blame it, too, for my only fear in life—to feel like I'm drowning. Do you ever feel that way, unable to breathe? To feel like you're going to drown, whether you're in water or in a perfectly oxygenated room?

However, moon or no moon, I think I was positioned headfirst and then, at the last minute, had doubts about being born and did an acrobatic flip to go the opposite direction—where it was safe and warm, where collapsed fetal lungs pose no threat and a solid heart isn't required to get through the day. I'd like to know whether my heart fluttered as it tried to redirect blood flow, whether it hurt, and whether I struggled to breathe the moment I was out in open air. But such memories are never really experienced during birth, are vaguely registered in our infant brains, are impossible to recall, or are simply not of significance in the scope of one's life. But if birth is our jumping point, why wouldn't those memories be of significance? Are we meant to be reeducated throughout life on everything that we learned in utero and at the moment of birth? The memories and learning I'm referring to are the making of the human heart and lungs and the three lessons that would make life so simple, if we stuck to them.

THE THREE LIFE LESSONS

I can only imagine how it happened, based on what I learned in nursing school about the transition from utero then out into the world.

A fetus, in its cozy womb, has a heart resembling a miniature golf course, with holes and surprise outlets here and there. Despite having these holes, the heart is able to keep its pace at 110–160 beats per minute. The lungs are like delicate sheets of origami paper yet durable enough to hold an appropriate amount of fluid that neither drowns the fetus nor gives it a sense of drowning. Instead, the fluid keeps the lungs distended at just the right pressure to keep them patiently waiting to expand and to sustain life.

A basic lesson in anatomy: The heart is divided into four chambers. The top chambers are the left and right atria. The rooms directly below are the left and right ventricles. The atria are connected by super thick, sturdy, and wide vessels (similar to a boba straw)—some bringing blood up and down, some in and out of the heart and lungs. On the right side, the heart contains the veins of the inferior and superior vena cava and the pulmonary artery, while the left side of the heart contains the strongest vessel of them all, the aorta.

Now that we have the anatomy down, let's begin learning the fetal blood route. The placenta rushes blood through the umbilical vein to the inferior vena cava and delivers it straight into the right atrium. Then, instead of heading directly below to the left ventricle, as it's doing right now in your post-birth heart, the blood is in a mighty hurry and is prompted directly *across* the heart into the left atrium through a hole. This hole in the heart is called the *foramen ovale*. The blood then flows down to the left ventricle to allow the great aorta to supply the head and heart with blood that's lavished in oxygen and nutrients.

Are you still with me? Hold tight!

The blood has just taken the speedway passage to be propelled up to the head and heart, bypassing everything else. Why? Because in the womb, the head and heart are the most demanding organs. They expect, and they receive, no less than what they demand—the very best that their environment has to offer.

There's a profound lesson to be learned here, so permit me to repeat it.

Lesson Number One: *Even in the womb, the head and heart are the most demanding organs. They expect and they receive no less than what they demand.*

To settle for less, or to allow some other physiological process to compensate, would place these organs, this precious life, at a high risk for demise. Yes, there's a deep lesson to be learned here that I either missed or must have slept through while in utero.

After the head and heart have devoured all the oxygen and nutrients from the blood, the depleted blood momentarily returns to the heart. A very small fraction of this blood will find its way to the lungs, enough to give the lungs a taste of what life will be like after birth. The majority of that blood, which is now starving, will be granted a shortcut back to the placenta in order to refuel.

Another self-created escape hole, this one between the pulmonary and aortic arch, called the *ductus arteriosus*, will act as a detour. You see, right now as you read this, the pulmonary trunk is taking blood back to your lungs to pick up oxygen. In utero, your lungs aren't at work yet. The ductus arteriosus allows the lion's share of the blood to bypass the fetus's nonfunctional lungs to make its way back to the placenta. The placenta is like an immaculate pantry ready for war, fully stocked with everything the fetus needs—oxygen tanks and fresh superfoods.

Upon arrival, the blood *knows* to rid itself of any waste collected along the way. It's like sanitizing your hands prior to serving the royal feast to the king and queen, the head and heart. The blood enters the pantry and bathes itself giddily in oxygen and slurps up nutrients before beginning its journey back to the head and heart.

Lesson Number Two: *The blood knows to rid itself of any waste, any toxin, collected along the way before heading back to the head and heart.*

This process, these lessons, will repeat time and again until birth, until the umbilical cord is cut.

Now, the moment of birth has arrived. It's only been a few seconds, but the heart and lungs have to get serious, fast. For the blood, there are new routes to be learned. There will be no more zigzagging to easily and loyally serve the head and heart. And the lungs, which were holding fluid and had no sense of drowning while in utero, will now search frantically to catch their first breath.

The perfect recipe of physiological adjustments begins to unfold with the initial breath. Pressure in the left side of the heart drops, while power from the right side amplifies. Aortic force rises. Pulmonary circulation augments. Blood oxygen content increases. All this orderly chaos causes the holes and passageways in the heart to begin closing. Why? So that the heart can start off whole and unscathed. So that it and the lungs can function in their new surroundings. Welcome to the world; this is life. Now learn to breathe.

Lesson Number Three: *Learn to breathe.*

I was left in awe when I learned all of this during nursing school. "Wow, isn't that amazing?" I asked my nursing school buddy, Alicia.

"What?"

"How the baby's heart has holes in it and then begins fixing itself at first breath."

"I guess so. It's just physics."

You guess so? It's just physics? I guess I'm easily impressed. I don't know physics, so whether it is or isn't physics is beyond me. But I've made up my mind. It's not just physics. It can't be. It's more than that. What it is, I didn't know and still don't know, but it has to be more than that. It's one of the physiological processes that have kept me in awe since nursing school. I want to tell everyone I know about it. I want to rush into every delivery room, and while the parents are looking at their newborn, stupidly counting fingers and toes, I want to scream, "Who cares about the toes? Do you know what's happening to your baby's heart right this instant?" I want to educate—no, not educate—I want to enlighten them on the closing of the foramen ovale and ductus arteriosus, on the new blood pathway that we take for granted.

And the mother would look at me and say, "Wow, isn't that amazing? I never knew."

And I'd reply, "Yeah, it's amazing, truly amazing."

But by the time I could rush into a delivery room and explain what was occurring, the heart would be well on its way. Although permanent closure can take a few months, functional closure is accomplished almost immediately, unceremoniously, without a sound, without one appreciative witness. The only time this conversation will ever take place (at least in my head, to myself) is the day I give birth, to a baby that I've named *Joaquin*.

Joaquin was the reason I'd changed careers. I'd been working as a music publisher in Los Angeles for eleven years. I'd outgrown LA and knew my job, and my pay, couldn't really afford me the lifestyle or the flexibility I wanted for myself or my dream of having a baby. As a nurse, I'd be able to afford a home, work less than forty hours per week, and raise the baby I was planning for. Nursing took me one step closer to my greatest desire, becoming pregnant.

So, needless to say, my greatest desire is to experience birthing Joaquin and to visualize this precise moment, the completion of his heart and lungs. Screw the number of fingers and toes, the color of hair or eyes, and the question of whether he looks like me or the biological father. I'll be waiting to hear that first breath in and wonder if what I can't see is properly taking place. Did the holes close completely? Will there be a murmur, a wrong direction of blood flow? What's his lung capacity now? It's true: a little bit of knowledge is a dangerous and worrisome thing. During pregnancy, everyone's excited and focused on the fetus's heart, the heartbeat rate and rhythm. Then once the child's born, the heart's almost immediately neglected. We instantaneously forget that seconds prior, it was (and remains) one of the most demanding organs, accepting no less than the very best that its environment has to offer, accepting no toxins.

 After three years working as a floor nurse (and not anywhere near labor and delivery), I still haven't memorized the normal range for arterial blood gases. But the fetal heart, I got it down.

 It's fitting that the one thing that imprinted on my brain from nursing school is a matter of the heart and breathing. And I don't just remember it; I can dictate it, visualize it, and feel it. Perhaps it's because I can feel my heart, its location, its size, its missed beats, its breaks and self-reparation. The adult heart, so much more complicated than the fetal heart—its emotional behavior, such a mystery, such lack of control. The adult heart and lungs run amok all over the damn place, beating uncontrolled and gasping for air, for no evident reason, so unlike the fetal heart and lungs.

 I can't help but think that it isn't only at birth that the heart transforms. The heart is manipulated and molded, tweaked and twisted, mishandled and manhandled. Maybe it even temporarily reopens those holes to keep you alive when you feel like you're drowning and your lungs can't seem to stay faintly open. We're in a constant state of transition—from one utero out into another new world, literally and figuratively speaking. It's unstoppable. I'm convinced that the heart goes through many alterations and, without question, many altercations after birth—with every event and encounter wherein we forget and have to be schooled again.

Lesson Number One: *The head and heart are the most demanding organs. They expect and receive no less than what they demand.*

Lesson Number Two: *Rid yourself of toxins.*

Lesson Number Three: *Learn to breathe.*

It's as easy as one, two, three, isn't it?

But this is about life, how I forgot those lessons, and how I had to be taught them over and over again.

JOE

TAHITI, HALLELUJAH!

It was the end of April 2006. I arrived in Stockton, California. This was my hometown, where I was born, where I was raised, where, according to *Forbes* magazine, I had a high probability of being killed and then, by my request, being cremated, and God forbid, where I had a chance of being reincarnated. I hadn't vowed never to return to Stockton when I left in 1994 for Los Angeles; I thought I'd never have a valid reason to live there again. But now I did. I was to start summer school at San Joaquin Delta College to begin my prerequisites for nursing, a career change at age thirty-four. Mentally, I had to acclimate to living back at home with my mom and brother Neil. I had to adjust to going back to school and working a part-time job. I got home, unloaded a car full of books and clothes, and made a trip to Target.

The entire nine months I'd been in Chandler, Arizona (I left Los Angeles eighteen months prior and this was the end of my whirlwind gypsy days), my cousin Diana had been telling me about this guy that worked at a local coffee shop in Stockton. She'd go on about how good looking he was and how I had to meet him. She and I had different taste in men, so I never took her opinion of men as something to consider. She said he was maybe half black and half something else. She wasn't quite sure what mix he was, but she was certain I'd like him. I was known for dating primarily black men up until that time, but because a man was black didn't mean I'd like him. Now that I was in the same town as him, she wanted me to meet him. I told her, "I'm tired of everyone thinking I'd like any guy because he's black or part black."

"No, you've got to see this guy. He's gorgeous, Julie. Where are you right now?" she asked.

"Leaving Target."

"OK, you need to come to this coffee shop. That guy I was telling you about is working. I'm going through the drive-through."

"OK, order me a drink. And also, I want to show you a picture of Jonathan. He's got beautiful eyes."

Jonathan was a guy I dated while in Arizona, and we were attempting a long-distance relationship. There's a saying in Spanish for long-distance relationships—"*Amor de lejos, amor de pendejos,*" which roughly translates as, "Long-distance lovers are dumb asses." And I vouch for its validity. Jonathan was one crisis after the next, and he was lacking one testicle because of testicular cancer as a teenager. But that's neither here nor there, because Jonathan—aka Arizona-Boy-with-One-Testicle who worked in the plumbing department at Lowe's—and I never worked out. I thank my lucky stars for that shitty, down-the-drain relationship. No pun intended. But at that point in time, I still found him attractive, and he was still my romantic interest.

Unlike most drive-through establishments, this one had no intercom system to order at prior to driving up to the window where your drink would be handed to you. This place that Diana had beckoned me to had one window; you drove up, you ordered, you paid, you watched them make your drink, and then they handed it to you. I pulled up next to Diana's car, placed my car in parked position, and jumped out to show her Jonathan's picture and get my drink.

Then I saw *Joe*.

Then, I saw *Joe*.

Then I saw…*Joe*.

All I saw was *Joe*. All I felt was *Joe*, looking right at me, looking me over. My head and my heart demanded to know more about this man, Joe. The head and the heart are the most demanding organs. From here on out, it would be all about *Joe*.

Joe.

Joe.

Joe.

How can I describe him? Some things are so remarkable that they're nearly impossible to explain; you have to view and experience them for yourself. But let me try. If you want the stats, he was six-foot-three, his complexion was as light as mine (fair, a Clinique Concealer #3 Moderately Fair, to be more precise), he was completely bald, and he had a mixed brownish-blond goatee, profound, dazzling green eyes, full lips, high cheekbones, and a strong build. And if you examined him long enough, you'd see a slightly crooked nose. Not the kind of nose that one is born with, but the kind that's earned after a fistfight with that punk-ass kid you've always wanted to beat the shit out of. As his beauty gods would have it, his displaced nose had set and healed at the perfect asymmetrical location to give him the shadow of roughness that every woman wants to see in her man. His imperfections were flawless. His imperfections worked to his benefit. And he knew it, or he had to know it. One couldn't look into a mirror with that exquisite beauty and not know it. He was as beautiful as a mythical creature, like a unicorn. I could have spent a lifetime on that dirty pavement staring at him through the coffee shop window.

    I can think of only two words that could remotely encompass everything that he exuded and that I fully wanted: *Tahiti* and *hallelujah*. First, *Tahiti*. No, he wasn't from Tahiti, nor did he resemble a Tahitian. In my mind, in my vocabulary, he was as exotic as the word *Tahiti* or *Tahitian*, which I'll use interchangeably here. I've never been to Tahiti, but the word alone evokes thoughts of the exotic and of pure sensuality. By vocalizing the word *Tahitian*, I can smell coconut oil, I can feel the heat from a beach bonfire send goose bumps up my spine as cool sand runs through my toes, I can see a glorious sunset fading over the Pacific Ocean, and I can hear the locals speaking French about a particular spice in a cream sauce from last night's meal. He was all of that and more in one solitary glance. I lived in Los Angeles, the mecca of beautiful people, for eleven years. I've traveled and lived abroad, seeing facial features of the French, Thai, Panamanian, Peruvian, Brazilian, and so on. I've seen a wide array of good-looking people face-to-face throughout my life, but an exotic, mysterious, intoxicating man, literally the most stunning, magnificent man I'd ever seen with my very own eyes? It was the first (and probably the last) time.

Second, hear me say *hallelujah*! This is my favorite word in the world. Now let me hear ya break it down: H-A-L-L-E-L-U-J-A-H! I thoroughly enjoy the way that word rolls off the tongue and the spiritual exultation I feel. There's relief in its surrender. There's a solid affirmation it gives when it's said. I rarely use this word as I refuse to let it be watered down the way the word *love* has become. I *love* him; I *love* those shoes; I *love* bean burritos. *Love* is overused. *Hallelujah* remains powerful, and I'd like to keep it so. If I could enact a law that forbade religions—or any person, for that matter—to use it so casually, I would. But for this man? Hallelujah.

Something ignited in me when I saw him. I wanted to do a Candomblé spirit dance to Oxum, the Orisha god of beauty and intimacy, and the only word I'd chant as I wildly danced in circles would be *hallelujah*!

The moment I said this word, I immediately wished to take it back, to enact my self-made law upon myself. I wished not to make him so special. I love (and I do mean *love*) this word, and I always wanted to reserve this word for a man that would be my knight in shining armor. Would it be possible for me to use the word *hallelujah* for two different men the way you can use the word *love* for one man and then years later *love* another man and hate the first? Only time will tell if all this analysis is even necessary. But for now, him. Tahiti, hallelujah! Are you getting somewhat of a depiction of him?

And what I couldn't believe was that there, in the stinking, hairy armpit of Stockton, California, was the most alluring man I'd ever seen. Holy shit! He was like a precious lotus flower, blossoming out of the muddy waters of a city listed by *Forbes* magazine as "The Most Miserable City in America." Stockton consistently made the top ten list of *Forbes*'s "America's Most Miserable Cities"—scoring number one twice. The honorary title is granted based on crime, unemployment, the economy, and the housing market, to name a few of its bad points. And Stocktonians brag that their city was mentioned in *Forbes* magazine! "We might be in the most miserable city, but you can't break our spirit," as one man from Stockton said to a news crew covering recent shootings and stabbings.

Don't get me wrong. There are things in Stockton that I miss when I'm away and that I always visit when I'm there. There's Yen Du, my favorite Szechwan restaurant with the crispiest, spiciest, and freshest kimchi ever; Siamese Street Restaurant, whipping up pad prik king the way I like it; and Tigers Yogurt's swirling raspberry tart. But I knew that this little coffee shop, or rather the man running this little coffee shop, would supersede every craving I had for kimchi, pad prik king, or yogurt. My eyes had seen the unreal, my palate had been wiped clean, my taste buds had changed, and regardless of how corny this sounds, I instantly knew I wanted a sip of any flavor java he could serve. Let my cup runneth over. I felt my heart skip a few beats; my breathing was shallow. What the hell was happening to my heart and lungs?

My next thought after seeing Joe: *He's completely out of my league. Don't even think about it.* All these thoughts of beauty, flavor, and my chances ran through my head in a split millisecond. I forgot what I was there to do. Diana was waiting at the drive-through window. I had stepped out of my car, parked alongside hers, in order to grab the drink she ordered me. When his back was facing Diana, I mouthed "Oh my *God*!" to her. Let me emphasize the word *God*, hallelujah. She nodded in a way that said, "I told you so."

I never did show Diana that picture of Jonathan. It may have fallen to the ground, along with my jaw and drool upon seeing Joe. It would be fitting that I didn't think about Arizona-Boy-with-One-Testicle while in front of Joe, as it was Jonathan dumping me for the *n*th time that would lead me directly to Joe.

I tasted the mocha Frappuccino with whipped cream made by the most breathtaking man to exist, while daydreaming on my drive back home. Diana followed in her car behind me. I knew, once back at my house, Joe would be the topic of our conversation now and, possibly, forevermore.

"Wow! How can anyone be *that* good looking?" I asked.

"I have no idea. Good genes, I guess. Didn't I tell you?"

"There's no way you could have ever described his look. He's the most beautiful person I've ever seen."

"I know, for me, too. He was staring at your ass!"

"He was?"

"Yeah, when you got out of the car to get your drink. I told him, 'I see you staring at my cousin's ass.' He smiled and then asked me what your name was."

"Did you tell him?"

"Yeah, I said that you were my cousin Julie and had moved back to town."

He asked my name? "What's his name?"

"I think it's either Dante or Diante. Something like that."

"I thought you *knew* him."

"Not really, just from driving through to get a coffee every morning. We make small talk and he knows my name because I have my work ID on my scrubs. I think he likes Latin girls."

"How do you know that?"

"I think his girlfriend is Latin or something."

"Oh, he has a girlfriend?" *Of course he has a girlfriend; he probably has many of them!*

"Yeah, she's all right. She's cute. I've seen her a few times. But he's way better looking than her."

"That doesn't mean anything. He's better looking than everyone."

"True. So true. You should go in there by yourself next time."

"What for? He's too damn hot. And he has a girlfriend. And I know the level of hotness I can attract, and he's way above it."

"I think he liked you. He sure was looking you over."

Could he have found something in my looks—the way I walked, the way I looked at him—attractive? I went to sleep that night secretly hoping he had.

***

Even though I wouldn't allow myself to believe that a perfect-DNA specimen like Joe could find interest in me, it didn't stop me from driving to the coffee shop every morning before summer school to buy coffee. I wanted to view him. That's all. I'd have a look, like window-shopping without showing any intent on buying. After all, I was, technically, still seeing Jonathan.

Most mornings Andre waited on me. Dante or Diante would say, "Hello, Julie," nod his bald head to further acknowledge me, and make eye contact with those eyes of his for what I considered a lengthy one second. I'd look away. He loved attention from women, I concluded, and I refused to be another one drooling in front of him.

"Do you have a punch card?" Andre asked.

"No, I didn't know you guys had those."

"Joe hasn't given you one?"

"Who's Joe?"

Andre nodded toward Dante or Diante and said, "Yeah, Joe."

Joe? His name is *Joe?* Yes, he looked like a Joe, like a GI Joe, a cup of Joe, my morning Joe, oh Joe, Joe, Joe. Oh my, Joe. *My* Joe. Joe DiMaggio and Marilyn. I have a hopeful imagination. Yes, that's what I can hear myself calling out to him, Joe.

Joe continued listening the whole time, smiling to his cocky self, not making any comment.

"No, he never gave me one. How rude," I said, joking.

"You're just bitter," Joe replied, not joking.

Bitter? I'm not bitter! I've never been called that before, much less by someone I've never spoken to. This was perhaps my fifth time ever in the coffee shop. I'd never had a conversation with this man and he called me bitter? *Bitter, like bad coffee?*

Andre watched our exchange. I whispered to myself, "I'm not bitter." I took my coffee and vowed never to return.

"Have a good day, Julie," Joe said as I left, knowing he'd struck a nerve.

I called Diana before I reached my car. "He's an asshole. He called me 'bitter'!"

"Who?"

"Joe!"

"Who's *Joe?*"

"The coffee-shop guy. His name isn't Dante nor Diante; it's *Joe*."

"What? When? Why? What exactly happened?"

"I don't know. I went in there to get coffee and he looked at me and said I was bitter."

Diana began laughing uncontrollably. "What did you say?"

"Nothing. I can't stand him. He doesn't even know me and he's making comments like that? Who does he think he is?"

"Wow, you're really worked up."

"Am I bitter?"

"Oh, no, not at all bitter. No bitterness in you," she said sarcastically.

"I'm never going there again."

"Yes, you will. They have good coffee. Don't let him get to you."

What got to me was that maybe he was right. How could someone in one week, without having spoken to me, have me pinned? Did his beautiful green eyes have X-ray vision into my head and heart? He can't be gorgeous *and* right. He could only be one or the other.

The following day Diana called me. "I saw Joe today." I remained silent. I figured there was a story coming. "I asked him what the hell happened to get you all worked up."

"Oh, great, now he thinks I actually care."

"He said to tell you sorry and that he'd apologize in person next time he saw you."

"Screw him."

"Wouldn't you like to?" she teased.

"Shut up."

"I told him that he scared you off. He said for you to please come back. I told him to be kind to you, that it's taken a lot for you to come back to Stockton, after traveling the world, and now doing a career change and everything."

"You told him all that?" Oh God!

"Uh-huh. Yeah, I bragged about you."

This was childish! But I'd return—to show him that he didn't bother me. I waited a few days to build up my courage. I walked in, very nonchalantly of course, and ordered my usual, a nonfat iced latte, medium. He was alone. I felt silly. Everything I felt seemed to come from my high school years. There were emotions I didn't know what to do with. I was the new, nerdy girl in town with a major crush on the popular boy. I felt so juvenile. It was to the point of my wanting to run home and write: *Dear Diary, The other day I met this cute boy and now he's calling me names for no reason at all. I don't know what to do!*

But there I was, standing in front of him, acting like I didn't have a care in the world about him or his perception of me.

"I'm sorry if I offended you the other day," he said in his most delicate voice. Lord, he was sexy!

"None taken," I lied.

"Your cousin said you were quite upset." Oh, she's in trouble!

"No, it's that you don't even know me to make such a comment."

"I don't need to know you," he said softly, directly, and matter-of-factly. Was this still part of his apology? I hated his self-assured way with me.

I peered at him in disgust and didn't reply. *I'll get my drink and leave as soon as he hands it to me*, I thought.

"But I can get to know you," he suggested, saying no more, and looked right at me. Oh, Lord, he was smooth! Is this how he does it? Bruise the ego first and then provide the remedy to heal it?

I had no comeback. I had no personality at this point. I felt there was no blood flow to my brain; I couldn't think straight.

"Don't be mad. Stay and talk with me for a bit."

"About what?" I whispered, more to myself than to him.

"Anything, whatever you want to tell me." He sensed my hesitation. "You're a very sensitive person; I can tell," he said gently. "I won't bite," he promised and smiled.

Aren't those the exact words the serpent said to Eve? Oh no, I'm wrong; the serpent said *"Take* a bite." Oh Lord, save me. As I mentally tweaked his words to reveal his underlying intention, or my hopeful fantasy, my mouth watered in anticipation and my teeth were ready. This is how I walked right into temptation, shyly sipping a latte and biting the straw to contain myself.

A nonphysical, non-flirtatious connection carried on between us for an entire six months. He was a great listener. He thought before he spoke. He was calm, never rushed, never "biting." I'd get my caffeine high and mind stimulation during our simple exchanges. When Joe was working alone, he'd always say, "Stay, talk to me for a while."

"About?" I'd repeat as if it were our first time interacting.

"Anything. Tell me what you're studying."

I'd tell him my school plan—anatomy, physiology, and microbiology at Delta and then nursing school the following year in Oakland, if I was accepted into the accelerated bachelor of science program. He'd tell me he was close to getting his bachelor's degree in accounting.

An accountant? Hmm, he could have been a model, but he had a brain. I was intrigued. I found myself even more attracted to him.

Whenever I had a book in my hand, he'd say, "Tell me about what you're reading."

One day I carried in printouts on research articles and a book about iguanas. I saw him trying to eye the cover's title.

"I'm researching the marine iguana," I said proudly.

"Why?"

"Physiology project. Did you know that the marine iguana is the only vertebrate that can shrink its actual bone structure up to twenty to twenty-five percent during El Niño season?"

"Um, I can't say that I do. Go on."

"Yeah, so they shrink in order to survive the famine."

"Why is there a famine during El Niño?"

"Because the water temperature around the Galapagos increases, killing the nutrients in the algae that the iguanas live off of. Once the El Niño phenomenon passes, they grow back to their original size. They're the only vertebrate that can do that! Isn't that cool?"

"Fascinating," he said in equal wonderment as I. "So are you gonna do a presentation?"

"Yes."

"You're so smart."

"Not really."

"That's why I like talking with you. I feel like I learn something every time—and I love to learn."

Little by little, I, too, was learning that he had both beauty and brains. During the week, I went to the coffee shop before class; on the weekends, I went whenever I woke up or was driving by. I always found time in my day to get there. One Saturday, my mom and I were driving near the shop, and I figured I'd make a quick stop. I'd never mentioned Joe to my mom, which wasn't unusual. A week after I'd finally decided to introduce Jonathan to my mom, he'd broken up with me, only to return a couple weeks later. So I'd vowed not to get my mom involved in my stupid love affairs until it was drastically serious enough to do so.

"Oh, the guy that works at this coffee shop is really good looking. And I'm positive he knows it, so make sure you don't compliment him," I advised her as I parked the car.

"Why not?"

"Because I'm sure he's conceited and we shouldn't feed into it any further."

"OK," she said.

I considered Joe my friend, but I refused to be openly giddy in front of him. It was a control thing.

Joe greeted us warmly.

"This is my mom," I said.

"Hello," he said and gave her a smile.

I looked at my mother; she was staring at Joe. She didn't say hello back to him. Instead she said, "You've got the most beautiful eyes I have *ever* seen!" OK, Judas! This would definitely be The Last Coffee between mother and daughter.

Hadn't I explained to her less than one minute ago that she was *not* to compliment him? I knew she heard me. She had her hearing aids in place and had said OK. Had she misunderstood me? Had she heard the opposite, "Make sure you compliment him"?

I rolled my eyes involuntarily.

"Thank you," Joe said, smiling, "but obviously your daughter thinks otherwise."

"I didn't say they weren't," I said.

"Well, you can't deny that they're the most beautiful eyes you've ever seen, Julie!" said my mother, Judas, as she continued to betray her agreement not to compliment him and began melting under the spell of this barista, too!

"I'm sure he's used to hearing it all the time," I said sweetly, yet *bitterly*.

"It's always nice to hear," he declared to me. He looked at my mother and replied, "Thank you. I really appreciate it."

Walking back to the car, my mom went on and on about how good-looking he was. *Yes, I know!*

"And he seems really nice, too," she added.

"Yeah, he is."

I realized then that Joe probably could attract every kind of woman—young, middle-aged, old, decrepitly old, lesbian, asexual, anything from a nun to a whore. I wasn't jealous. I couldn't be. He was beyond anyone's league as far as looks went. As far as brains went, I knew that was something I had the upper hand in as long as we were alone, having our private talk sessions.

For months our conversations were about education, languages (he spoke some Spanish), traveling, places we'd like to visit, world events, and religion, Buddhism and Taoism primarily. I told him my ultimate goal was to go to Africa on a medical mission trip once I had enough nursing experience under my belt. He was engaged in every conversation we had.

After a lengthy conversation about behavior and Eastern philosophy, the next morning he said, "I was thinking about what we were talking about, how in that book it says not to judge something as good or bad but as just *being*. I like that. Makes me feel better about myself." He laughed.

"What do you mean?"

"All my faults, no matter how much I'd like to change, it's who I am. It's in my DNA."

"What nationality are you anyways?"

"Black, white, and Native American."

If there were a nationality called "perfect phenotype," he'd be it. "So you blame your DNA for your actions?"

"Kind of. For example, it's well known that Indians are alcoholics; it's in their DNA, and I like to drink! And I'm a lot like my dad, even though I don't want to be. It's in my DNA."

Sounded kind of lame to me, but I understood. I blamed my motherly, nurturing ways on being Latina. "You need to take responsibility for your own actions," I preached.

"I do! I know I behave certain ways because that's how I was made, and I accept me."

***

I gave Diana a rundown of our conversation.

"Wow, he must be bored at home if he's having these conversations with you," she said.

"He's actually really smart and a deep thinker. You know how I love that. He really has it all. What the hell is he doing working at a coffee shop?"

"He doesn't even realize that he has it all. I mean, he knows he's good looking, but he could be even more than that. At least he's going to school. He's gonna outgrow his girlfriend. Has he mentioned her?"

"Yeah, he's very open about her. Says he doesn't have much time to study or read once he's home with her and her kid. They live together."

Joe's girlfriend had a young son when she and Joe met about six years earlier. When they first got together, according to Joe, he was trying to earn a quick buck by selling marijuana. Big deal. Remember: this is Stockton, where nearly all of its inhabitants are tempted and close to dealing drugs at some point in time! Needless to say, he got caught; the girlfriend bailed him out, stood by his side, and provided some stability. He said he never meant to have a relationship or help raise her son; he fell into it and never left. He said he was amazed that it had lasted so long when he never thought he'd commit to anyone, but he did love and care for her. He said that if he could have his way, he'd like to be alone, that he was selfish ("Like my dad. I have his genes," he'd say), but that time had passed quickly and now they were like a family. "You can get accustomed to anything," he said.

I always found it odd that he felt he had no choice in the matter, thinking he had to stay forever. I'd have to explain to him the plain fact that nothing lasts forever. Nothing. Not that I was trying to break them up or anything. I knew he was far more than I could ever handle. And he never outright showed that he was physically attracted to me—he wanted to pick my brain, and I wanted to share it with him on a silver platter.

I'd seen his "lady" (as he referred to her) a few times when

I'd gone into the shop. She was thin, pretty, not very friendly with anyone there; she rarely smiled, from what I observed. But she loved him. I could tell. Her eyes never looked around or down. From the moment she walked in, she was focused on him entirely. Or maybe it was her way of marking her territory, her man, to the many women observing. Some days she had her little boy with her, and he'd call Joe "Dad." I'd observe him playing this role of boyfriend, of dad, of the other side of him that I didn't know. But what do we really know about anyone?

DNA 101

When I think about Joe's beauty and how it all came together, as he marinated for nine months in his mama's belly, I imagine him as a kaleidoscope. The outside of him was no ordinary cylinder, as any passerby could easily notice. And if the outside was so beautiful, then it had to contain amazing gemstones inside. Joe's body, his frame, and his looks were simply the container that held his exceptional genetic code. In essence, that's what we all are, but some, like Joe, are exquisite, and with every rotation, the reflection of the gems inside transfixes, if not tricks, the eye.

Imagine with me, if you will, a huge, magnificent kaleidoscope that represents the human body. Inside, there are close to one hundred trillion cells, or preciously cut pieces of rich gems, waiting to create a colorful helix of a pattern.

With the exception of our red blood cells, within each cell lies a complete set of DNA. The DNA is made up of four molecule bases named adenine, guanine, cytosine, and thymine. To continue with our colorful kaleidoscope analogy, let's think of every molecule base as a different precious or semiprecious stone. Inside us are vibrant stones ranging from axinite and emerald to maw-sit-sit and mystic topaz, to ruby and zircon and every other gorgeous gem in between.

The unique sequence of our multicolored stones is lined up

on two separate strands of DNA, waiting to be turned and mixed for the first time. Picture each gemstone as having a tiny hand, grabbing its mate, and then doing a graceful, waltz-like twirl as the kaleidoscope is rotated, forming the double helix. There are up to three billion pairs, dancing, functioning, in each human being. The order of these pairs, where they stand in the lineup, and how they decided to sequence themselves are completely unique in every human being.

We receive one set of genes, or gemstones, from our mothers and one set from our fathers. The possibilities of what genes we do or don't inherit and how they'll all line themselves up are infinite. But it all comes down to the same thing: We never know what we'll get. Nothing is guaranteed or predictable in the making of a human being. We can't calculate which one of the millions of sperm will reach the mature egg, and we have no idea what each is holding in terms of genetics. With every twist of the kaleidoscope, we can't even guess as to what pattern will appear.

All we know is that priceless genetic information will pass down everything from complexion to gender, all contributing to the formation and operation of the human being it's designing.

We're judged by our phenotype, the genes that become our characteristics. In others, we're lured in or repulsed by them. We might not choose a mate strictly based on them, but they're the first thing we notice. And if you're searching the sperm bank websites, reading through profiles, phenotypes are *everything*. They're the sperm bank's treasure. A donor who's six foot one with blond hair or even dark hair and blue or green eyes is going to sell far faster than a donor who's five foot six with any color hair and brown eyes. That's the way it is.

Will environment and experiences play a role in one's ultimate behavior? Of course they will. But isn't it easier to blame DNA? Everybody else seems to use his or her DNA as a scapegoat, even someone as physically magnetic as Joe.

Kaleidoscopes work based on the angled positions of mirrors contained inside and the reflection they give. But if you stare long enough at one pattern, you can find chips on the gems, irregular shapes, and imperfections that are all too often ignored.

CRESCENT-SHAPED SEX

I'd been in Stockton seven months. I was breezing through my classes, working part-time at the hospital as a clerk, and spending time in the coffee shop having thought-provoking conversations with Joe. He was my one-stop fix. I made no other friends. I didn't need to, nor did I want to.

My on-again-off-again, so-called boyfriend, Arizona-Boy-with-One-Testicle, was to visit over Thanksgiving. The one-testicle problem wasn't a genetically inherited trait, but the cancer that took his testicle was. His whole family was dropping dead of cancer. Diana asked why the hell I'd choose to go out with a boy that could never provide me with the baby that I wanted. Good point—the only thing I really wanted in life was to experience pregnancy and become a mommy to Joaquin. I hadn't forgotten that this desire had been the driving force behind changing careers from music publisher to nurse. So I didn't have an answer to Diana's question. It was the end of October, and I was going to visit Arizona-Boy-with-One-Testicle's grandma, who happened to live in Stockton. She also happened to be dying of lung cancer. I bought her a pumpkin pie and thought I'd go to the coffee shop beforehand. It was a mildly cool Sunday, and Joe didn't work Sundays, so I went through the drive-through with no thought of seeing him. But there he was. He popped his head out the window.

"Hey! I didn't expect you here today," I said.

"Yeah, they needed someone to work. What are you up to?"

"Going to visit my boyfriend's grandma."

"I thought he broke up with you over the summer."

"He did; now he's back." I never mentioned my relationship with Arizona-Boy-with-One-Testicle to Joe during our endless conversations. Probably because I never thought of him when I was with Joe.

"Why did you do that? Never take a guy back. He'll just dump you again."

"Thanks a lot."

"I'm just saying. You're a beautiful girl, and you have a nice body. He's just going to break your heart again." Then he placed his elbows on the window seal and leaned his head out the window toward me. He looked me dead in the eye and said, "You know what you need, Julie?"

"What?" I heard a lecture coming.

"You need a *buddy*."

"A *buddy*?"

"Yeah, a *buddy*. You know what I mean."

I knew *exactly* what he was referring to—a *fuck buddy*. Who the hell was he to tell me that I needed to get laid? "I can't even get a date."

"Well," he said, "if you want a *buddy*, you can have one. I'm telling you, you could."

"Who?" I didn't want to assume that he was referring to himself.

"I think you know," he said without flat-out mentioning his own name. And that's what I needed him to do. Otherwise, I didn't want to assume.

"I have a boyfriend," I said in disbelief.

With that, Joe's demeanor changed. For the first time then, and in the days that followed, he didn't make much eye contact. He was cordial, but there was no in-depth coffee-shop talk.

"I'm sure he's never been rejected before," Diana said when I sought out her opinion on the situation.

"He has a girlfriend!" I said, like that ever stopped anyone.

"You hurt his ego. I think you should take him up on the offer. You'd be crazy not to."

"Do you really think he was referring to *himself* as my buddy?"

"Yes, of course it's him. He isn't gonna waste his time setting you up with a friend of his!"

I was completely unsure of this. I knew the facts: he had a girlfriend, and they had been together quite a while. I had no desire to cause problems, to interfere, or to think that I'd be something special or different. The other simple fact was he wanted to fuck around, and this time he wanted it to be with me. I felt guilty for wanting the same. Yet part of me didn't want to do it, in fear of ruining the friendship we'd been slowly establishing over seven months.

It was a few weeks before Thanksgiving. Jonathan texted that he wouldn't be visiting after all and, as a matter of fact, he thought it was best if we ended it, again. I was angry, but my next thought was

Joe. I'd been tempted and life was short. No use in crying over Arizona-Boy-with-One-Testicle. I got in my car, and all logic flew out the window as I drove with fervor to the coffee shop. Did I mention that the adult heart runs amok?

Joe was there.

I'm guessing there's no guideline on how to approach the topic of a suggested affair that you rejected only days prior. I have no idea why I decided to go through the drive-through window to discuss this, maybe because that's where the situation was first offered. I should have walked in with a bit of pride and confidently said, "Yeah, I'll take you up on that sexual offer. And make me an iced latte to go."

Instead, this is how it happened.

"What we talked about the other day…you were right," was my opening line to him at the drive-through window. I delivered this one-liner without a greeting, without any segue, and without any foreplay. I delivered it like breaking news that couldn't wait for the appropriate news hour.

"About your dude breaking your heart?" *Did* this guy have mind-reading capabilities?

"That…and a lot of other things."

"Yeah?"

"Yeah, like what you said about the *buddy* thing."

He turned his head slightly in an attempt to hide his surprised smile. It was almost an "Ah, she's gonna come around after all?" look.

"Is there something you want to tell me?" he asked.

I was stunned. How could he put me on the spot like this? "No," I whispered.

"Well, it looks like there's something you want to say."

"No," I whispered again. Why was he doing this, making me say it? He was turning it around so that when I finally explicitly said it, it would be my idea and not his.

"Well, when you're ready to tell me, you know where to find me."

"So it's with you?" If he was going to make me spell things out, then I was going to make him do so in return. I didn't want to be mistaken that it was he and not any other person.

He laughed. "I'm sure your cousin told you that I've been attracted to you from the first day I saw you."

"No, she never told me."

"I think you're beautiful, Julie."

And because it was difficult for me to take compliments, especially from a Greek god, I blurted out, "I've seen your girlfriend. She's beautiful."

"Yeah, she's all skinny!"

What did that mean? That I was all fat? She was a stick, like a model. I had breasts, a butt, and thighs. I'd always wanted to be a little flat chested, like her, as I thought it would make me look thinner. But enough talk and thoughts about her; he and I had a secret encounter to arrange.

"So, we'll have to come up with something," he said.

"Yeah, let me know."

"We'll talk," he said as he handed me my usual drink with a wide smile across his beautiful face. The cold shoulder he'd had toward me days before was gone. He was back. He was warm, ready, and able.

I finally made it inside the shop a few days later. He started the conversation. "My only reservation is that I wouldn't want you to have any regrets. You're very sweet and sensitive, and I have to keep that in mind."

"I know what I'm getting into. There won't be any regrets," I said. How could I proclaim that I'd have no regrets about something yet to be experienced? I said it to ease his worried mind.

"So if this is a one-time, two-time, five-time thing and that's it, you won't be hurt, and we'll still be friends…?" He was testing the waters.

Thinking back on this now makes me laugh. A one- or five-*time* thing was a sheer drop in the bucket of what would become a one-, two-, three-, four-*year* affair.

"You don't need to worry," I reassured him.

"You know, I don't want to get all caught up either, get fired from my job."

"Fired? From here?"

"No, not the coffee shop. I don't care about that. With my lady. I call it a job because it's a whole lot of work."

This was getting real romantic. Did we need to have a whole list of rules going into this? Was this his way of ensuring that I wouldn't hound him, fall in love with him, and attempt to ruin his relationship with his "lady"?

"Sounds like you're having doubts," I said.

"No. I'm excited about it!"

"Me, too."

"I want to kiss you."

"We will."

"No, right now. I want to kiss you right now," he said.

"Now?"

"Yes. Nobody's here; nobody's coming through the drive-through. I'm excited. I want to kiss you before we meet up."

This was a side of him I'd never seen. He was always so collected, never giving away too much at once. He'd finally stopped nibbling; he was ready to go against his word, ready to take a bite. "Come here," he said and guided me to a tiny hallway that led to the back bathroom. He pinned me against the back wall. "You're so tiny."

"Petite," I corrected as he bent over and I stood on my tippy-toes to kiss.

"I have coffee breath," I said.

"Me, too," he said. But he didn't. He had gum in his mouth, Wrigley's Winterfresh flavor. It was cool and tasty. God, he looks and tastes good, too?

He had full lips like mine, and he moved his tongue the right way, in a nice, circular, clockwise motion. It had been a long time since I'd French kissed. Arizona-Boy-with-One-Testicle never used his tongue when he kissed. He believed French kissing should be reserved for fucking. Huh? I needed French kissing to get me started. It must have been his lack of testosterone that kept him from kissing. I didn't have to worry about any of that with Joe—he had plenty of testosterone and, I bet, two testicles. It was only a matter of time before I could confirm that.

"Mmm, you kiss nice," he said.

"You, too," I whispered.

We got a taste of each other and returned to the front of the shop. I cut to the chase. "So, when and where?" I asked boldly. Either he wanted to or he didn't. I wasn't going to have another conversation to help him feel safe with his decision of infidelity. If he wanted to do this, which I was sure he'd done before, then he knew the risks. He was a smart man.

"How about here? Before I open shop?"

"Here? The coffee shop?"

"Next door."

The coffee shop was connected to a tattoo shop. Both shops were owned or partially owned by Joe's family. The idea of having sex in a coffee shop/tattoo parlor really didn't excite me. It seemed dirty, low class, and oh-so raunchy! But where could we go? I was living at home with my mom and Neil. I was sleeping not on a twin-size bed but on a single, which is much narrower than a twin bed. Think of an army cot. It was fine for me, a five-foot girl, alone, but not with a lover who was six foot three and probably two hundred pounds of muscle.

And because this man could read my mind more easily than a third-grade schoolbook, he said, "I'll be here an hour early on Sunday. If you decide to show up, I'm here."

In a tattoo shop? I've never even stepped foot into a tattoo shop, I thought. But it was Joe. I knew he'd be waiting. I couldn't let him wait through a wintry morning, alone in a tattoo parlor, so I showed up. It would have been rude not to!

It was cold and strange. First, I never snuck out of the house as a teenager, but here I was, thirty-four years old, quietly leaving before the crack of dawn to have sex in, of all places, a freaking coffee shop/tattoo parlor! My mother was 75 percent deaf and loved to sleep in, so I knew she'd neither hear me leave nor be awake when I returned. Second, why do people do such stupid stuff like this for sex?

He opened the front door. He, too, was bundled up in sweaters and a beanie cap. "I wasn't sure if you'd come," he said.

"Yep, here I am," I said shamefully.

He opened the door that led to the tattoo portion of the shop. "So, is this your love shack where you bring all your women?" I asked jokingly.

"Ha-ha," he responded; he didn't like my inquisition. I knew then that it was. He'd done this before, many times. He was calm, confident, and quiet. But then again, he always was.

We sat on a yellow crescent-shaped couch. He kissed me again with his Winterfresh mouth. "I'm tired," he said. "I went to bed really late."

"You could have canceled," I said.

"No, I wanted to meet up with you."

The couch, because of its shape, was our biggest challenge. My entire body, although only sixty inches long, fit nowhere on its crescent shape. I couldn't crescent-shape myself, so my upper torso would be on the couch and the rest of me dangling to the floor. If I wanted the lower portion of my body on the couch, then my head would be hanging down to the floor, rushing with blood, my face turning red. We moved clumsily. "I'm nervous," I confessed.

"Me, too, a little," he said. But he didn't seem nervous.

I'd always wanted to see his chest; I'd fantasized about it. Because he was half black, for whatever reason I wanted to see his chest, and the rest of his body for that matter, to confirm if his complexion was as white as mine. I made him take off his sweatshirt, even though it was freezing. His chest was broad, warm, strong, and yes, as white as, or even whiter than, mine.

"Joe." I whispered his name as he lay on top of the part of me that was badly positioned on the crescent couch.

He chuckled.

We ended up on the floor. It didn't last long. If I had to use one word to describe the whole scenario, it would be *awkward*. It wasn't bad, just awkward. Two unknown bodies, trying to come together in a set amount of time, in a strange location, in Popsicle-making temperatures, and on an unconventionally shaped couch.

We dressed and returned to the coffee shop. He made me my drink. "On the house," he said.

"For services rendered?" I asked jokingly.

"You OK?" he asked.

"Yeah!" I said. And I was fine.

"You know my name really isn't Joe, right?"

After seven months, were we finally having this conversation? We'd already had sex. Did we need to have this conversation? It made me feel cheap, having sex with someone after seven months of knowing him, but never using his real name.

"Isn't it Dante or Diante?"

"You know that it's Dante," he said.

"I didn't know for sure. How come you told me it was Joe?"

"I never told you it was Joe. Andre did. We came up with that because girls are always asking my name, and I really don't want them to know my real name."

"That's the most arrogant thing I've ever heard!"

"No, I don't want certain people to know my name; they don't need to."

"Oh, so you didn't want me to know your name?"

"No, I do want you to know my real name."

"You're conceited. And I think of you as Joe. You will always be Joe to me. Always."

"If that's how you want to keep it. So all of this"—referring to our sexual rendezvous—"isn't ever real. It's a fantasy for you."

"I don't like your arrogance."

"I'm not being arrogant. I think you call me Joe to keep things separate."

"That's not true." Or was it?

"Maybe I should come up with a name for you. Like…Darla?" he joked.

"That'll be Dr. Darla to you, if we're gonna play make believe."

I couldn't believe how quickly he'd analyzed the whole situation. Perhaps he had regrets. I knew, nickname or not, he wanted to, he needed to, and he'd keep things *separate*.

***

"So how was it?" Diana later queried.

"Awkward," I said.

"Ooh, are you disappointed?"

"No, not at all. It wasn't bad, it was strange." I explained the crescent-shaped couch and how cold it was in the shop.

"So is that it or what?"

"I don't know…."

"You should get knocked up."

"What?"

"Julie, you're never going to meet anyone who's better looking. Do it for the genes!"

"I could never do that, change his entire life like that without his consent."

"He doesn't have to know. You get pregnant right before moving to Oakland; he'll never know. Then one day you come in for coffee carrying a baby that looks exactly like him with those eyes."

Didn't the rock group Heart have a song about that called

"All I Wanna Do Is Make Love You"? The girl in the song meets some stranger in the rain, drives to a hotel, and gets knocked up on purpose because her husband couldn't provide viable sperm, and then later she runs into the guy she used and he sees that the baby has his perfect blue eyes? Only in a song, only in a song.

"I could never do that. I'd want to tell him if I got pregnant. And we used a condom anyways."

"Poke a hole in it," she said. She had an answer for everything.

"That's not my nature," I said. I unfortunately didn't have the DNA required to be so manipulative.

"Too bad; you're going to regret it. So would you have sex with him again?"

I thought back to my friend Dahlia, who told me she hated bad sex, as it made her go back time and again until it was good. She said that after having bad sex, she'd think, *No, it* can't *be that bad. It has to be better.* And once the sex was good, she could walk away on a good sex note. Or she'd keep returning because the sex was finally good and she'd invested so much effort in getting to that point. She wanted to reap the benefits of all her hard work. I was starting to see her point. Joe wasn't bad; we were both awkward. And I knew we could do better. If offered, I'd return to better myself and give it a second chance.

"Yeah, I need to have sex with him at least one more time," I told Diana.

***

I waited three days before returning to the coffee shop.

"I thought you weren't ever going to come back," he said.

"I've been busy," I said.

"I thought you were regretting it."

"No, not at all. And you?"

"No. I want to see you again."

We met a few more times in the wee hours of the cold morning. Then we moved on to Diana's house (at her suggestion) when she wasn't home. Our bodies learned one another's ways, and the sex got much better. So I kept meeting up with him. The eye contact became more intimate, and he handled me like a precious china doll that might break. It scared me. I thought I better stay away. He noticed and questioned me about it.

"I've been thinking of you too much and thought it was best if I kept a distance," I admitted.

He seemed bothered by that. "So you can't even come around to say hi?" he asked, and I caught the irritation in his voice. He reeled in his tone and said gently, "I know I have to respect that, though. I'm trying to be good, anyway. You know, my dad always cheated on my mom. I have his DNA. I'm trying to be good."

He need not have worried. My strike against him didn't last very long, and neither did his good behavior attempt. Most times DNA is stronger than good intention. And it was in my DNA, obviously, to allow this, too. My time was winding down in Stockton. I'd be leaving for Oakland by the end of May. We knew we had a short run left, and we were going to make the most of it.

Some days I would sit there with my coffee, reading the paper or studying, and watch the stream of women coming in to flirt with him. I was accustomed to it. I'd observed this for a year now.

"See that girl that passed through the drive-through?" he asked one day while I was hanging out.

"I didn't see her."

"I don't like her. Every time I hand change to her, she tries to hold my hand practically."

"I want to hold your hand!" I squealed.

"You do? Well, come over here and hold it."

"I thought you didn't like that."

"I don't like it from her, but you I care about."

I went over, and we held hands. Oh, I was digging myself deeper. This was more intimate than sex! *Dear Diary, That cute boy I told you about? We held hands today! Oh, I forgot to mention, we had sex a while back, too!*

"So it's a curse to be good looking, huh?" I asked.

"Just strange. Sometimes it makes me uncomfortable. I don't know what to do when people gawk. That's why I walk away. People think it's arrogance."

"They're admiring or jealous."

"I find that because of my looks, people expect very little from me, like I have no brain. Or they expect way more from me, like I could solve all their problems."

"You have to find a way to make it work to your advantage."

"I don't know. I don't think about it too much. I had nothing to do with how I look. I can't take credit for any of it. It's how I was born; know what I mean?"

"I can't relate." And I couldn't. My looks were fair, decent, and cute. Striking I was not. Beautiful was a stretch. That was my friend Liliana. She was pretty but was accustomed to being called *beautiful*. I remember when she overheard her boyfriend's mother describe her as "cute." She wasn't just shocked but appalled. "Cute?" she asked me. "I've never been described as cute. People describe me as beautiful but never cute." I couldn't relate.

I'm not sure at what point I stopped being in awe like most women who first see Joe. I started to see him as a man, a friend, and someone I wanted to get to know, someone I wanted to see happy. I wanted him to get out of the coffee shop and flourish. I wanted him to reach beyond the ordinary.

For Joe's birthday I gave him *The Alchemist* by Paulo Coelho and *Tao Te Ching* by Lao Tzu. I'd given this exact gift to others before. It was my way of pinpointing how open they were. Open to what, I don't know, maybe to following their dreams and to self-reflection. It was my secret way of judging someone, and I disliked myself for that. *If he never reads them*, I thought, *then he isn't as special as you're giving him credit for.* I secretly hoped that he wouldn't read them or would call me and say, "This is nonsense!" If he did that, then I'd have a solid reason not to like him. I admit I judge people by whether they read or not.

He called me and said, "Thank you for these books. I read the *Tao* already. I'd never have been introduced to this if it weren't for you." Damn it, he'd read it, and he went on to quote a section of Chapter 49 as his favorite. It's about goodness and the trustworthiness of people.

"You know how I interpret that chapter?" he asked. He was excited; I could hear it in his voice. He was speaking fast as if he had to hurry and tell me all his new revelations. He didn't wait for me to respond. "To me it says she knows who isn't trustworthy; she isn't trying to change or believe that they'll be trustworthy. Instead she trusts in what she already knows; therefore, she knows what to expect from that kind of person. And she's not disappointed in their behavior."

I knew he was relating this to himself and his unfaithful ways. Expect what you know. Joe always used his DNA, what he was, as the reason for his cheating ways. It was truly his one fault. It gave him justification to accept not only being unfaithful but remaining with this girl, only to cheat on her. Instead of leaving, creating the bachelor life he wanted, he could easily play the DNA card and not have to make hard choices and go after them.

Two days before I was to move to Oakland for nursing school, Joe called. He'd finished reading *The Alchemist*. He wanted to discover his personal legend, the way the character in the book did.

"And you can," I encouraged.

"I feel like I've had an epiphany. And you're part of it. I want to learn again. I want to travel…."

"You will, Joe. I have no doubt."

"You're a good friend," he said.

"I hope we can be friends for a long time to come."

Then there was a momentary silence. I knew he was gathering his thoughts about something he should consider not saying, something he'd never said out loud before.

"You know, we never know where we'll end up. Things may not work out with my girlfriend, and—" he said.

"Stop," I interrupted him, "let's not talk about that. I meant what I said. I want us to be friends for a long time."

"We are friends."

I couldn't bear to hear him talk about *What if I'm no longer with my girlfriend? What if things don't work out?* I was afraid to dream that it could be a possibility. That's what I wanted, him. But I didn't dare listen to the what-ifs. I'd been disappointed in the past with others, and with Joe, I didn't want to ruin what we did have, a friendship. I valued it more than anything.

I went to see him the day before I was to move. We hugged for a long time. "You're gonna do great," he said.

"It's only a year," I reminded him.

"Yeah, I probably won't be working here much longer."

"I know. Let me know?"

"Yeah, of course."

***

It was the end of May. I moved to Oakland and started the nursing program. People say you can't think of two things at once. I beg to differ. The first month, I learned the basics: blood pressure, lung sounds, bowel sounds, electrolyte values, how to start an IV and how to insert a Foley catheter. I took all this in as an eager new student *and* I thought of Joe the entire time. Who said you can't think of two things at once?

I figured that as school got more complex, thoughts of him would fade to the background. But they didn't. I reminded myself that I needed to stay focused; it was only one year. I counted the weeks the way a newly pregnant woman does: how long it had been and pretty much how long I could hold out. Six weeks. And in those six weeks, I concluded I'd tell him that I missed him, that I wanted him to think about what he told me in regard to him and his "lady" not working out, that I had a lot to offer and I hoped he and I would one day have a shot at something. That was the speech I'd say to him, that was the plan, and that was the truth.

I made the hour drive home to spend a few days in Stockton. It was July, perhaps my birthday week; I can't recall. I went to see Joe. The moment I walked in, I knew all had changed. The planned speech dissipated into oblivion. He could barely make eye contact with me.

"What's new and exciting?" I asked, bracing for a dreadful response. My instincts told me that my silly high school girl crush was about to end with some very adult news. And it came.

"Lots. I'm gonna be a dad…and I'm going to marry her," he said, looking down into the latte he was stirring.

My heart gushed, and my lungs filled with disappointment. Holes opening, holes filling, holes, holes, holes, everywhere in my heart. And the collapsing of my lungs. Confusion throughout. And no redirection of blood flow. Chaos inside my heart. A heartbreak isn't a jagged crack down the middle, separating itself left from right. It's more like a spray of bullets hitting every artery and valve, every wall. It's a well-traveled ricochet to ensure destruction. This is where heartache resides, in the frayed, silent spaces of the heart, and in the winded, compressed spaces of the lungs—in the unseen organs that the survival *of anything* is dependent upon. I tried to put things in perspective and said to myself, "This is just heartache, nothing more, nothing less. It isn't war, it isn't death, it isn't torture, and it isn't a violation of my human rights. It's everyday heartbreak. It isn't the end of the world." Nonetheless, I felt that I deserved a consolation prize for this great loss.

I reminded myself of Lesson Number Three: *Learn to breathe.* And not drown.

They say the best way not to drown in rushing water is to relax the body and go with the current. How do you relax a racing mind, a hole-patterned heart, and shallow breath? You pretend—that's how.

"Well, congratulations," I whispered with the last speck of air in my lungs.

"I've been meaning to call you," he said, "but I've been so busy since finding out."

"I can't believe you didn't."

"It's not like you didn't know, Julie," he said in the most defensive tone he'd ever used with me. "You knew I was in a relationship, so I don't know why you have a sad face."

Yes, I did know. And all the crap about his fucking epiphany and my being a part of it were just that—crap! An epiphany doesn't call for commitment or a relationship, but a baby usually does. The girl he never intended to be with was pregnant, he was going to marry her, and he was going to be a father. There was only one thing I could do—accept it. And learn to breathe.

The five notable stages of grief are defined as denial, anger, bargaining, depression, and acceptance. Although I'd silently said to myself, "Accept it," I knew I wasn't strong enough to jump to the final stage of grief and ignore the remainder. I felt all stages, with the exception of denial, all at once. I was angry at him, at myself. I wanted to bargain with the universe for my consolation prize. I was so sad, yet I knew I had to accept this. What had I expected? It was an affair and these were the consequences.

"I can't fuck this up. It's way too important," he rambled. "I don't know what's taken me so long to marry her in the first place. I'm not going to be like my dad. I'm gonna break the cycle. I'm not going to allow my child to be raised without its father."

From rambling he went on to advice giving. "You need to find someone who's interested in the same things you are, like art and reading and going to Africa for medical trips. You need to date a square."

"Yeah," I responded in a daze.

"You know it's gonna be hard to find someone to wait for you to go to Africa and do your thing and then come back. People don't wait around, unless they do that kind of stuff, too."

Is that what it was? He couldn't imagine waiting around for me? He couldn't think outside the box and imagine joining me in some capacity? Perhaps the same way I couldn't allow myself to think he'd ever want to join me in some capacity beyond infidelity?

I'm not even sure how I left that day, besides disappointed and, dare I say, *bitter*. But what had I expected? That my six-week absence was going to make his heart grow fonder? Isn't that what we're taught, "Absence makes the heart grow fonder"? Or is it "Out of sight, out of mind"? All I knew was that I had to remain focused, pretend that nothing was bothering me. And I was very good at that in front of other people.

I returned to school, went through the motions like everyone else. I learned about congestive heart failure, acute renal failure, respiratory failure, liver failure, and my personal favorite, failure to thrive. I thought of all the failures I could study and analyze about myself, and that only I could cure. All the while, I did my best not to think of Joe. I was definitely a failure in that, too.

The end of August rolled around, six weeks from the last time I'd seen Joe. Diana called me, and the first words out of her mouth were, "Joe's girlfriend lost the baby."

"What?"

"Yep, I just went to the coffee shop and Mandy told me. I bet you that she wasn't even pregnant. She probably did it to get him to marry her."

"Hmm, I don't know. How's Joe doing?"

"She didn't say."

"I can't believe it."

"I bet you'll be hearing from him again."

"Not sure about that. He seemed pretty adamant about changing his ways. I'm sure they're already married."

"Like that means anything. Men like him don't change," she concluded.

I didn't know what to think or feel about this news. If she really had been pregnant, I felt very sad for him. This was a life, his child, and despite my feelings for him, I didn't want him to hurt. I cared about him. If she'd been lying about the pregnancy, then they were both one and the same, selfish liars attempting to get out of life the things they couldn't obtain through being honest. But who was I to judge? I was the one falling in love with another woman's man. She was just trying to progress their long-stagnant relationship. And whether it was 1940, 1950, or 2008, this was the way a lot of women still seemed to do it!

In September I had a few days off from school and headed to Stockton. I wanted to see Joe. I wanted to see if he'd tell me, if he was still the new and improved version of himself. I headed to the coffee shop. We made our cordial, "How are you? How have you been? I'm fine, thank you," to one another. Andre was there and gave me my coffee. I waited for Diana to show up. I seated myself at a table approximately twenty-five feet away and perused the newspaper.

"She's just brokenhearted about the baby," I heard Andre say to Joe.

"I know, but she called me a loser the other night," Joe voiced loudly.

"That's not right," Andre responded.

"Yeah, she just blows my money on all this girlie shit she buys. She got mad when I asked her for the receipts. She said she didn't have the receipts! How can you not have the receipts?" Joe had graduated with an accounting degree, and like all good accountants he wanted the receipts! He continued, loud enough for me to hear, "I felt like leaving. But I can't do that. I care. I don't know why, but I do."

"Give her time," Andre advised.

Had he said all this so that I could overhear? I don't know, but the timing was incredible. At that point, I'd imagine she'd miscarried two months ago. And with the history he and I had, I knew he was a smart enough man to have either waited until I left or spoken in a lower tone that my radar ears couldn't pick up.

What my ears couldn't pick up I invented. I figured they were having problems and thought maybe he'd finally leave. Why I thought that, I don't know, considering I overheard him say that he couldn't leave. Regardless, I thought, *What do I have to lose by telling him how I feel?*

The next day I said to him, "There's something I need to say to you."

"What do you have to say?" he said, as if he knew or he thought I was going to give him a lecture.

"The day you told me your girlfriend was pregnant, I'd come

to tell you that if one day you should ever find yourself alone, I feel that I have a lot to offer…." Then my words became inaudible until they got stuck. Joe had called me out on this before, saying he could never hear me when I became shy or afraid. But this time he didn't encourage me to say what I was hiding or afraid of telling him.

"It's not like I don't care about you. I appreciate what you're saying and everything you've done, Julie. I'm just trying to grow up."

"I understand that," I said, realizing he didn't directly respond to what I said.

"I didn't mean to hurt you."

"I hurt myself." I never planned to say that, it just came out. And it was so true: *I had hurt myself.*

Despite my self-realizations, I couldn't stay away. I saw him again in November when I went home for Thanksgiving break. He was friendly and flirty, calling me "sweetheart" in our conversations. After months of tension, he seemed relaxed, back to his old, natural-DNA self. The self he blamed his faults on, the self that I fell in love with.

"I think you'll like this," I said as I handed him Deepak Chopra's *Buddha* book.

"You're perfect," he flirted.

"Far from it," I responded.

"You know medicine, music, spirituality," he said.

Now if I could just put into practice what I know and believe! "How's your Spanish going?" I asked him.

"Badly. I have too many things on my plate, like finding a job in what I have a degree in, improving my golf game, and learning guitar."

"In a year we can do flute-guitar duets, if you keep practicing."

"We do make nice music together." *Here he goes.*

"Well, that's never going to happen again."

"It's just on hold," he said confidently. What did that mean? Was divorce imminent?

"No, I know you're married."

"I know."

"Congratulations, by the way."

"You've already congratulated me."

"No, I didn't."

"I guess I thought you had, since we're friends and that's what friends do."

"I congratulated you on the baby."

"My baby isn't coming anymore."

"Oh?" I feigned a shocked tone.

"She lost it, nothing that she did wrong."

"I'm sorry. I know you were excited about it," I said.

"I guess it just wasn't time."

I didn't have the right words to respond. What was I supposed to say? "Go try again! Get her pregnant again! You can do it!" I wasn't that good of a friend, mistress, or actress. So I nodded my head in agreement to nothing in particular.

"Do you still want to have a baby?" he asked.

"Oh, yeah!"

"Why don't you just go find a sperm donor?"

"That's the plan."

"You need to date a square."

"So you've said before."

"I'm selfish. Just the way I am. But I've been good since getting married."

Wow, a whole couple of months as a newlywed and he's praising himself for being "good"? Did he want an award for this good behavior?

"Too bad it's taken so much."

"Change doesn't happen overnight, Julie, and I was used to doing whatever I wanted."

I waited for his tagline: "That's how I am. It's in my DNA." But it didn't come this time.

SPILL YOUR GUTS BUT WIPE UP YOUR MESS

It was December, and I was halfway through the nursing program. I started my perinatal rotation. Not only did I learn about, but I also witnessed, cesarean sections, a boggy fundus, sitz baths, episiotomies, contraction stress tests, colostrum, and chloasma. Oh, and my personal favorite, circulation of the fetal heart and lungs. Phew! That's not even the tip of the iceberg of the before, during, and after of pregnancy and babies. It was my favorite rotation. I was speechless the time I was allowed into the neonatal intensive care unit to hold three-pound premature baby twins. Why I didn't become a perinatal nurse is still beyond me. Maybe it was all too overwhelming. Maybe I loved misery—infections, trauma, cancer, and broken bones. To me, nursing signified helping the ill, injured, and dying. That's what I was signing up for, and hanging out with happy parents, precious babies, and scared first-time mothers was something I could do after I got burned out with diseases.

The day before winter break, I shadowed a labor and delivery nurse who was assigned to a heavyset woman giving birth to her first child. The birthing mother's heavy legs and feet were in stirrups, and she was on her back with her buttocks close to the edge of the table, lithotomy position—no gravitation help here. *Isn't this birthing position considered outdated?* I thought. The nurse, also a heavyset, strong woman, stood solid in a semi-squat between the mother's legs as she held the mother's extended arms and hands, giving the mother support with every contraction and push.

"You try it," she told me.

I positioned myself in the same manner, a foot or two away, facing a vagina that was distorted, unrecognizable, and scary. Yet I kept my eyes transfixed on it. I was determined to see the baby's head peekaboo through the tumbleweed of a mess. I offered my small, sweaty hands to the calm woman, who stated she couldn't feel a thing, thanks to an epidural. I braced myself in the semi-squat position; she was far too large (close to three hundred pounds) for me to be supporting. The nurse and I were all she had for now. Her husband was useless, standing to the left of her shoulder, pale, diaphoretic, and only able to say, "Oh God!" in perfect synchronization with her every contraction appearing on the monitor.

"Get ready, hold her hands tight…and…*push!*" commanded the nurse.

I pushed, too, bearing down like I was going to have a bowel movement after months of constipation, and exhaled with great force while tightening the few abdominal muscles I had. I'm glad she couldn't feel a thing; otherwise she might have felt the breath of my exhalation reach her vagina. And that's weird and disgusting. My abdominal muscles held tight through the contraction. Basically, I was doing the Valsalva maneuver. This technique really is used when it's difficult to poop. During this maneuver, all the force causes the pressure surrounding your heart and lungs to rise and doesn't allow as much systemic blood to return to your heart. Your blood pressure rises quickly due to the force, and then drops quickly due to the decrease in circulation back to your heart. Ah, another heart circulation matter. The only problem with the Valsalva maneuver is that such strain can loosen a blood clot, cause a stroke, or cause one to faint, have a heart attack, or die. I thought how embarrassing it would be to faint between this lady's legs. Then I thought about how Elvis died, on the toilet, most likely bearing down, constipated from all the pills he was popping. I continued to "help" this lady with a few more contractions, and then the nurse said she'd tell the doctor it was time.

The doctor came in and gave some words of encouragement to both Mom and Dad. She made small talk to kill time during the last minutes of this routine birth. She went on about how many women were in labor right now, how many boys and how many girls had been delivered. I was still thinking about Elvis and the Valsalva maneuver. The head was now crowning. The husband was raising his eyebrows and stretching his neck to get a peek, then turning away to take deep breaths. The mother kept asking the dad, "Are you doing OK?" The top of the head, the forehead, the nose facing her right inner thigh, the doctor supporting the head, full face out and now the shoulders, and before I had a chance to blink, the whole baby was out. And Max, as they named him, was born.

The nurse rubbed the bottom of Max's foot to stimulate a response; he hadn't made a sound. They didn't spank his bottom like they do in the movies. They rubbed his foot again. My heartbeat accelerated. Max let out a good cry and everyone clapped. My thoughts of Elvis dying on the toilet were quickly forgotten, and my mind immediately turned to the circulatory changes in this baby's heart and lungs. I wanted to cry at the thought of this. My eyes watered. I looked at the new mother and wondered what she was thinking. It *must* be some profound thought, as this was her firstborn. She looked at my face, I gave her a smile, and she said, "I'm hungry! Do you think I'll be able to have something to eat soon?"

I ended that rotation warming up a food tray for her and her husband. I asked the nurse if it was normal to be so nonchalant after giving birth to your firstborn. "Everyone's different, but I believe the epidural makes you less connected to the whole process. But that's a personal choice, too," she said.

I wish she'd never told me that. I vowed that I'd never get an epidural during childbirth. How could I possibly vow that, though, when I had zero tolerance for pain? At least I had time to contemplate my options.

***

During winter break my mom would be getting married. It would be a short week off from studying; instead I'd be prepping for the wedding, getting ahead with some of the required reading for school, and of course, seeing Joe daily.

Priorities first—see Joe.

"Hello, my friend," he said when I walked in. He told me he'd read the *Buddha* book I'd given him. He said it really helped him and he liked it. He never mentioned how it helped him. "It made me miss you," he said.

This doesn't help me, I thought.

"You're the only one who has ever cared for me beyond the physical. I realize you're interested in me learning and knowing the world."

Here he goes again, and there I went again. "I miss you, too. I do care about you."

"How long will you be in town?"

"A week."

"I want to see you before you leave."

I said OK. I thought he meant "see" me at the coffee shop, so I returned the next day.

Again he said, "If you want to see me, I'd like to see you."

"In *that* way?" I asked. I was starting to realize he wanted to see me naked, not drinking a latte in the coffee shop.

He nodded.

"You're married!"

He paused for an instant and gave me a look that said, "Fuck, I'm married." How about that for an epiphany? After that light bulb went off in his head, his expression changed. He looked mad!

That night, after not helping my mom with her big day and not reading anything about nursing, I wrote Joe a two-page letter. I scribbled it all out, that I was no longer offering booty call, that I cared about him too much to be having random sex with him, that everything I had to offer him was now out on the table, and that if he wanted it, we had to do it the right way: no more secrets, a divorce, and a new start. We hadn't had sex since days before I moved to

Oakland, yet we were still so emotionally involved. I saw no point in carrying on pretending that all I wanted was to be an emotionally charged mistress. I had nothing to lose in spilling my guts to him.

"Read it after I leave," I said, handing him what felt like a teenage love letter.

"I have a feeling this is going to make me sad," he said as he folded all my silly emotions written on that paper and placed them into his back pocket.

I was trying to do what was right, not have an affair. I knew my letter would be considered an extreme option for him. The odds were not in my favor; I felt sad. I stood there before him, waiting to discuss anything other than our emotions. The letter was already weighing heavily. Perhaps he was waiting on me to start talking about something random and not related to "us." Melancholy drifted between us, and he started his justifications.

"I married her because she was pregnant. Now I'm in a marriage, and the family unit I thought I was gonna have isn't going to be. And the family unit I do have"—meaning her and her son from a previous relationship—"isn't mine!"

I knew he'd continue if I just listened.

"I'm both happy and unhappy. I'm never satisfied," he said. "I still miss you. You seem to know what I want. Your gifts, those books, are sentimental," he went on.

He was emotional and I could see him getting lost in thought. He contradicted his words. "If you knew me, Julie, you'd understand my actions better. You know, my mom's bipolar, and I, too, wake up depressed for no reason, which makes me think I'll never be satisfied in life," he said. "It's the way I am—it's not a choice," he concluded.

I disagreed. Either he wasn't listening to himself or he was refusing to put two and two together. *You're depressed because you're in a marriage you don't want to be in and a job you couldn't care less about! It has nothing to do with your mother's being bipolar!*

I could have said this, but then he changed the subject. "You know, I wasn't mad that day I said I wanted to hook up with you," he said.

"You looked mad."

"I think I offended you. I'm sorry for asking you to meet up. That would have just brought you back to deal with all those emotions. I shouldn't have done that. I can't offer you what you want," he said, as if he'd already read my letter.

And your wife isn't offering you what you want, I thought, then added, *You're not offering yourself what you want.*

"I think you're going to shut me out once you read the letter," I said.

Andre came into the shop, and we changed the subject. I left briefly thereafter, as my words waited in his back pocket to be read and then rejected. And then, for safety's sake, shredded and thrown out with coffee-shop coffee grinds and garbage before he went home.

And then something incredibly psychosomatic occurred.

Later that evening, I went to my mom and Robert's wedding rehearsal. I was the only bridesmaid, so I just had to stand there and hand my mom Robert's wedding band when the time came. The rehearsal dinner followed. I felt nauseated. I had no appetite. I figured it was because of everything that had happened between Joe and me earlier in the day. I had spilled my guts to him and now I'd lost my appetite. With every bite, I could literally feel the chewed-up food traveling through my stomach, attempting to make its way through the small intestine. A small pain would come and go in my gut.

 The next evening my mom and Robert, widow and widower, were married. You see, genuine love is easy. Wishful love is complicated. I felt happy but still a bit nauseated. I hadn't eaten all day. I sat down to eat, and again, with every bite came a bit of pain and the feeling of the food trudging along through me. Maybe my girdle was too tight, so I took it off. But my stomach felt better with the support, so I put the girdle back on.

 When I got back to my hotel I took off the girdle and the pain increased. I tossed and turned all night trying to find a comfortable position. In the morning, I took a shower and ran my soapy hand over my stomach. And there it was, a lump the size of an egg. A hernia. I recognized it immediately.

 It was December 30. I unfortunately had to call my mom the next day and ask her to call Dr. Mark, her doctor for the past hundred years. She told him I wasn't feeling well. Maybe I forgot to mention that I was sure it was a hernia. He said he could see me the next day. The pain was tolerable if I didn't eat, laugh, cough, sneeze, or remove my hand from supporting my stomach.

The next morning Dr. Mark sent me to the surgeon's office upstairs. The surgeon palpated my stomach, although the lump was visible to the naked eye.

"No, no, no, no!" I yelled out in pain as he tried to apply pressure over my lump.

"It's a hernia. Why didn't you go straight to the ER?"

"I don't know. I thought I could tolerate it."

"It could be strangulated," he said.

Great, a strangulated hernia. A hernia occurs when the wall that's supporting the organ is weakened. In this case, my abdominal wall had weakened enough to create a hole big enough to allow my intestines to push through. A strangulated hernia occurs when the intestine is getting strangled and its blood supply is cut off. All I could think of was that I couldn't afford to miss weeks of school recovering.

"You're going to need emergency surgery," the doctor said.

"OK." What else could I say?

I was sent to the hospital and had surgery on New Year's Eve 2007. The doctor asked if I'd done any heavy lifting or overexerted myself in some way. I couldn't think of anything. I told him I have always had weak abs. "Well, it could have been congenital and waited all these years to finally break through," he said.

Congenital, a condition existing at birth. I thought about my ass-first birth and wondered if that was it. Ah, yes, it was from birth, this hernia. But not my birth—Max's birth. I'd probably strained myself way too much assisting in the birth of Max during my last rotation at the hospital.

Diana came to visit on New Year's Day. "Joe was working today. I wasn't sure if you wanted me to tell him that you're in the hospital."

"No," I said, "I spilled my guts to him the other day and haven't heard from him."

And then shortly thereafter, my guts literally spilled out of my abdominal wall. So psychosomatic! So dramatic, like a Hispanic soap opera! At least my intestines could be pushed back in and my abdomen repaired with a simple mesh and some stitches. Why couldn't things with Joe be fixed that easily? Because there's no haberdashery department in the world that can fix a love affair, that's why. I now have a 4.5-inch diagonal scar above my belly button to remind me about spilling my guts both figuratively and literally. Little Max had left his mark; he was worth it. My emotions for Joe left their mark, too. I'm not sure if they were worth it.

Ten days after, I returned to Stockton to have my stitches removed. Of course, I saw Joe.

"Hi, my friend!" he exclaimed in an extra gentle and sweet tone as if I were super fragile because he now knew for sure that I had feelings for him.

"Guess what happened after I spilled my guts to you?"

"What?"

"I ended up with a hernia!" I lifted my shirt for him to see my war wound.

"Oh my God! Are you OK?"

"Yes, no big deal." I brushed it off as if I hadn't scrutinized it all. We spoke about the operation, healing time, lifting restrictions, and how he, too, had been born with a hernia and it was only a matter of time before it ruptured! Maybe that's the day he would spill his guts to me. I wouldn't hold my breath, like I had in utero. This was real life, and the odds were slim.

"Your letter made me feel really small," he said.

"Why? What part?"

"Where you said you thought I only wanted to get with you because you were 'safe,' quote unquote, and thinking you were only a booty call."

"Why would that make you feel small?"

"I've never used those words with you."

"But that's what I am, right?"

He couldn't or wouldn't answer that.

"It is what it is, Joe."

"I feel like a very small person if you think that's what I think it was."

Am I confused? So I'm not just a booty call? He's confused!

"It was never my intention to make you feel that way," I said.

"We'd pretty much discussed everything that was in that letter. It was just longer," he laughed.

"You mean I babbled on and on?"

"No," he said gently.

"I figured if I was gonna go down, I was going to give it my all."

"And you did!" And he gave me that smile he'd given me many times when he was proud of me.

If I'd expected a better outcome or response to my letter, I'd have been sadly mistaken. I guess that's why I'd felt all the disappointment the moment I gave it to him. Like I said, I knew I was the underdog in all of this. The friendly conversation and wide smile through that fucking drive-through window was the most he was able to give.

***

The next day that I saw him, he opened the window all the way and stuck his head out. "So I can hear you better," he said, anticipating another grand proclamation from me.

"I didn't say anything," I said.

"In case you do want to say something," he said. Was he looking for my exact instructions on how to leave his wife? I doubt it.

"I don't think there's really much left for me to say after that letter," I said laughing.

He chuckled. He knew I was right.

Neither one of us would get what we wanted from the other. He wouldn't have me as his lover, and I wouldn't have him as my boyfriend.

"I won't be seeing you much anymore," I said. I figured if I said it, I'd stick with it.

"Why?"

"I'll be busy with clinical rotation until graduation, and I need to buckle down and study to pass." And I needed to learn how to focus and do only one thing at a time. I couldn't continue going through life doing a million things *and* be thinking of Joe the whole time.

"I wish you good luck in everything, not that you need it. I shouldn't be here too much longer either."

"If you quit the coffee shop, let me know."

"I will. Take care."

"You, too."

That was yet another one of our good-byes. I went back to Oakland to finish the last four months of the nursing program. I stuck to my word; I didn't return to the shop until after graduation, a whole five months later. I concentrated on the last of my rotations, I meditated more, I read more, I drank more wine, and I went out more with my nursing friends. I kept busy every minute, and I counted down the weeks until graduation.

BEFORE MOVING ON

When I moved to Oakland, I'd bought twelve new toothbrushes to represent a countdown of every month that I had left until beginning my new nursing life. In May 2008, when I opened the very last toothbrush, I knew I was only mouthwashes away, not from deciding which hospitals to apply to but from deciding whether to see Joe.

The day after graduation, I moved back to Stockton. I'd live with my mom and Robert until I took the NCLEX (the nursing license exam) and got a job. I had applied to hospitals in Sacramento and had one interview lined up. I felt stronger, better, like I could resist Joe. It had been a whole five months since seeing him, a record for me! My heart felt so strong and whole, like it knew Lesson Number One—*Demand the very best. Don't settle for anything less.* Yet I couldn't resist going to see him. And I had to see him to test whether I'd truly learned Lesson Number One. At least that was my justification. I hoped that he was stronger, better, in his marriage. Or I hoped he was single and waiting for me. I wanted an absolute, one way or the other. I didn't want our previous mixture of marriage and infidelity, wanting and repressing. And since it takes two to tango, it would require only one of us not wanting absolutely anything from the other to keep us apart.

One week after arriving in Stockton, I made my way over to

the coffee shop. I parked my car, and I knew he saw me walking across the parking lot. He was tending to someone at the window, making small talk. He then turned to me, smiled, and said, "Are you all done now? A nurse now?"

"Almost. One more exam in three weeks." It was good to see him. I took a deep breath. The holes in my heart felt like they were healed. It was so good to see him. I took another deep breath. I saw him take a deep breath, and it was like he sucked the air out of my lungs to do so. Reminder to self: Lesson Number Three is *breathe*. Don't get sucked in.

He started making my drink before I even asked. He seemed nervous. He was. I saw his hands literally shaking. His adrenaline must have equaled mine. Then he started to ramble, as he did when he was nervous. I knew we were in *big* trouble. His mishmash of sentences made no sense. "I've been thinking of you, wondering how it's going. You forgot my birthday. You know I'm trying, trying to be *just* friends, and then you come in here."

"First of all, your birthday was a month ago. I did remember it. I was in Oakland taking a test."

"Yeah, but you didn't wish me a happy birthday."

"Happy birthday. How was it?"

"Thank you. It was the same old shit."

"Second, I just got back into town, and I thought we *were* friends. If you don't want me to come in here, say so."

"No, I do. That's the problem." He knew we were in *big* trouble.

And it was a problem that I could remedy by staying away. But this was Joe. Tahiti. Hallelujah!

"If you keep coming in here, we're going to end up wanting to see each other more," he said. It was his way of telling me to make the choice for both of us and to stop coming in so that this craziness would finally end, so that we could both move on, he to other lovers and I to…? I ignored his request.

We held out for three weeks. I was staying at my mom and Robert's home, in their guest room. If he came over and we were caught, I knew my mother would be livid and have me shot. But then I thought maybe once she saw with whom I was having sex, she'd say, "Oh, *him*, the guy from the coffee shop, the one with those beautiful eyes. I understand. Carry on, my daughter. Carry on." With that fantasy in my head, I gave him directions to the house.

The months apart only made everything far more intense, needy, and intimate. We talked and visited for a while. He was in no rush. I knew I needed him out of the house by half past five.

"You're beautiful," he said.

I giggled. I always felt silly being called "beautiful" by someone whose face defined the word. And aside from relatives, he was the only man to have ever called me beautiful. I believed he meant it. I thought about all those so-so women who were with hot men…but how did they *keep* them? That was my question.

"How come you've never once told me you find me attractive?" he asked.

"I haven't?"

"Never."

"Because every girl has already told you."

"But I want to hear it from you."

"I show you with my actions, not my words," I said.

"It would be nice to hear at least once."

I waited. It had been over two years since we'd met. I wanted to withhold my one last compliment about him from him a moment longer. It was the only control that I'd had since meeting him. We kissed. He smelled and tasted just as I remembered. We took a breather. We both remained silent, thinking.

My left hand rested on his chest, attempting to get as close to his heart as possible. My right hand caressed the back of his head and neck as I drew my face close to him.

"You are very handsome, Joe," I finally whispered into his right ear.

"Yeah?"

"You know that. I find you incredibly attractive, unlike any other."

He smiled, rubbed his nose against mine, and took a deep breath. Was he, too, learning to breathe, reminding himself to do so?

Somewhere in the middle of sex, I can't remember when or how, he removed the condom. I knew what he was thinking. I blurted out, "I'm ovulating." My mother was right; I was always either on my menstrual cycle or ovulating. My body let me know. Every month I had a deep, dull, and increasingly sharp pain in my right quadrant when I ovulated. I could literally feel that egg pushing its way through. "I'm not on birth control and you know I want a baby." *That will scare him!* But no, he nodded, kept silent, and then slipped himself into me as if there were nothing to fear. I looked at him. I didn't move. I was stunned by his naked gun. Perhaps he needed a few seconds to realize what he had done. So I remained completely still. I gave him time to remove himself. He was looking at me; he didn't say a word but closed his eyes and pulled me as close as he could to him. We had crossed the ultimate line. Sometime toward the end, he said he'd pull out. I trusted he would.

And how was sex with Joe sans condom? When you combine great conversation, intimate eye contact, comfort level, the many months of waiting, *and* sex with Joe, and the only thing missing was a condom—well, it was *decadent*. It was like being hand-fed a twelve-course gourmet meal, morsel by morsel. The French have a saying, "*Fromage ou dessert, mais pas les deux,*" meaning, "Cheese or dessert, but not both." It's gluttony to have both, yet I'd indulged in both. I was cruising my way through the list of cardinal sins—lust and gluttony, targeted in one shot. Then there were the Ten Commandments regarding infidelity. I felt like I had a bucket list of sins, and I was successfully checking each one off. It was wrong. It was true. It was Joe. My own private Tahiti. It was my own personal, resonating hallelujah.

I was drowning in a chorus of breathless, hauntingly melodic hallelujahs. Hallelujah. Hallelujah. He was serene. I was blindly lost in this turn of the kaleidoscope.

Five minutes later, in the shower, he was freaking out! "We

should never have done that!" he said.

"You put it in," I protested in my defense.

"I know I did!"

He grabbed the bar of soap and kept washing over my stomach, as if he could now wash away any possible conception occurring within me.

"What are you doing?" I ask.

"People can get pregnant with precum!" he said.

"Calm down! I knew you were going to regret this. Calm down. Don't worry. If anything happens, I won't bother you with it."

"No, we'll both deal with it."

"I told you, Joe. My God, you know how to ruin a good moment."

"We've crossed every line of inappropriateness...." I saw him there, aging with worry, or regret, naked and soapy in the shower. My beautiful Joe was aging under the running water right before my eyes. His DNA wasn't fighting back the worry. His kaleidoscope of gems slightly dulled under this bathroom light.

Two weeks passed before either of us mentioned our "inappropriateness." When I saw him, I said, "My period's due today."

"It would be an unfortunate situation if it doesn't come," he said.

Unfortunate? Of course it would be unfortunate—for him, for his family! He was only thinking of the consequences for him, not me, not the potential baby. Just him.

I was disgusted.

We changed the subject. He said he and his wife were looking into buying a house. He said it was her idea. He spoke about her like she was a pain in the ass.

"Does she get everything she wants?" I asked. I was in a foul mood.

"She expects and demands a lot. I go with the flow."

She had Lesson Number One down: *The brain and heart are the most demanding organs. They expect, and they receive, no less than what they demand.* I briefly allowed myself to admire her. "Don't you have a say? I mean, it's your life, too!"

"You'd think that's how it works. But if I don't agree, then I might as well get a divorce."

I didn't dare open my mouth. I had nothing nice to say. I knew I'd regret my words, which would be, "Then get a fucking divorce! Fucking get a divorce! Get a goddamn divorce! And get a backbone while you're at it. You have the fucking courage to have an affair without using a condom, but not stand up to what you want and don't want with your wife?" I was riled up inside. *I don't believe in love*, I thought. If he loved her, as he said he did, then no wonder I was no good in relationships. My idea of love was so far from his and hers. I could feel my period coming on; I didn't tell him. Let him ponder one more day on the possibility of my being pregnant. This was me with my hormones in command—mentally, emotionally, and physically enraged.

The next day I was even worse. Part of me wanted him to

know I was pissed off. I refused to make eye contact with him. Eye contact was a big deal for us, and I knew avoiding it would tell him exactly how I felt.

"What's wrong?" he asked.

"I have a lot on my mind."

"Sit down. Talk it out with me," he said as I started to leave. "You're gonna run away?" he asked.

"I'm not good company today. I wouldn't be a good listener for your stories today." *Stories, or excuses, of why you will never leave your wife.*

As I walked to my car, he stuck his head out the window. "Psst," he said, trying to get my attention.

I turned to look at him. He looked so sad and worried. I felt bad. Was I aging him?

"Have a good weekend," I said in my most upbeat voice.

He called me an hour later. "Are you OK?" he asked.

"I'm just having a bad day."

"I've never seen you like this before. You're always so bubbly. I've never seen you like this."

"I'll be fine," I reassured him.

"I just want you to feel better. I want you to know I'm here if you want to talk or not talk."

"You know how you have your bad days where you don't want to talk to anyone about anything?"

"Yes," he said.

"Well, I'm having one of those days. It'll be over by

tomorrow."

I know that what he was really worried about was that maybe I was pregnant. "I started my period, FYI, so you don't need to worry anymore," I said.

"I wasn't worried," he said.

Liar.

***

I was hired as a nurse after my first interview. I got a job at the hospital Diana worked at in Sacramento. She worked in the ER. I'd work on the fourth floor. I passed NCLEX and would start my new career, in a new town, in four weeks. I was relieved. I knew moving away would be my saving grace. It had to be.

Joe was happy for me and flashed me his proud-of-you smile. "Let's get together before you leave," he suggested.

My rage had subsided as it always did. It was the weakest link of my DNA. A little bit of lasting rage is always good, but I couldn't ever hold on to it that long. I was happy and feeling free-spirited, like I couldn't be hurt. Or rather, I felt I could protect myself from getting hurt.

""Sure. Since this will truly be our last time," I said, trying to convince myself.

"You never know what's gonna happen," he said suggestively.

But I did know. I would move away. He would move into a new home with his wife and her son, they would eventually have a baby, and they would learn to live with one another, or he'd continue to live in his self-proclaimed misery. I'd be a nurse, I'd eventually have a baby on my own, and I'd learn to live alone in my happiness. The only thing we would have in common would be that the past two years becoming but a nice memory to recall.

THE LAST ROUND, BEARING PARTING GIFTS

It was to be the last rendezvous between Joe and me before I headed a whole twenty-eight minutes north to live and work in Sacramento County. We were acting as if I were moving to Timbuktu with this celebratory going-away get-together. I knew my life had to start away from him and without him. Although we didn't officially term it "the last good-bye," we know that all good things (or even bad and naughty things, as it were) must come to an end at some time. Considering how comfortable we were becoming, how many lines we crossed, it was better that it ended now. He said he'd be about fifteen to twenty minutes late as he had an errand to run beforehand. I was impatient and hungry when it came to him. As far as I knew, it would be our last time together; I wanted those fifteen to twenty minutes. He was calm and smiling, arriving fifteen to twenty minutes later than our usual time.

"Where's your guitar?" he asked, heading straight to the living room, eyeing the guitar in the corner, and grabbing it.

Really? He's going to play guitar right now?

He sat down, still smiling. "Sit next to me," he said and motioned me to his left side, close to his heart. "I've been practicing and have learned a few songs." He started to strum some chords. I wanted him to strum me! This was our grand adios, our sweet au revoir, our last chance for romance!

"Greensleeves!" I called out quickly. *Let's get this game of Name That Tune over with ASAP.*

"Oh, you recognized it!" he said, proud of either his playing or my recognizing it.

Of course I recognized it. My first bachelor of arts was in music, and every musician, from an oboist to a pianist, learns "Greensleeves."

He started again with another song, the first few chords classic. "'Money' by Pink Floyd," I casually said.

"Look at you, naming out all the tunes so quickly."

"Well, that's an easy one. You play it very well." I grew up listening to Pink Floyd, Rush, and Zeppelin. I knew these songs better than anything currently on the radio. Yet I was impressed by my Joe.

"I've been practicing every night," he said, still smiling.

Is this how our last day was going to be? He could read my mind as always. He bent down to give me a kiss on the lips. "Be patient," he said, smiling.

"I am," I whined. Maybe the moment would last longer if we delayed the final crescendo.

I pulled out the book I bought him, *The Four Agreements* by Ruiz. "It's something we both need to start practicing. We've been bad," I said.

"Look, I have something for you. This is why I was fifteen minutes late." He pulled a thin rectangular box from his back pocket. It was a guitar tuner.

"I love it!" I was smiling now. "That was very thoughtful of you."

"Just a little going-away gift," he said, then started instructing me on how to use it. So this was an official "going away"? My heart missed a beat with the reality of our separation setting in.

I'd only been given two gifts by men before. And those two gifts were also parting gifts. My very first gift was from my first boyfriend. A month before breaking up with me, he gave me a long rectangular box. It was a one-handed blender for making smoothies. I should have known then that he didn't plan to stick around, as the one-handed blender was designed for single people to make exactly one smoothie right inside the glass you were going to drink out of. I was twenty-one years old at the time. I think I used the one-handed blender a couple of times and then donated it to Goodwill. If I'd known I was going to be single for decades, I'd have kept it! Maybe that boyfriend could see my future better than me.

Jump eleven years later to age thirty-two. I'd been dating Jon, a fireman. Jon was thirteen years my senior, and our relationship was a great friendship but even more so a father-daughter relationship. When he took me to Dodgers games, I always felt like he was taking his little girl to the "big game," treating me to garlic fries and a Dodger Dog. We always had a great time but never in an intense, romantic sort of way. I almost felt like he was simply looking for a companion, the way a seventy-nine-year-old widower looks for a companion. A week prior to my leaving Los Angeles to study abroad, we met at a coffee shop during my lunch break. He handed me a little box. Inside were square diamond earrings. They were beautiful, delicate, and not flashy. I liked those earrings and thought he was incredibly generous. He mentioned how proud he was, "going off all by yourself to another country." I felt like a daughter graduating from high school, headed for college. And then he said, "I'm going to miss my friend." And there you have it. I knew that's all we were—friends. I'd entered the friend zone with this man, as I would with so many to come.

Do I still have the earrings? No, unfortunately I lost one somewhere in my cousin's home whose wife has the real deal, big, flashy diamond earrings. I'm sure that either their housekeeper vacuumed my sweet little earring up or my cousin's wife came across it and thought, *I don't remember buying these little earrings. Is this even a real diamond?* and tossed it aside.

I've never cared about gifts as much as how I felt with someone. And that's what always made Joe stand out. With Joe I felt like a woman and like a little girl; I felt smart, sexy, silly, and strong. That's when a woman feels like a complete woman, when she can feel the full spectrum of what makes up the very nature of being a woman. *This is what Cleopatra must have felt like with Julius Caesar or Mark Antony*, I thought. Joe always told me how much he believed in me, no matter what I said I wanted to do. When he was with me, I knew that was where he wanted to be, that he wouldn't be wasting his time otherwise. And yes, he did leave me each time to return home to a wife. I didn't need to be reminded of that. But when we were together, he was present. He made eye contact (big on my list), he listened, he was patient with me and my crazy thoughts that I rambled on about. And that look in his eyes when he wanted me, or when we lay there not saying a word—those moments can't be bought, and those were the gifts I wanted from him, from anyone.

But for now I accepted his going-away gift, a guitar tuner.

"Maybe the next time I see you, I'll know how to play guitar as well as you," I said. My heart was weakening. It fluttered like it couldn't make a full beat; it started to worry. It needed to know if there would be a next time, needed a reason to beat normally again. It needed to know if those holes it was feeling would be repaired. I still stick to my belief that the heart makes adjustments to keep you breathing and the blood flowing. That's compensation. Mere compensation.

He laughed and said, "And maybe I'll speak Spanish as well as you." These "maybe" predictions sounded more like "and maybe there will be no next time. Or maybe when pigs fly."

If this was our last time, I didn't want to be sad. Or at least I didn't want to show him that deep down I was crumbling. I'd never touch anybody as beautiful as Joe. How could anybody compare? No one could compare. Joe remained out of everyone's league as far as beauty and the calm quiet soul that he carried.

He placed the guitar down, grabbed my hand, said, "Come on," and led me to the bedroom. I was an impatient little girl at this moment. I wanted him all to myself, to hold him close, to stare into those eyes and keep my face as close to his face as possible. I didn't even want to share him with the rest of my body, if that makes any sense. He was for my soul, not my body. I placed his beautiful face in my hands. I used the tips of my fingers, my eyelashes, and my nose to trace my favorite bilateral bones on him, the zygomatic arches, his cheekbones. They were sturdy, high, and strong. They were so typically Native American, and I was drawn to them. It was all I could do not to break down crying. I wanted to remember every moment. And when we're in the moment, we really think we'll remember how every touch feels, the sound of the other person's laughter, exactly how his mouth looks smiling—but we don't. The brain only remembers glimpses, and imagination fills in the remainder. That's why all history is truly historical fiction. I wondered what I'd remember, what I'd forget. For the moment, I tried to appear happy for him.

We'd promised to use a condom. And it started out that way. Not even midway through, he removed it. "I want to really feel you," he said.

"Are you sure?" I was giving him an out.

"Yes, it's okay," he said and proceeded.

The final good-bye wasn't mushy, not weepy, not even visually sad. It was lighthearted. I didn't receive a lecture about pregnancy. We embraced at the front gate.

"See you later," he said.

"See you later," I whispered, more to myself than to him. We'd had so many good-byes in this relationship that I thought they would have been getting easier.

A few months later, Diana ran into Joe. The topic turned to

us, and she gave him her time and again a speech of how he let the best thing walk out of his life. He mentioned that he and I ended things well and that we both were moving on fine now.

"How do you know she's fine?" she said to purposely raise doubt in his mind.

"What do you mean?" he questioned. "She seemed fine that last time. She seemed happy." That's what he remembered, what I wanted him to remember.

My cousin added, "You don't know that for sure, though. You never asked her."

But any last-ditch effort on her part or my part didn't matter. I wanted to let go. I wanted to move on. I didn't want to have an affair ever again. I'd have to work through what I felt for him. And I hoped I could.

JARED

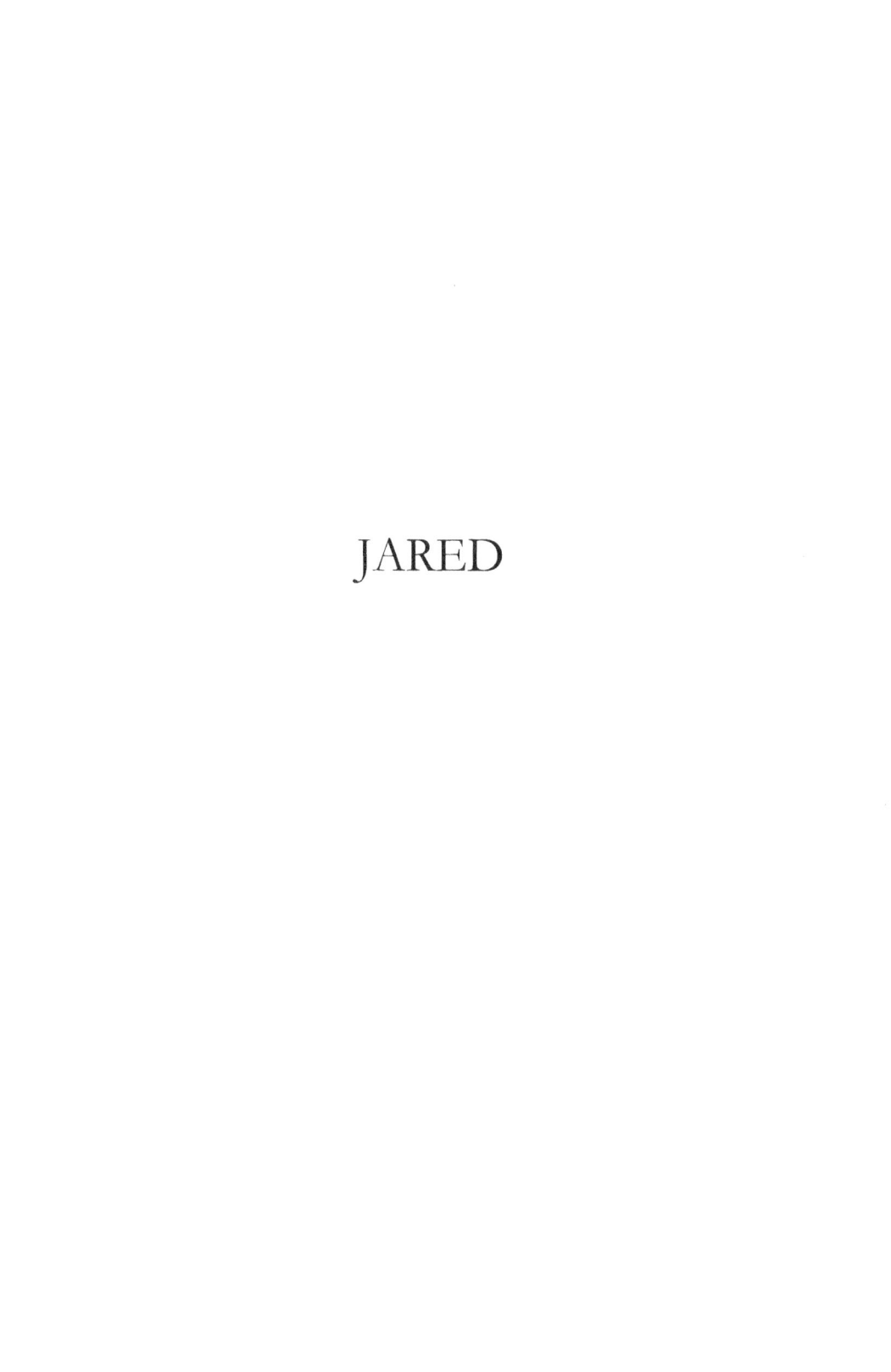

WOW!

I met Jared in September 2008, within weeks of starting my nursing career. I was on day-shift orientation and stopped by the emergency room to pick up some Costa Rican coffee beans Diana had bought me. When I saw her, she said, "Oh, I want you to meet this doctor. He's newly divorced." This was her way of saying he was available. I hated being introduced to people "to see if you guys might like one another." Jared, a thin, young-looking guy, came up to us and said, "I hear you're quite the gypsy."

"I was, but not so much anymore," I said.

My cousin had obviously told him that I'd lived in Los Angeles, Brazil, France, Mexico, Arizona, Oakland, back to Stockton, and now Sacramento, all in a matter of four years. Either I *was* a gypsy, or I was completely lost.

Then there was some small talk about nursing up on the floor. I can't recall much thereafter. I had no initial thoughts about Jared or lasting impressions. I was sure he felt the same way. Several days later Diana said he'd asked, "So what did your cousin say about me?"

"Nothing," she'd told him.

"But what about my blue eyes?" he'd asked.

"What about them?" she'd asked, knowing full well what he meant.

"Did she like them?"

"She didn't mention anything."

He'd seemed confused at the thought of this, according to Diana. I couldn't recall his blue eyes. He told her he'd like to take me out. This went on for a few months. Finally, in January, I told her to give him my number. I couldn't remember what he looked like, and I didn't know why I wasn't going out. I knew I needed to get out. I knew I'd never find another Joe. I knew the time to move on was well overdue, and here I was, not doing so. She told Jared that I didn't know Sacramento, so I'd enjoy going out with someone who could show me around downtown. Why did I need someone to show me around downtown when I'd shown myself around everywhere from *les arrondissements* of Paris to the Pelourinho district of Salvador, Brazil? Because I needed to start behaving like a girl in need, needed to be taken out and needed to put Joe in a far, locked corner of my heart and mind. It was about time I started living Lesson Number One: *The heart and brain are the most demanding of organs.*

I didn't receive a phone call from Jared but rather a text asking if I'd like to go to Second Saturday in downtown Sacramento. Second Saturday occurs, well, every second Saturday of the month. The art galleries stay open late and are free of charge. It's a great way to walk the streets and have drinks between art galleries. I thought it would be a nice first date. He texted me that he'd meet me on some random corner downtown and I was to "wear something sexy."

I was immediately turned off and wanted out of the date. First of all, would a quick phone call to touch base have taken too much time or effort? I knew I was behind the times when it came to texting. I figured this was how dates occurred now and I needed not to be so picky! And while I was overlooking things, I had to overlook that he wouldn't be picking me up but would instead be meeting me on some corner. This was nothing like my hook-up arrangements with Joe, which were simple. Dating married men was so much easier, but I had to go on this date. I took into consideration the little tidbits Diana had told me about him: he had three children, he had lots of female friends, he had a great sense of humor—be ready to laugh all night. I figured the "wear something sexy" comment was his sense of humor, and I texted back, "I'll wear what I want."

Diana was working with him when he received my text. She said he laughed at my response. I really didn't want to meet him on any corner. My old-fashioned ways overruled, and I told Diana that I felt odd meeting him downtown on a corner, especially because I couldn't remember what he looked like. Despite my worldly travels, all of a sudden I wanted this to be like a real date, wherein he'd pick me up and drive us to wherever we were going. Diana told him that I didn't know downtown and that was the point of my *going out* with him, not *meeting up* with him. He agreed to pick me up.

***

It was now Saturday. I'd yet to speak with Jared by phone. He texted me that he was on his way. I went down to the parking area of my complex, and he jumped out of his car. My first impression: *He's not my type (he's not Joe), but he looks like a really nice guy.* He seemed so small compared to Joe, but I really didn't want to think of Joe. So I put those thoughts away and said to myself, *You want to have a good time tonight, and this man deserves to have a good time, too. Let Joe go, at least for tonight.*

Within five minutes of our being in the car, Jared told me that he didn't have as much money anymore due to his and his wife's separation. I wanted to say, "No worries, I can pay my own way." But I refrained. And separated? I thought they were divorced. I checked him out while he drove. Light skin, brown hair, thin lips, and a cute nose. I liked his nose for some reason. The tip was round, which gave him a boyish look. It was too dark to see his blue eyes that he was so proud of. But I saw he had some bushy, caterpillar-looking eyebrows! But I did, too, up until the eleventh grade, when I discovered tweezers.

We reached downtown and entered a few art galleries. He was easy to talk to. I liked him. He had a very casual way about him, and he loved to talk—nonstop. Despite the fact that he told me all about why he and his wife split, how I was his third date this week, and how he could always use the "I have to get home so the babysitter can leave" excuse to get out of a date, there was something I did like about him. He was witty and sincere in a naïve, boyish sort of way.

We were enjoying a nice glass of wine when he said some friends of his were over at a club, walking distance from where we were, and since he hadn't known whether this was a date or not, he'd told them he might join them. This wasn't a date? I thought it was. OK, I'd been out of the dating scene far too long. No phone calls, had to ask to be picked up, and even my date wasn't sure if this was a date. I was confused—and a bit disappointed. I thought he'd been asking me out all this time. Had my cousin arranged this? Had she told him I wanted a tour guide and asked if he was available to lead the way for one Saturday evening? Did she want me to have a night not thinking of Joe? I felt like a fool. "I thought it was a date," I admitted.

"Oh, OK. And if it was a date, I wasn't sure how much alone time I wanted with you before having to meet them, so I told them I didn't know."

"OK." But was it OK? I was thoroughly confused about this date that I might or might not be on.

Walking through the streets, Jared would on occasion place his hand on my back and guide me through the crowd. I liked that. Joe and I weren't able to touch in public; that's why our eye communication was always so intense. That's why he had the ability to read my mind. But here, being guided by a man—this was new to me. We didn't have to hide. Jared touched me and didn't seem afraid to do so. He was comfortable, but this wasn't or isn't something that I can claim for myself. I'd later learn Jared was comfortable with anyone, anywhere. I was glad that at the time, I didn't know that it was his nature.

When we crossed the street, he wrapped his arm around my

waist to hold me back until he thought it was safe to cross. "I can use saving you from an oncoming car as a reason to touch you. Do you mind?" I thought his openness, his inability to keep his thoughts secret, was funny. No games, I hoped.

"No, I don't mind at all," I reassured him.

There were two moments in the course of the night that I started to find him attractive. The first was at an art gallery showcasing photography of men's and women's bodies. I asked, "So what kind of art do you like?"

He replied, "I don't know, but I do know that I like boobs," as he stared head on and wide-eyed at a photograph of a lady's bare chest. His delivery was perfect, funny. I knew he meant no harm. What man doesn't like boobs?

We met up with his friends at the club. I guess he'd had enough alone time with me. They flocked to him to joke with him, to whisper something in his ear, to ask medical advice. He was the center of attention, and he knew how to be. He worked the crowd like a hummingbird, moving from one flower to the next, getting the most nectar out of each, making each feel like he or she was the sweetest or funniest. But I could tell that he wanted to be the most clever and amusing.

And when the hummingbird, Jared, finally found a small space to perch next to me and entertain those seated, I placed my hand on the small of his back, due to lack of space and maybe to signal that I liked him. I can still feel the texture of his shirt. It was brown and made of eyelet fabric, and I liked the feel of it against the palm of my hand. I don't know why, but feeling it gave me a sense of security—I've never demanded much. It was my Linus blanket. The shirt was rough and soothing to the mild anxiety that I'd catch myself having. Yes, there was mild anxiety in knowing that I was having a good time without Joe.

I was observing Jared's profile; he was laughing out loud (LOL, literally) at one of his own witty remarks and smiling widely. I liked what I saw. He looked at me and kissed me lightly on the corner of my mouth.

He took me back home, parked his car, jumped out, and said, "And yes, I'm coming up to your apartment, even though you haven't invited me."

I was excited about it. Finally, someone who wasn't afraid, someone who had his shit together. How lucky was I? I poured us a glass of ten-dollar Mark West Pinot Noir, a favorite from nursing school. I was nervous; I knew he knew his wine, or so I'd perceived throughout the course of the night, and for me, this was my go-to wine. But I thought it was fabulous and hoped he did, too. I gave him my disclaimer: "It's only a ten-dollar wine, but I like it. If you don't like it, don't feel you need to drink it." He swirled it around in the glass the way they do in the movies and, I'm guessing, at wine tastings. I wouldn't know; although I was only two hours from Napa, I'd never been wine tasting. He held it up to his boyish bulb-tipped nose, inhaled deeply, and took a delicate sip.

"It's nice," he said.

I breathed a sigh of relief.

"You seemed a bit nervous about the wine," he said.

"I was," I admitted.

"It's good."

Good.

I had the smallest sectional couch in history, similar to my army-cot-sized bed in Stockton. The couch wasn't even six feet long, yet it was a sectional. The chaise lounge part couldn't have been more than three feet. It was an odd couch, but it fit nicely in my apartment, and I'd bought it with me in mind. I'm five foot (on a great day), so it was a petite couch for a petite lady. Now this couch was to hold me *and* Jared. I thought he might have been five foot nine (on a good day). He was definitely on the smaller side of the men I've dated, but without a doubt on the more aggressive side.

We made out that first night on my tiny couch. All clothing remained on and intact. He loved to bite, and there was no disclaimer promising not to, unlike the way Joe had promised. Jared liked kissing and to be kissed on the neck.

"I love necking, it feels so good," he said, "but there's such a stigma with hickeys."

"Right, so don't give me one," I said.

He bit me on my shoulder, leaving a pinkish-red bite mark on my white skin. "You have such soulful eyes," he said.

"Like a jazz singer?" I asked. Why I think of jazz singers as having soulful eyes I don't know; I just do. Now I was close enough to notice that he did have blue eyes.

"Yeah, I guess," he said. "It's just the way you look at me

with them. Soulful."

I liked the compliment; it was different.

"I like your nose," I said.

"My nose?"

"Yes, it's cute."

"Oh my God, it's one o'clock in the morning! I lost track of time. I have a babysitter and said I'd be home in a few hours! I gotta go." Was this true? Earlier hadn't he told me he could always use the babysitter excuse as a reason to get out of a date?

"OK."

No lingering kisses at the door. No, "I'll call you later," just a, "Thanks, I had a nice time," from me to him.

And he left. But I was certain I'd hear back from him. And I did, the next day.

He'd spent the day in San Francisco with his kids and was home now. The kids were asleep, and he invited me over. He told me to walk in. I felt completely uncomfortable doing that, but he refused to answer the door when I texted him from the porch. I walked in; he never rose to greet me, not then, not ever (a pet peeve I'll always have). He was resting on his couch, his legs outstretched and his feet on an ottoman.

"I've poured you a glass of wine," he said. "Come sit next to me."

He showed me pictures of his day at the museum with the kids. He told me he told his best friend about my soulful eyes. I laughed. His friend had said, "You've never had a girl look at you like that before?"

He told his friend, "No, this is different."

I saw Jared every day that first week. He came over after work; I made us an early dinner. We met in the surgery waiting room during my lunch break at four in the morning when he was working the overnight shift, too. He said he told his best girlfriend, a coworker, about me and she told him to slow down. I didn't laugh. Must he obtain a consensus from all his friends? I'd yet to call any of my friends to let them know about this guy named Jared that I might or might not be dating.

I learned more about him, as he was open about everything. He said he bought the house a few houses down from his for the ex-wife. "That way the kids can go back and forth. It makes it easy, and she and I are on good terms."

Hmm, an ex living only a few houses down? "You must be on good terms, if you don't mind her living so close."

"No, no problems. She was actually the one babysitting the first night we went out. I'd told her I'd be home at an appropriate hour, like eleven. So she was pissed off when I walked in past one in the morning. She said, 'This isn't an appropriate hour, Jared!'"

I said nothing. What did I know about marriage or divorce? I'd had neither, and they only go hand-in-hand.

At the end of the week, he had to work an overnight shift and said he could sleep at my place after. I said that was fine. I didn't have to work that night, but I'd stay up through the night so that I'd be tired and fall asleep with him in the morning.

We texted throughout the night. I felt like a young schoolgirl again, but this time, with my emotions unbroken. It felt great. He said that coming over gave him something to look forward to after a long night. He texted me not to feel any pressure to do anything that I didn't want to do, that he didn't expect anything.

He came over and immediately hit the shower. I waited in bed. He came out and said he needed to turn off his phone. He had a missed message from his ex-wife, he said. After listening to the message, he said, "Let me text her real quick. She said she drove past my house and didn't see my car and is worried. I'll text her I'm fine, or else she'll keep calling." Really?

"She must still care deeply about you," I said. *Great*, I thought.

"Of course she does; I'm her cash cow. That's the only reason."

He made his way over, naked, but I didn't have my contacts or glasses on, so he was one big blur approaching me. If he meant to impress me with his manhood, I wouldn't have known—my vision was a negative 8.00, bilaterally. He continued talking about the different life insurance policies they'd had when they were married. "I commuted to the Bay Area a lot, so if I'd been killed while en route to work, this one life insurance would have paid her very well," he said.

"Interesting," was all I could say. My mom's friend says that when you have nothing nice to say or when you don't know what to say, just say, "Interesting." It fits all situations perfectly.

"Interesting," I repeated. He got in bed and snuggled close to kiss.

"Do you think we should, so soon?" I asked.

"I know women think that if you have sex right away, then the relationship won't last. I don't believe in that. When you decide to have sex has no bearing on how long a relationship will last. It either works out or it doesn't."

I agreed with him to an extent. I knew girls that ended up marrying their one-night stands.

"Don't compare me with your previous guys," he said. Then he added, "I don't want to use a condom with you."

"Aren't you afraid of having unprotected sex?"

"No, I'm careful with whom I choose and I don't just have sex with anyone. I might kiss anyone, but I don't have sex with anyone."

He spent the night—or morning rather—and we did have sex. Immediately after, I said, "Well, you got what you wanted," meaning unprotected sex.

I could tell he didn't like this response. He was quiet, then said, "What can I do so you're not sad? Can I hang that frame on the wall for you?" referring to a large *Ashes and Snow* framed print that sat against my wall.

Then he fell asleep, and I did, too. In the afternoon, we woke up and he got dressed. I walked him to the door.

"So will I hear from you later?" I asked jokingly, or not.

"Yes," he said. "Then I'll start distancing myself, and you'll ask your cousin who I'm dating now."

Are you kidding me? I couldn't tell whether he was kidding. I didn't find it funny. "No, I won't," I said in response.

"You won't?"

"Absolutely not," I insisted.

"I'll call you later," he said and walked out.

And he did. I visited him at his home, and we went out to dinner the following week. But something had changed. He repeated how his friend advised him to "slow down".

"Your cousin told me that you want a baby and that it's a deal breaker for you," Jared mentioned one night on the phone.

"Ask me, not my cousin, what's a deal breaker for me," I said.

"Well, do you want a baby?"

"Yes, I do. It's all I ever wanted."

"I wish it wasn't. But you should have a baby if that's what you want. I wouldn't change having had my kids for anything."

Where this conversation was going was unspoken, but I knew: he was done having kids, a wife, a marriage, now or in the immediate future.

He stopped calling daily. This was the distancing he'd forewarned me about. He had not been kidding. A few days later, he mentioned he threw a poker party and hadn't invited me because he didn't think I liked poker. He made that assumption without ever asking me.

He finally mentioned he wasn't ready to be in another relationship. He was newly divorced—or separated, whatever—and he didn't want to get tied down. He wanted to date around and mentioned how surprised he was when one girl said no to his date request simply because he had kids. He was already asking out other women? I later learned he was; it was a nurse that worked in another unit at the hospital.

"Have you kissed another girl already?" I asked.

"Not yet," he said nonchalantly.

I felt disappointed, not in him but in myself. Was this the best I could do? Date a few weeks?

"Well then, I guess that's it," I said.

"Well, we can still be friends, go out to lunch," he said.

Yeah, friendship and lunch—was that the booby prize?

He called later that week asking me out to dinner.

"Why? I thought you made your choice already," I said.

"Do you have to be all or nothing?" he asked.

"Well, I know what I want." And I did. After two years of being stuck on Joe, I wanted a real relationship. *The head and heart should not settle for anything less, damn it!*

"Let's just go out to dinner."

We did, and it was nice. We went to a French restaurant and then after went for a drink and foie gras, which I didn't like. I didn't like the idea of those poor ducks, and I didn't like the taste. I felt he liked it only because it was French and I felt bad for having tried it. He came over afterward and we started kissing.

"We can't have sex," he said.

"OK, why?"

"We just shouldn't," he said.

We were lying on the living room floor. We got up and headed to the bedroom. We were now naked. "Just touch and rub, no sex," he said. I didn't say anything. This guy was a tease! We started having sex.

"OK, we can't have orgasms," he said.

"What?"

"No, we shouldn't orgasm, just sex."

That had to be the most ridiculous statement I'd ever heard. Sex with the intent of *not* having an orgasm? I was a woman, and women had to take them whenever they came, literally and figuratively speaking. I wasn't sure if I even would have one, but I wouldn't try not to not have one. Is that right? Not try to not have one? Correct, that's what I'd do, *not* try to *not* have one. It's confusing trying to formulate the sentence, much less understand the reasoning. He provided no reason, but he wanted me to *try* to not have one, to hold back. He was crazy.

Despite all the instruction from him and confusion in my brain, we both failed. It was one of the better episodes between us.

Jared said he wanted to make me *moules et frites* for dinner the following week. He was obviously fascinated by French cuisine. He said he had a recipe that was great and went on about its simplicity yet outstanding taste. He mentioned several times that the "simplicity to taste ratio is amazing." I picked up premade French fries on the way to his house.

Like clockwork, the kids were fast asleep. The awesome-simplicity-to-taste-ratio dinner was nearly done. We popped the fries in the oven for heating. We prepped our places at the counter and made small talk. He was quieter than usual. I knew his mind was brewing, but with what? Another girl? Or how to tell this girl, me, something? I was getting mixed cues. He'd kiss me here and there. We served ourselves; he fed me French fries. Jared thinks it's acceptable to feed women from his own hand or fork. It's a personality trait he shows *all* his women, and it means nothing. Well, in *Jared-pedia*, it means, "Open your mouth so I can put this piece of food in it, and I'll make you feel special, even though I do this with every woman." And it works every time!

We watched television, drank wine, and headed for bed.

"Do you like my lamp?" he asked as he ran his fingers through the strings of small circular shells that hung from it.

"Yeah, it's pretty."

"I like the sound it makes when the air from the ceiling fan hits it."

"Nice," I said.

We'd been in bed maybe twenty minutes, having pillow talk, listening to his lamp beads make their soft noise.

"On a scale of one to ten, how would you rate yourself?" he asked.

I gave it a thought, taking a moment to calculate my features and personality.

"Never mind," he said. "I don't want to hear your self-deprecation."

"I was just thinking," I said. He never gave me a chance to respond.

"I think I'm about a seven and a half, based on looks. But with personality, I give myself a nine," he said.

He was confident.

"What was your first impression of me?" he asked. I knew he was fishing for a compliment.

My first impression of him was that he wasn't my type. That wouldn't be nice to say, so I told him what my second impression of him was. "That you looked like a really nice guy. What was your first impression of me?"

"That you weren't my type," he said with no brain filter.

Likewise, I thought.

"So we weren't each other's type," I stated.

"Well, as the night progressed, I found you more attractive."

Likewise.

There was a small knock and voice outside the bedroom door. "Daddy," a little girl's voice said. It was his daughter. He jumped up and threw on his shorts.

"Hold on! I don't want her to see you," he said.

"Do you want me to hide in the closet?" I suggested.

"Yeah, it'll take me just a second to put her back in bed."

I'm not sure if I meant it when I asked him if he wanted me to hide. But I jumped up anyway and ran into his walk-in closet. He opened the door and picked his daughter up to take her back to her bedroom.

This was an ultimate low point.

I stood there, naked, with his shoes, hanging shirts, pants, belts, and some scrubs. I passed the time looking at his different shirts. I found the brown one he wore our first night out, the one made of eyelet fabric, and caressed it against the palm of my hand for comfort. I wanted to cry but didn't. I reminded myself that I'd been through worse with Joe. But Joe never made me feel humiliated. I had to hide with Joe, too, but never naked in a closet.

"She's fine," he said when he returned. "Looking at my shirts?" he asked.

"Yeah," I said and was glad it was dark enough that he couldn't see my expression.

We got back in bed. *The night will get better*, I tried to convince myself.

There we were, lying next to each other, naked. I felt it—something—coming.

"I just want someone that I'm *wowed* by," he said.

Where this comment came from I can't recall. This "What the fuck?" moment wasn't what I predicted.

"And I don't do that for you?" I asked, afraid of the answer.

He looked me right in the eye and, without a blink or second thought, said, "No, you don't *wow* me."

Crushed, shattered, devastated? I don't know. In moments like this, you can't focus on anything else but the words, the structure, the tone, the delivery. *Did he say that I don't* wow *him? Yes, he did. Did he say this after we made out, as I'm lying next to him completely naked in his bed? Yes, he did.*

"Then I should leave," I said.

"Why?" he stupidly asked.

"Because I feel like a fool." *Why the fuck do you think?*

"Don't."

"I'm gonna go."

"No, I'm not going to let you. It's late. Sleep here tonight."

"I don't feel comfortable now," I said.

"But then I'm going to have to walk you out, and I don't want to get out of bed."

Wow!

"No, you don't have to get up," I said as I rolled away from him to leave.

He pulled me close. "Just sleep here tonight," he said and held me closely.

I felt trapped in the arms of the man that I didn't wow. I could barely breathe. I couldn't sleep. He fell asleep quickly. I stared at him, then the ceiling, then him, and back again.

The words, "You don't *wow* me," were on repeat in my head. Had I heard it right? I heard nothing else, not the fan spinning above, not the lampshade made of dangling seashells, mother-of-pearl, or some other noisy crap that he loved, not his breathing right next me, not my own breathing. Was I breathing? I was suffocating, drowning, in his words of rejection, which repeated heavily as an endless, torturous echo.

It's known that there's a fine line between love and hate. I'd like to add there's also a fine line between a man telling you his honest feelings and a man being an asshole. I'd yet to determine on which side of the line Jared stood.

    It's in moments like these that you know you will never be the same. You try to digest what you've heard, try to analyze what it means. What *will* it mean as you carry on? Words and jabs like this were not the first, nor the last, to come out of this man toward me. Out of all the things I've ever been called by anyone—needy, picky, uptight, sensitive, too giving, cold, over-analytical, motherly—this phrase would become the most memorable. I'd walk out on the street, see strangers, and think, "I probably could never wow you, or you…or you."

    The W Hotel has a service called Whatever/Whenever. Guests can call this concierge hotline to get help from something as basic as getting a preferred toothpaste delivered to his or her room to arranging a private jet to take his or her friends to a private beach. The hotel's intention is to wow its guests with its customer-service ability. I wanted to squirm myself out of Jared's peacefully sleeping body and call the Whatever/Whenever hotline and demand a few things. First, a quick lesson on how to wow a man. Second, a therapist to deal with this ego blow.

    The following week, Diana spoke to Jared's best friend, who also worked in the ER, about the whole situation. He mentioned to Diana that it sounded like I had some emotional issues. I was pissed! The audacity! If pissed off was the emotion he was referring to, then yes, I had some emotional issues. Diana said that Jared had the gall to break up with me as he was still inside of me.

"Oh, I wasn't aware of that," the best friend said.

I then received a pissed-off telephone message from Jared saying how dare I lie about being dumped while having sex, that (a) it wasn't true and (b) it made him look really bad. I didn't call him back, but I did send him a long e-mail stating that I never said it was during sex. I guess he forgot that it was while we were in bed naked, though. But I guess *that* didn't matter. I simply wished him the best. I mentioned that I didn't appreciate that he told his friend that I had "emotional issues." He didn't respond.

Looking back at Jared, I realize he never wowed me either. But he had convinced me he had through his charm and charisma, because he was full of it, literally and figuratively speaking. He'd convinced me that he was fascinating, that he spoke of interesting topics, that he was hilarious and quick witted. He worked hard at it, and he was good at it. It's all in the presentation, baby! And his presentation was right on. I bet he'd be great on a debate team, and I really couldn't debate him on the topic of himself.

He reminded me of the commercials for the Mexican beer Dos Equis. They're a series of tongue-in-cheek commercials about The Most Interesting Man in the World, who prefers to drink Dos Equis when he does drink. My favorite of the many commercials is the one where the police pull over The Most Interesting Man in the World, for no legitimate reason, just to question him because they find him that interesting. Jared thought that highly of himself. I didn't know whether to fall for or be turned off by his arrogance. Maybe it wasn't a matter of either at that point but more of a matter of repairing my damaged ego.

Even if Jared was the most interesting man in Elk Grove, if not in the world, I couldn't help but take the "You don't *wow* me" phrase so deeply personally. What was I supposed to have done? Speak every language I knew to him, write him poetry, serenade him, laugh at his every joke? What? So he thought I had emotional issues. I must have, for putting up with all that shit!

I thought I'd hear from Jared after the "You don't *wow* me" episode subsided. *He doesn't know what he's missing*, I thought. But when you're a young, confident doctor, and girls, nurses, emergency room patients are all potential dates—well, there would be no follow-up phone call, e-mail, text, or related conversation between us. I wouldn't get to know his friends, and I probably wouldn't get to know Sacramento. I knew I was a homebody; I was a typical Cancer, a crab stuck in her shell, and I had been counting on him to drag me out to enjoy the city. Now that I felt like I couldn't entice anyone, I had even more of an excuse to stay home. My nightly outing was arriving at work at 10:40 p.m. Thank God I worked the night shift. It gave me additional reasons to stay home on my nights off.

I parked in lot eight and saw Jared's Passat parked in the physician parking area. And then I saw it—the Yakima car rack mounted on his car. I'd always noticed it, but now I really saw it. I had an epiphany, a mild one, but yet an epiphany. I *was* too plain Jane, as my brother calls me, for Jared. A Yakima car rack on anyone's car makes a statement. It says, "I'm athletic, I climb rocks, I own a bike (and I use it!), I possibly kayak, canoe, camp, and I definitely have a season snow ski pass, and"—like the Yakima website proclaims—"I *ride off into a different sunset every weekend.*"

I, Julie, didn't do any of those things. Not one. I was boring. I wanted to do all those things, I really did. But I couldn't imagine going to some lake and renting a canoe for one and paddling myself out into the water. I'd feel even more pathetic doing it alone—and I could only imagine the exhaustion. It's not the same as eating dinner alone, which I have no problem doing. Birds of the same feather flock together; I had no friends who'd plan such a day of activity and go through with it.

I needed new friends. I thought back to the night at the club, with Jared surrounded by friends, laughing, having a blast. That's what I craved, not a new social network but an active one. I wanted to discover the hiking trails. I wanted to ride a bike and justify buying the helmet, water bottle, and little backpack for trail mix and energy bars. These were the reasons I didn't impress him, or at least that's how it clearly seemed to me at 10:40 p.m. as I was walking into work. My socializing, activity level, and weight lifting consisted of running between patients' rooms on 4 West. It was stretching high up to hang an IV fluid bag. It was rolling a 245-pound patient to his left side status-post total right-hip replacement to place him on a bedpan. It was hearing a patient talk about anything from her grandchildren to her chemotherapy treatments.

I'd never have a reason to buy a Yakima car rack. Just as other girls loved Louis Vuitton handbags to make a statement about money, fashion, or whatever (I've yet to figure that one out), I wanted a Yakima car rack to pretend that I had an active lifestyle. But that would make me quite the fraud. But like the saying, "Build it and they will come," maybe, somehow, if I placed the rack on the car, I'd attract active opportunities—like being invited to go parachuting. Without it, I'd continue to drive my four-door Toyota Camry, which to me states, "I care about reliability and my family," although I was now feeling reckless and had no baby to place in the backseat. And, I reminded myself, a baby is what I wanted, man or no man.

I called my friend Liliana and told her my Yakima-car-rack epiphany.

"That's not true," she countered.

"But it *is* true. He and I are two different people. He's active and I'm not. I'm boring. I can see why I don't wow him. If he were to go skiing with me, he'd have to spend the whole time on the bunny slopes teaching me. And you know how I hate the cold."

"If he liked you, then he'd want to teach you."

"Then that goes back to the fact that he doesn't like me. Hence, why I'm at home and he's God-knows-where hauling his fun equipment on that Yakima car rack, with some exciting chick in the passenger seat."

"Then he's not the one."

"But that's the lifestyle I want, and I don't know anyone else who does all those things and has a good job and is smart."

"You have to do it for yourself, Julie."

"I feel like such a loser, so fucking pathetic. Seeing that rack on his car put everything into perspective."

"Julie." That was all she could say, my name, in a sad, I-don't-know-what-to-tell-you kind of way.

It was tough being my friend; I knew that. There wasn't anything further she could say to make me feel better. I remember one time I got stood up by a cop I was dating named Michael Jackson, of all names. Funny now, being stood up, but it wasn't then. I remember he was to pick me up at work to go to the movies. He never showed up, never phoned until two years later. Yes, two years! That night, waiting, I'd felt like the fat girl who gets lied to and never picked up for prom. That's how I felt again with Jared, like the fat girl who never gets invited to go on a mountain hike because people knew she'd tire out after one-sixteenth of a mile. Although I wasn't fat, it was worse: I wasn't fun. Holy shit, I wasn't fun, and hence Jared wasn't inviting me to poker parties or skiing.

To this day, when I go somewhere, if I see a car with a Yakima car rack, say at the coffee shop, I can instantly pick out to whom the car belongs—usually the lesbians sitting outside, having coffee, wearing the Merrell-brand hiking shoes. And they always look so happy. Or it belongs to the good-looking white man with the prosthetic leg—even he remains active. He probably lost his leg in a freak dirt-bike accident, which he overcame, and is now training to climb Mount Everest, and any money he raises will be donated to the Special Olympics. I needed a life like that. And I'd take either one, the happy, active lesbian life or that of the white man with the prosthetic leg.

Two months later, when I was going to work one night, I was running behind my usual time. I parked and started walking toward the hospital. Jared had just arrived, too, and waited for me.

"I thought that was you. How are you?" he asked.

"Good. Yourself?"

"Good, thanks. Keeping busy with the kids and work."

We walked in silence for a while.

"I never told Diana you broke up with me while having sex," I blurted out.

"I know you didn't," he said. "I think my friend likes to stir the pot."

And just like the rage I'd momentarily had against Joe, this rage, too, was now nonexistent. I wish I could change this aspect of myself. A few days after this run-in with Jared, I called him. "I want us to be friends," I said. I had no pride.

"Sure," he said, as easily as if I'd said, "Would you like a piece of chocolate cake?"

We said we'd keep all conversation only between us.

I'd go to his home every now and then. We'd talk and sometimes we'd kiss. We never had sex (at first), and he never promised to call (never), or spend time with me (never ever), or anything (nothing actually). We enjoyed the night.

One night, he invited me over for a get-together dinner with some of his friends. I'd only met a few of his friends, so I was excited. As usual, he didn't answer the door to his house. I never expected him to kowtow to me, just answer the door and greet me to show some acknowledgment of my arrival. Was that too much to ask? I knew what the answer was, so I walked in and saw two girls there. An Asian girl and an all-American girl were putting poker chips away. Another poker party I wasn't invited to? They introduced themselves and were friendly. Jared was cooking in the kitchen. He greeted me with his usual kiss on the cheek and poured me a glass of wine.

The white girl came to the kitchen. She wore a long, thin cotton dress. She looked flushed from a day in the hot sun. She didn't have on a bra, and didn't need one, but she looked nice nonetheless. I felt the sexual tension between her and Jared. *He's fucking her, or soon will be*, I thought.

Why had he invited me here?

I must say she was nice. I liked her. I gathered, from the conversation she initiated with him, that she worked in a lab somewhere. I could tell they'd been hanging out with one another. She used what I call Jared Vocabulary, Jared-isms, which are also part of *Jared-pedia*. He always used phrases like "coddle" and "technically speaking," and she strategically placed them into the conversation and looked at him for a response, for approval. Was this the skill I was lacking?

I made it through dinner. The other dinner guest had to run off after eating. Lab Girl and I remained with Jared. We went out to the backyard to finish our drinks. She went inside briefly to use the bathroom.

"She seems like a free spirit," I said, offering my unsolicited opinion.

"She is."

Is this what wows him? I wondered.

He said no more. I indicated that I better get going home, and she momentarily returned and said the same. He walked us to the door, and she suggested that she and I should exchange numbers to do something together. I gave her my number. *She must not know, or maybe this is how she plays her cards*, I thought. Was this another skill?

I was about to walk out of the house with her when she abruptly said, "Oh, I have to use the restroom. Go ahead."

Ooh, skill number three. She's good. Her bladder couldn't be that tiny. I left and she stayed behind. I'm sure they fucked. *This is what wows him*, I thought.

The skills to wow.

Fucking skillful bitch.

HONEYSUCKLE BREASTS

In the few months that followed, Jared would call me at ten or eleven at night and say, "Come over for a glass of wine." I'd learn later that he'd had a dinner party. Everyone had left, and he was presumably lonely and still wide awake. I imagined him scrolling through the contacts on his iPhone (today's little black book) and coming across my name. Thinking, *Ah, Julie, I haven't seen her in a while. She doesn't expect much, and better yet, only a couple miles away and always available.* And there I was. I always swore I'd keep to my side of the living room. I'd make him beg for me to come closer. That was always a botched plan.

This time, it was July. I wasn't over him, or rather, I wasn't over my inability to wow him or my wanting to do so. My gut told me he was dating the Lab Girl with skills. After a long glass of wine, I was ready to leave; he asked for a shoulder massage. No problem. But this was Jared's way. Before I knew it, the man I couldn't wow was on top of me. We made out like teenagers on his living room floor. I made a comment of, "If I'd known, I'd have shaved my legs."

"We can't have sex. I'm seeing someone."

What the fuck? But kissing and a massage at eleven at night are kosher? "Is it Lab Girl?" I questioned, knowing the answer.

"Yes."

"I knew it. Then why are you on top of me?"

"Because I know it's not gonna last. I've already been distancing myself from her."

"Does she know?" I'd experienced his "distancing," and I wondered how she was handling it all.

"No, we haven't spoken about it. She's created such a ripple in my little circle of friends. None of them like her. There are little things in her personality that I see that tell me it'll never work."

Ah, there was a glitch in her skills. She stood no chance if the friends didn't like her. Jared relied on his circle of friends to make decisions.

"What is it about her that made you like her?" I remembered her, and all her skills, vividly. When the man you're interested in has sexual tension with another woman, you always remember that woman vividly! She'd had a free-spirit look that disguised her true nature, a clingy spirit, I concluded based on that one encounter with her. She'd worn a thin, flowery cotton dress that hung loosely over her flat chest. She'd looked a bit sweaty, in a sexy, hot-day sort of way.

I thought it funny that I remembered her breasts because Jared's next words were, "I like the smell of her breasts. It must be her pheromones or something." Excuse me? Hold on! I can't learn *that* type of skill! He elaborated, "Her breasts have the best smell I have ever smelled." *What, patchouli?* I thought. "It's so sweet and subtle, like honeysuckle. And it's not soap or anything. Her breasts naturally smell like that, and I can't get enough of them. Being a doctor, I can't help but be intrigued by the whole pheromone attraction." And because I hadn't learned my lesson the time he told me that I didn't wow him, I asked, "And I don't have those pheromones?"

I tempted fate.

"No, you don't. I already smelled your breasts…and nothing."

He lowered his head down into my cleavage to give me another whiff, a second chance, took a deep breath, came back up, and shook his head, "No. But see, you have perfume on, too. It's not natural."

I was mortified and shocked at the up-front, unfiltered response.

So the answer to the question, "What does that girl have that I don't have?" is obviously the pheromones of honeysuckle scent that exude naturally from her breasts. I should have acted out of character and run around with my big rack out, woken up his kids, and made a fucking scene.

Instead, I lay there on his carpet, on which he'd probably lain down with dozens of women to smell their breasts. Again, this man rejects me in the most inventive ways.

I don't wow him. I don't have honeysuckle-scented breasts. What's next on the list?

This fucker wowed me, and not in a good way. My friends later asked, "How could you just lie there and listen to him? Why didn't you get up and walk out?" The lyrics to Pink Floyd's song "Comfortably Numb" come to mind.

PHEROMONES 101

The first time I ever heard the word *pheromones* was in Long Beach, at one of those Latin boutiques that sold everything from candles of the Virgin de Guadalupe and incense to tarot cards and dried rooster claws for homemade voodoo spells. I was with my cousin Victor, aka Victoria, an all-knowing and loving transgender who was simply born in the wrong body. She was quite religious in that she believed in prayer, the rosary, the Virgin Mary (and any sightings thereof), holy water, and God's divine intervention. She was also very experimental, in case the aforementioned Catholic beliefs failed for unknown reasons. She'd try any white or black magic spell, if she could find the called-for ingredients, which is why she knew of this store that sold such talismans. She could read your fortune with a deck of playing cards, loved interrogating the Ouija board in the dark, and knew every zodiac sign, its traits, strengths, weaknesses, and compatibilities with the other signs.

"Oh my God, I need to purchase a bottle of this!" she exclaimed while whimsically walking the narrow, four-foot-long aisle of this sacred shop. She picked up a one-ounce vial that contained a red liquid that looked exactly like what I put in my hummingbird feeder.

"What is it?" I asked.

"Pheromones!"

"What's that?"

"Girl! No wonder you don't have a boyfriend! Pheromones are what you naturally exude to attract the opposite sex. They make you irresistible!"

"But how?" I was twenty-two years old but felt eleven, asking questions that she obviously thought I should know the answers to. But this was Victor Victoria, and everything she expressed was highly animated, so I could never decipher what was truly important.

"Didn't you pay attention in science? You, your cells, your sweat glands—they communicate to men as you pass by them. If they can smell you, then they want you."

"If it's natural, then why do you need that? How did they get that in the bottle?"

"You want to enhance what you have so it's stronger. How much is this? I need some! Three fifty? That's a deal."

"Does it really work?" I had my doubts.

"Girl, scientists have studied this! Yes, it works. I had some before, and girl, if walls could talk! Know what I mean? Every man from my neighbor's husband to the local firemen was chasing me down! Then someone stole my bottle, probably some jealous tranny, and I've been having trouble finding where to buy some more! It just takes a dab behind the ears. *Just* a dab," she said in a forewarning tone and motioned how she'd place it behind her ears.

Her eyes were wild; she was vivacious and elated, but I wasn't buying it. If holding the vial in her hand made her this crazy, I was afraid I might be raped by passing men if I dabbed any on.

"You better take some, too," she advised. She wore flip-flops, cutoff jeans, and a loose white tank top, which innocently showed a training bra underneath, with budding breasts barely scratching the lining of the cup. Her fashion matched her blithe attitude. She positioned her arms just right to allow her jangling bangles to keep time with her swaying hips as she made her way to the cashier. She may have not been born a woman, per her birth certificate, but she sure as hell knew how to be one—better than I.

We'd planned to play Ouija later in the evening, and according to Victoria, we needed new white candles to protect us from bad spirits while we played such a devilish game. I planned to purchase only the white candles and no bottled pheromones. It's not that I didn't believe Victoria. She stated everything as a fact, not as a "maybe" or "I think." She didn't say, "I think I might be a woman." She proclaimed, "I am a woman!" I admired her convictions on all matters from candles to womanhood.

"I don't think I need any," I said.

What little I knew.

Alas, Victoria was correct. Pheromones were a recently new finding in the science arena, but primarily with insects.

There are different types of pheromones: some to claim territory, some to act as defense, and some to lead the way to food (I'd probably be great with the food pheromones). Then there are sex pheromones, the ones of interest here, the ones I had little knowledge of, and the ones that Jared obviously needed for bonding.

Studies show show that female insects can release chemicals to attract males for breeding. A butterfly can smell the pheromones of another butterfly from up to six miles away. It's not just a locater of the opposite sex, but it's a catalyst of the arousing type! What's the point of finding a potential mate if he's not aroused? But Jared wasn't an insect; he was a human being. However, he did have those caterpillar eyebrows. And caterpillars do metamorphose into butterflies. It was a long shot, but I needed a rational explanation for all this rejection from him and his pheromone need!

So what about pheromones in humans?

There's much debate on whether pheromones in humans exist. I'm sure Jared is 100 percent certain that they do. And I am, too. I know that certain scents are picked up in the brain, and *bam!* Just like that, a flood of emotions in connection to a certain person, place, or event are brought back like you're seeing the person again, visiting the place again, reliving the experience. I suspected that honeysuckle played some comforting role in Jared's childhood.

It was already difficult to meet a man, to wow him, and to build something profound with him. I didn't want to think of all the hormones or pheromones that could possibly make or break a relationship. I was glad that most people didn't know about pheromones.

I could hear Victoria's voice telling me to buy that bottle of pheromones. From the street smarts of Victor Victoria to the Ivy League doctor, attraction and seduction come down to the most basic human components: chemical reaction. Pheromones. Which I apparently didn't possess and had been too smug about purchasing when I'd had the chance years earlier.

But smells fade, do they not? I lay there on Jared's carpet floor, worried of what might come next. To pour salt on my wounds, Jared went on about how sometimes it felt like he had another kid to babysit when Lab Girl was with him and his children.

"She met your kids?" I asked. I overlooked the part about how he felt she was behaving like another child. I could still envision the interior of his closet! Men have a high tolerance for bullshit from women they like and zero tolerance for women they don't. Boy, her skills and honeysuckle pheromones sure worked magic on someone who wasn't that interested in her!

"Well, yes, by accident. She spent the night and forgot her car keys. When she sneaked back in to get them, I was downstairs fixing breakfast for the kids, so they met her. I'm not sure if that was manipulative on her part or not," he explained.

Oh, but it was! What's this? Skill número seis? Does he not know that plenty of women do shit like this? And how do you not remember your car keys as you go out to your car?

"I can't believe you already introduced her to your kids." I felt so insufficient.

"It's not like I'm going to hide her!"

Yet I had to hide in his fucking closet? This is what's wrong with me. Gays are coming out of the closet while I, a single, straight Latina female, am getting ushered in. Lab Girl was squirming right into his family life. She had the pheromones and the technique. I was fucked.

And of all the things I liked about Jared, I liked his nose first—only to discover that his nose didn't like me.

JACOB

BLINKING & CRYING

A pair of human eyes. Are they really the window to a person's soul? Sad eyes, bloodshot eyes, Paul Newman piercing-blue eyes, *mal de ojo*, bedroom eyes, snake eyes, and let's not forget, soulful eyes. Then there are the pupils, changing size however they please. The pupils will dilate, an involuntary physiological response, when our adrenaline is high. If you can catch it, there's a subtle betrayal by the pupils to the poker face you're analyzing.

Oh, all that the eyes can give away, disguise, or avoid. The eyes can be indicative of so much, such as one's actual soul, with just a momentary connection (or lack thereof) with another person's eyes. Is it possible that a great deal more can be disclosed with the actual function, or mechanism, that the eyes can or can't perform?

On average, a person's upper eyelid blinks fifteen times per minute. That's approximately one blink every four seconds. We'll never be able to obtain a definitive figure of how often a man cries. However, we do know two things: One, the frequency of blinking and crying isn't correlated. And two, our tear gland produces three types of tears: basal, reflex, and emotional.

Basal tears, made up of primarily water, are a constant stream of fluid that's released onto the lining of the upper eyelid and that helps keep your eyeball moist and clean. Reflex tears, concentrated with antibodies and enzymes, fill the eye up with fluid to wash away irritants, like pet dander. And finally, emotional tears are produced from, well, emotion.

Although all tears are important and special in their own chemical composition, it's the emotional tears that I want to zero in on. Emotional tears are the ones that many people try to suppress or have no ability to suppress.

During times of stress or pain, a variety of hormones are released into the bloodstream. Without this release, we wouldn't be able to mentally cope with the simplest of life stressors or pain. By the same token, we don't want our blood filled up with hormones once we no longer need them. Hence, we need to cry.

Crying releases these stressful, emotional, pain-induced hormones. It decreases tension levels and helps a person's system avoid accumulating hormones to a toxic level. Crying helps us cope, makes us feel better after it's released; it helps us be less toxic.

Remember Lesson Number Two from utero: *Rid yourself of toxins*. The blood knows to rid itself of any waste, any toxin, collected along the way, before heading back to the head and heart.

All of us should be open to having a good cry every now and then to help rid ourselves of toxins. But what happens if you can't.

... AND THEN ALONG CAME JACOB

It was the last week of January 2010. I'd completed one of two goals. I'd bought my first home two months prior. It was a one-story with four bedrooms and three baths—my dream home. The house was spacious and probably a bit too large for me. The second goal was to begin artificial insemination in February 2011 and fill the remaining bedrooms with one baby and a live-in nanny. I had one year to work nonstop and save a nice nest egg prior to getting pregnant. I wanted to do this as responsibly as I could, since I was doing it alone. I also wanted to get in shape. I went back and forth on whether to join a gym. I made an appointment with Gold's Gym to get a tour of the facility prior to heading to work.

I met Mike, manager of membership sales for Gold's, at the front. He pointed out all the equipment and said, "This is the busiest it gets, and you'll always find an open machine to work out on. Most people sign up and don't use the membership after about a month." They had a promotion for "$19.99 per month for life." I figured I spent more per month on coffee, so I went ahead and became a member.

He said the gym granted one free personal training session, if I was interested. I figured I could learn exactly how to use the machines and perhaps get a better workout. The free session would be in a few days with a trainer named Jacob.

I approached the trainer's station on the designated day, and a white guy was sitting there talking to another client. He looked like a Jacob but didn't acknowledge my standing there until he'd finished his conversation. Why do workers do that? I obviously wasn't standing there to eavesdrop. Why can't workers acknowledge your presence and say, "I'll be right with you"? Salespeople usually are overbearing and constantly trying to upsell you something, or they completely ignore you as you stand there. This guy didn't even make eye contact.

I introduced myself when there was a break in his conversation and said I had an appointment at three. He confirmed that he was Jacob and that he'd take me through a quick workout to see what my level of fitness was. I stated I hadn't been working out and that I was a complete beginner. He never acknowledged what I said. He walked twenty steps ahead of me, grabbed a big round ball (that didn't bounce), and headed to a small corner. I was bothered that he walked twenty steps ahead of me and kept thinking about how he didn't make eye contact.

Suddenly that little voice, my conscience, was speaking to me, my gut intuition telling me something. I instantly created a story as to why he walked ahead of me and didn't look at me, and that story was that he felt superior and didn't respect women. Why was I thinking such thoughts? It's not like I was going to have a relationship with this guy. Boy, was I judgmental! Maybe he was having a bad day. But why did I care if he was or wasn't?

In a dry tone, as if he were reading inventory, he explained the workout sequence. "You're going to do ten wall balls and then ten burpees, and that will count as one set. You'll do this for fifteen minutes, and I'll be timing you. Try to complete as many sets as possible. You'll probably be able to do five sets."

He then demonstrated a wall ball. He grabbed the heavy round ball that didn't bounce, faced the wall, did a squat, threw the ball against the wall as he came out of the squat position, caught the ball, and repeated the exercise.

"You'll do that ten times and then you'll go straight into ten burpees," he said.

He then demonstrated a burpee. He did a fast squat to the ground and placed both hands in front of him on the floor, kicked out his legs into a push-up position, did a push-up, threw his legs back into the squat position, jumped up, clapped his hands over his head, and repeated the sequence in one fluid motion.

"Got it?" he asked.

"Yes," I said. This didn't look too difficult.

"OK, get into position and when I tell you to go, start."

I started with the wall balls and was able to do the first ten without too much difficulty. He corrected me on my squat, said to throw the ball higher, to "explode" out of the squat for more power.

I went straight into the burpees and immediately realized these would be my death. I was getting tired but was able to produce ten mediocre burpees. He corrected my push-up position; he reminded me to clap over my head when I jumped up or it wasn't going to count. I hated this guy; hadn't I told him I was a beginner?

I needed to breathe between my first and second set. I was sweating, my face was flushed, and I was short of breath. I couldn't believe I never fell flat on my face doing an off-the-beaten path-five-day hike to Machu Picchu in Peru, hiking at an elevation of over thirteen thousand feet above sea level, but was wondering how I'd make it through the next fifteen minutes.

"Come on, Jules, gotta keep moving. I'm timing you. You can do it. Focus."

Jules? Only my close friends call me that.

I started my second set of wall balls. Did this ball just gain weight? It sure felt heavier the second time around. My legs were wobbly. My squat was slanting diagonally due to shaky quadriceps. Oh my! I wanted to go slowly and hoped the minutes would pass quickly. I was never competitive when it came to physical abilities or endurance. I wished I'd had that natural competitiveness and that desire to physically push myself beyond what I thought I could do. But I hadn't been born that way; hence, I was always trying to get into shape. I was more mentally competitive. I wanted straight As and the ability to conjugate irregular French verbs with ease. If my leg muscles could strive to be half as powerful as my brain muscles, I thought I might be able to get through this exercise. Who said physical exercise is 99 percent mental? I beg to differ.

My second set of burpees was even more disastrous. My mind was a blur, and I kept forgetting to do the push-up. I'd get into push-up position and go back into my squat.

"Don't forget the push-up, Jules!"

Yes, yes, the push-up.

"Don't forget to clap at the top, Jules!"

Oh yeah, the clap. Is an overhead clap necessary?

"Come on, I need you to finish another set. You can do this!"

With every burpee, I wanted to lie flat on the ground until my heart returned to its comfortable, normal sinus rhythm of sixty-four beats per minute. But that wasn't to be. I had this guy named Jacob here calling me Jules and counting out my dwindling remaining time from his stopwatch. He was sadly mistaken; I couldn't complete five sets.

The third set was slow. I hugged the ball close to my heaving chest between throws. My Olive Oyl arms trembled with ache and fright while Bluto—I mean Jacob—hovered over me. I somehow finished the ten and started the burpees. When would my time be up? The burpees had no eruption or thrust to them; I wasn't like a newborn frog jumping but like an old toad in need of bilateral hip replacements.

I finished three dreadful sets, and Jacob called out, "Time. Three sets." I think I went over the fifteen minutes, but he was going to force me to finish three full sets, even if I died or if it killed him to watch me agonize through it all.

After I finished those three Olympic-worthy sets, he said, "Meet me back at the trainer's station and we'll go over your fitness level."

Did we really need to do that? It was obviously very low. I

dragged my limbs over to the table; I was already sore. I needed a potassium-packed banana fast; I knew I'd cramp. I needed some Epsom salt for a hot bath later tonight, too. *And if you have some Bengay, let's get that lathered up right away as well.*

"So how serious are you about getting into shape?" Jacob asked.

I gave him the spiel about wanting to lose weight to have a baby next year. He said he got one of his clients down to 11 percent body fat prior to getting pregnant.

"That's not even an optimum body fat percentage to get pregnant," I countered. I wanted to be fit, not a stick.

"Well, she did. I'm pretty sure it was eleven percent, but I'll ask her again next time I see her. But you're very curvy naturally. How many times are you able to work out each week?"

"I'm hoping three to five."

He opened a binder and gave me a breakdown of the cost of personal training. He painted an ideal picture of how much body fat his trainers could melt off me, how my stamina and energy would increase, and how my overall body would change. He suggested three times a week with a personal trainer and twice a week by myself. For one hundred sessions, he'd charge twenty-five hundred dollars.

"If you need to go home and talk to your husband about it first, that's fine. This offer stands until Wednesday."

I didn't correct him on the husband assumption; I usually don't. It's simpler allowing people to think I'm married. Otherwise I'm left to field the same old questions: "What's wrong with you?

You must be picky."

"Give me until Friday," I told him.

"Why? What's Friday?"

"My next day off, and I need time to think things out before I decide on something so costly."

In actuality, I'd have my taxes done by then and have a better idea of what my tax return was going to be. And I never made huge impulse purchases.

"I'll call you by Friday, if not sooner," I promised.

He agreed.

On my way out, I ran into Mike the sales manager.

"How did it go with Jacob?" he asked.

"He killed me. I told him I'd think about it."

I called my friend Meena and we went to dinner. Meena always gave sound financial advice, as she was a numbers girl. She knew how to place a price tag on everything, from products to people, for better or for worse. We discussed whether I should pay twenty-five hundred dollars for personal training. We both thought it was too much. By the end of the night, I decided I'd pay no more than two thousand dollars for one hundred sessions. If Jacob didn't take the offer, then I'd have to work out on my own.

I called Jacob when I got home to tell him that, if he agreed, I'd pay two thousand dollars for one-on-one personal training. He agreed and threw in two additional workouts with him and four additional workouts with my trainer. I thought he was going to be my trainer but was somewhat relieved that he wasn't going to be. He said he sold the personal training and managed the trainers. My trainer would be Sheila, a toned and sleek-as-a-leopard, beautiful black girl.

I met Jacob for two more workouts. He explained that he was teaching me a form of exercise called CrossFit and Tri-hemisphere Training. CrossFit wouldn't use the countless machines lined up at Gold's Gym. *What?* No machines? Instead, we would use kettle bells and medicine balls of various weights and do lots of jumping, a lot of burpees and movements that required squatting. The workouts would be short but intense. I didn't capture the full explanations of the methods and the reasoning. All I knew was that I was going to get my ass kicked like the last time. I did capture his eyes. I searched his face, forcing him to make eye contact. Every few seconds he'd blink his eyes hard, like a twitch. Was it a nervous twitch, a tic, or a spasm? I also captured how he came alive when he talked about CrossFit. He was passionate about it. He truly wanted to share his knowledge.

He pulled out a low, padded bench and showed me how he wanted me to jump up on it. I didn't feel confident jumping on it with my feet together; I thought I'd trip. I kept jumping up by placing one foot at a time, more of a little leap up rather than a jump.

"No, you have to do it with your feet together. I'll spot you," he said.

I was able to jump up on it but was unable to keep the consecutive motion of jumping on, off, on, off, on, off. I jumped on, stopped, jumped off, stopped, got my footing and jumped on, stopped. I couldn't believe my fear of jumping. What type of childhood had I had? I remembered climbing and jumping. I was in gymnastics at age sixteen! Had I grown this afraid? I felt a slight pull in my gluteus. I hesitated. I hoped as I warmed up the discomfort would go away.

"Don't think about it, hon. Jump with both feet. Make each one count," he said.

Did he call me *hon*? I thought I was "Jules" at our last workout session. Was he one of those guys that calls every girl "babe" or "hon"? Yes, he was.

I swear it was jumping on that padded bench that caused me to pull a gluteal muscle that plagued me for the following month. Nonetheless, I signed up to get in shape, and I was on my way.

I met Sheila three times a week. She made me do a million (OK, maybe a hundred, but it felt like a million) lunges and push-ups and workouts called Karen and Angie. Karen was 150 wall balls for time. I can't recall my time, but I finished. Angie was a hundred pull-ups, a hundred push-ups, a hundred sit-ups, and a hundred squats. I can't remember if this was for time; I can't remember if I finished. Jacob wandered around the gym in a T-shirt that said, "I love Fran" on it—Fran was another workout, one I had yet, and no desire, to meet.

In the first two weeks, I started to feel stronger, more athletic. If I could eventually do these workouts effectively, maybe I'd have the strength to kayak, ski, and bike. Maybe purchasing that Yakima car rack was around the corner after all. I was feeling great.

By late February, Jacob was a regular attendee of my workouts, making small talk here and there. He coached Sheila on what additional exercises she should teach me. He complimented me on making progress, saying that it was noticeable that I was losing weight. He said, "Your husband must have his hands all over you every night."

I smiled. *No*, I thought, *I haven't wowed anyone enough to marry me*. Goodness, did I know how to dwell on things or what?

My pulled gluteal muscle from the first sessions a month prior continued to nag me. I told Sheila that I thought I pulled my muscle when I worked out with Jacob. She told me to lay myself on the ground; she'd try massaging it out with a large foam roller. It hurt badly as she placed her weight on the roller and rolled it across my injured ass. I knew I couldn't scream out in the gym, so I let out nervous, painful laughter.

After I got up and composed myself, Jacob approached. "What are you girls giggling about?"

"Julie has a pulled muscle and needs it massaged out. She's laughing because it hurts so bad," Sheila said.

"Come by my office tomorrow, and I'll massage it out for you," Jacob offered.

I looked at him and Sheila.

"With my elbow," he added.

Sheila nodded in approval and said, "Yeah, you need a deep massage to get out the knot."

"OK, I'll see you tomorrow," I said.

"Do you still have my number? Text me tomorrow before you come," he added.

I arrived the next day to get my butt massage. Jacob instructed me to warm up for fifteen minutes on a cardio machine and he'd be in his office. His office was in the corner behind the trainers' station, but it was a full glass wall; anyone could see in. After my warm-up, he told me to lie on my side (good glute down, bad glute up) and bend my top leg with my knee touching the ground.

"I'm excited; I get to massage Julie's butt!" he exclaimed like a teenager, intentionally allowing Sheila and the other trainers to hear.

He dug his elbow into the knot, placed pressure on it. He was very close to me. He spoke softly now. "Mike told me he asked you out."

"Yes, he did."

Mike, the salesman who'd sold me my membership, had indeed asked me out. He'd taken my number, not given me his, and told me the precise hours and locations where we could meet. After he did finally give me his number, he'd take days to return a text. People live with their cell phones in hand. If you have time to take a shit, you have time to return a text from a girl you supposedly want to take out. Bill Clinton, while running the United States of America, had time to *call* Monica. So there's no excuse. Mike and I never made it past a phone call.

"You told me you were married," Jacob said.

"No, you assumed I was married. And I didn't correct you."

"He said you backed out of your date."

"I realized I wasn't interested."

"Hey, if you don't feel it, you don't feel it. You can't do

anything about that if it's just not there."

He was silent for a few seconds; his brown eyes blinked hard and frequently. Was it Tourette's syndrome? The signs and symptoms of the disorder ran through my mind: a motor tic (usually eye blinking), repetitive and sudden, and was a vocal tic absolutely required to constitute a true diagnosis? I thought so but couldn't remember. I'd have to look it up when I got home. He never shouted out words at inappropriate times, he never cursed, and he never grunted or cleared his throat, which were all manifestations of Tourette's. Could this be a very mild case of Tourette's?

I looked up at him. He looked down at me. He was handsome, despite all his blinking. Definitely not my type—he was an all-American boy. I liked exotic- or ethnic-looking men. At least I thought I did. I knew I used to, but I also knew that taste changes over time. After finding Jared attractive, I questioned what it was I did like. Jacob looked like a soccer player, but neither the hot-Latin-American kind nor the David-Beckham kind—he was somewhere in between. He had a strong jawline but a thin upper lip, which I didn't find attractive. *My lips could easily devour that lip*, I thought. But why was I thinking such thoughts? It's not like we were ever going to kiss. His eyes were small and round with short lashes. And when his eyes weren't twitching, I noticed tiny specks of amber and green hiding behind the predominantly brown color. He didn't have one blemish on his skin, and I could tell that with the right amount of sun, he'd be a nice golden shade of a man.

He whispered, "This is a very sexy position."

"Is it?" I was embarrassed.

Had he been reading my mind about his looks and his upper lip?

"It is," he said.

I got up and composed myself.

"Feel better?" he asked.

"Yeah, it does."

"I do have my massage therapy license, if you ever need a massage. I make house calls," he said with a sly smile and a couple of hard, quick blinks.

Was he trying to get business or trying to get action? I was so bad with men. I still questioned whether men were or were not hitting on me. I never wanted to assume. I needed it spelled out for me, confirmed one way or another.

"Yeah, maybe you can come over," I found myself saying.

"Yeah, maybe on Monday? Around noon?"

"OK, Monday at noon," I said nonchalantly.

Over the weekend I went shopping for Japanese ingredients. I'd be making a Japanese-themed dinner for my uncle's birthday in the coming weeks. I needed to practice making the Chilean sea bass in a sake marinade and spicy glazed eggplant. When I got home from the Asian market, I thought I better save Jacob's number in my cell phone. While attempting to save his contact information, I accidentally called him. I canceled the call immediately. Shit! I didn't want to call him. I had nothing to say to him. He immediately called back. I answered and apologized for accidentally calling him.

"So you couldn't say hello?" he asked.

"Oh, I didn't know if you had even answered. I canceled the call as soon as I saw it was calling you."

He said he was in bed, resting, watching a *Pirates of the Caribbean* movie. I told him I loved Johnny Depp and had tickets to see *Alice in Wonderland* on Sunday night. We made small talk about actors we liked.

He asked what I was doing. I said I was going to practice making some Japanese food and maybe I'd have some friends over for Japanese, but everyone had to come in a kimono or something Japanese.

"That'd be great," he said. "I'll come as a samurai, and I'll bring my sword," he joked.

The conversation was light, easy. He reconfirmed for Monday.

On Sunday night, Meena and I arrived early to stand in line at the IMAX theater for the showing of *Alice in Wonderland*. I told her about Jacob.

"How old is he?" was her first question.

"He's forty-four but looks much younger."

"And he knows you want to have a baby, right?"

"Well, I did tell him that was my reason for signing up for personal training."

"Does he have kids?"

"Umm, I don't think so."

"I have a good feeling about this." She was excited for me, I could tell. "No kids, older, knows you want to have kids, and he wants to come over and give you a massage! And he was home on a Friday night when you called him."

"Maybe it's just a massage," I wondered.

"No, he's interested."

"I don't know."

"OK, what if he is? What are you going to do?"

"I'm gonna go for it."

"Are you?" Her eyes lit up with every thought and possibility that she hoped for me. Meena was the type of girl who keeps a checklist of what one must accomplish in life (basically, all the things society deems appropriate), and I'm sure she believed I was way behind in checking off what I *should* have accomplished by then.

"Yes. I never have men that are interested in me and that actually take action. If he's interested, I'm gonna go for it," I reiterated.

"Good. Then you may not need artificial insemination!" *Check!* I heard her say in her head as she silently tallied up what his average gross earnings and savings should be at age forty-four, working as a personal trainer.

It's true that words have power. They can hurt, heal, confuse, and clarify. And I have always done my best to be a woman of my word, whatever it may be. Proclamations alone have changed the course of history. I chose right then and there to proclaim something positive about my chance with Jacob. "I'm going to give everything and try my best. He'll be my last-ditch effort before trying to have a baby on my own." I had created my own checklist. A checklist society would be proud of.

Monday came. I showered, shaved, and exfoliated. Jacob sent me a text around noon stating that he wouldn't be able to come over and could we reschedule? Already going against his word. He'd chosen this time and date, but I guess things do come up, and he was busy. I made excuses for him from the onset. There went my house-call massage; it was probably for the best. Yet I didn't send him a text saying I was no longer interested, the way I had with Mike. Instead, I flirted with him via text throughout the day.

I had a workout session with Sheila later that day. Jacob was running around the gym, moving equipment, creating a large open area for the trainers to teach CrossFit. He approached me and said, "Hey, maybe I can come by sometime after work, rather than in the middle of the day."

"Sure, let me know when."

"On your next day off?"

"Wednesday."

"OK, text me your address."

I called Meena and told her how he had to reschedule.

"And you probably exfoliated and curled your hair," she said.

"I did," I admitted.

"Ugh. Don't you hate that? Men have no idea how much work and thought we put into seeing them."

"No, they don't. They flake out or show up with no thought to it."

"So now you're going to have to do that all over again."

"Yep."

Wednesday rolled around, and since he'd be coming over after work at about seven, I decided I'd cook dinner. I made my favorite Moroccan chicken dish. Seven o'clock, and Jacob texted, "Still at the gym, see you in about a half hour."

A half-hour late now.

At eight o'clock, with no sign of Jacob, I put the food away. Screw him. I called Meena at eight fifteen. "He's still not here. I put the food away so it doesn't look like I made an effort to cook for him."

"Now you're learning," she laughed.

I pulled out my nursing bag to clean it out, to kill time, to preoccupy my fuming mind. I dumped everything onto the middle of the living room floor to sort and organize. It was a quarter to nine when there was finally a knock at the door. One hour, forty-five minutes late. He should have rescheduled. I should have called it off, but I didn't.

Jacob walked in wearing jeans and a light-brown zip-up hoodie, zipped more down than up, no shirt underneath. He pretended to be looking at his cell phone, not really making eye contact with me.

He took a quick look around. "You live in this big house all by yourself?"

"Yes," I said detachedly.

"Why aren't you married yet?" he asked right away. I hate

that question! If I had the true answer, I'd be a millionaire, because I'd write a book about it and sell it to every late-thirty-something who's wondering the same thing and tired of coming up with different, creative, justifiable responses to every person that asks. Hey, that'll be my next book!

"I don't know. Guess I put other priorities first, like career and traveling the world." Would that answer suffice?

"Oh, you're like me, a gypsy. I can't settle down in one city for too long either. What are you doing?" he asked, examining all the contents I'd spilled out on the floor.

Pretending like I wasn't waiting for your arrival, I thought. "Cleaning up my nursing bag," I said.

"You have needles in there?"

"Yes, are you afraid of needles?"

"Nah, I used to do steroids."

"You did?"

"Yeah, when I was really into body building. But I stopped. I didn't like how they made me feel."

"Were you angry all the time?" I remembered Arizona-Boy-with-One-Testicle was supposed to rub testosterone gel on his shoulders, but he rarely did it because, he said, it made him feel angry all the time.

"Yeah. I mean, I guess I have anger issues to begin with, but that made it worse."

"Anger issues with what?" I was getting nervous.

"With my mother. She used to severely abuse me when I was

little."

I nodded slowly as I felt my annoyance diminish. "Sorry to hear that. Do you have contact with her?"

"Hell no! I haven't spoken to her in years."

OK, this wasn't the start I expected. Let me lighten things up. "Hey, would you like a drink?" I asked. I needed one.

"Yeah! What do you have?"

"Red wine."

"No, I better not do red wine. That'll make me sleep so fast. My mom used to make me drink red wine when I was little so she wouldn't have to deal with me. So now when I drink it, I just go to sleep. Do you have anything harder?"

"Um, yeah, tequila, vodka…." I motioned to a high cupboard in the corner of my kitchen.

He opened the cabinet. "Feels like I'm breaking into a hidden stash." He chose a tequila I'd brought back with me after studying in Oaxaca, Mexico. He took a shot. "It's good. Do you have anything I can mix it with?"

"I have a young coconut," I said jokingly. I had coconuts from the Asian market on my kitchen counter.

"That'll work," he said and prepped himself a coconut-tequila drink.

We sat on the couch for a while, and he scrolled through the television channels. He stopped on a Spanish language channel and mimicked the news broadcast.

Surprised by his clear pronunciation, I asked, "Do you speak

Spanish?"

"A bit," he said. He started saying random words. *Panza* (belly). *Amor* (love). *Magnífico* (magnificent).

"Where did you pick up those words?"

"Oh, I lived in Costa Rica for a year, when I was younger."

"Really?"

"Yeah, I was a stripper there and did a little modeling."

"Did you like Costa Rica? I've never been. I've been to Panama, though, which is right next door."

"Yeah, I took a bus to Panama one week. That was crazy." No further details on the "crazy" part or being a stripper.

He continued to scroll through the channels and stopped on CNN. There was a story about a family being shot to death and a little boy witnessing it all. Jacob was transfixed on the story as the 911 audiotape of the little boy played.

"See, now that little boy is going to be messed up forever." He blinked hard several times.

I watched his stern facial expression and his eyes blinking quickly, harshly, repetitively. I immediately felt sad for both the little boy on the television and the little boy sitting on my couch.

"I ran away at age fourteen and lived in cars until an aunt and uncle took me in." He offered this information without my prodding.

"You're lucky you had them."

"Yeah, I've been on my own ever since," he stated proudly.

"Do you live here in Elk Grove or Sacramento?" I asked out of curiosity.

"I live in the hotel next door to the gym. It's easy. Walk across the parking lot to work."

Jacob was one big *red flag* from the moment he walked through my front door. Not merely a little red flag, gently waving in a mild winter wind. He was an exacerbation, screaming, oozing, aching, blazing, and blaring in every hue of red imaginable. I'd been more at ease seeing, and attempting to save, patients literally bleeding out in all different shades of blood-red than I was in this very moment. Jacob was an uncomfortable tone of red that I didn't know how to stop from bleeding.

And I should have run, even though I was in my own home. Still, I should have run, to a neighbor, to a friend's house, to the dark field across the street with roaming cows. I should have run in any direction away from him. But that would have gone against my *last-ditch effort*. That would go against my nature. *What, he's one big red flag? You're a nurse; don't you dare run. Stay and nurse those flags away. Don't you dare run.* My wanting to help, to please, was also one big red flag, equivalent to and ready for the challenge of his many red flags.

God, please help him. Anyone, please help me. I did want to run, but I was cemented by the weight of it all.

I believe he, or we, made other small talk, but my heart and head were swirling. I can't recall one iota of anything that we possibly spoke about after this mini-introduction. Instead of my brain blacking out things that might hurt me (all these newfound facts about him), it repeated them and blacked out all the normal interaction we may have had that night. In my confusion, I failed to realize that my brain *was* trying to protect me by *showing* me, right then and there, all the warning signs that would eventually hurt me. But why should the facts of his life have an emotional impact on me? Why was I taking it personally?

I later recapped the first fifteen minutes of his visit in my head. I learned he'd once done steroids that altered his personality and made him very angry, although he did have anger issues toward family since his mother had severely beaten him as a child. He couldn't drink red wine because his mother had made him do that to fall asleep as a young kid. He ran away at age fourteen but got back on his feet, had done body building, was once a stripper and part-time model in Costa Rica for one year, couldn't settle down in one city for too long, and currently lived in the hotel next door to the gym. I didn't want this to be his story, who he was, but he was showing me exactly who he was.

I should have appreciated this one conversation; I should have asked questions, listened more intently, nodded appropriately, made grimaces, and added, "Really? Tell me a bit more about that." I really should have, because it was the first and last time he'd be so candid. The months that followed would be filled with heartbreaking, red silence. I'd give up anything to have a conversation, to hear him speak. But my window of opportunity had passed without my knowledge. And I was wrong: I shouldn't have run, as I previously thought. I should have let him go. But I was already in denial about what could be.

"So you gonna give me a massage?" he asked.

"Sure," I said. *Let's make the most of this one night*, I thought.

"Do you have a table I can lie on for the massage?"

"No, but I have a spare bedroom with a mattress on the floor." I motioned in the direction of the guestroom.

"That'll work." He made his way down the hallway.

"You can get under the top sheet," I yelled out to him. "You can keep your shorts or underwear on," I laughed. Nervous laughter?

"No, I want it to be like a real massage."

"Naked? You're not shy, are you?"

"No, I'm not."

"Cover yourself with the top sheet."

"I think I'll have a glass of wine after all," he said.

"OK. I'll bring it to you once you're ready."

He disappeared into the back room and reappeared in my hallway with the bedsheet wrapped around his waist. He was naked underneath. So swift in undressing. Well, he *was* a stripper at one time.

"It's freezing in there," he complained.

"I'll turn up the heat."

I handed him a glass of red wine. He took a few sips. Was he going to fall asleep instantly like a person with narcolepsy? No, he wasn't. He lay down.

"Aren't you going to light some candles?" he asked.

Was he serious? "Jesus! You want the whole works!" I exclaimed.

"I'd do it for you if I were giving you a massage. I want it to be nice."

"You will be giving me a massage after! Do you want the sound of a waterfall, too?" I joked.

"Yeah!" he said seriously. "Do you have one of those?"

I laughed, because I did. "I do, but it's in my bedroom."

"Can't we go in there then? Please? I want it to be nice with candles and everything. Come on, babe."

Did he call me *babe*? He did. Fuck, I agreed, and we went to my bedroom.

I lit mini–tea lights and started my small waterfall fountain, which also had a mini-light on it. I turned on a little portable heater to warm him up. He took sips of wine and placed the glass on the nightstand. I took gulps of wine and kept the glass in my hand as long as I could. He didn't pass out like in his childhood. The ambience was created, but my head was still racing. *The head and heart are the most demanding of organs.* I'm sure my head was demanding an escape route. Instead, I was creating an entryway.

He lay face down with his arms above his head. "Warm up the lotion in your hands before putting it on me, OK? That's how the professionals do it," he instructed, if not demanded.

"I know. I get massages all the time."

"Yeah, but do you know how to *give* a massage?"

"I think so. You'll soon find out."

I started on his lower back and worked my way up to his broad shoulders. His physique was amazing. Joe had been very big and buff, too, but different. Joe was like a block of muscles. Jacob was cut, every muscle defined, like a well-illustrated anatomy book. His broad shoulders reminded me of the wingspan of a hawk, flying overhead. My brother says that hawks are lone birds; they don't socialize with other birds but only approach them to steal eggs or newborns from a nest. Great, a bird of prey, lying in my bed.

After the massage, he moaned and turned over. "Oh, you've done this before."

I smiled. "My turn," I said.

"If I must," he said with exasperation.

He started on my back; I still had all my clothes on. "You have to take your shirt off," he said.

I did. He lightly rubbed my back with the palm of his hand but didn't really massage me. "I hate giving back massages," he quickly confessed.

"You said you were certified."

"I am. That's probably why I hate giving them now. I did it for so long."

"So now I'm not gonna get one?"

"I need a massage table or else it's not gonna be good and it'll hurt my back," he complained. Goodness! This body building bastard was fragile.

He started kissing me. Not because he was ignited with passion, but probably because he didn't want me to complain and beg him any further for a massage. He kissed lightly, not deeply, not passionately, but it was still very nice at the time. We made out. My thoughts were still racing.

We fell in and out of sleep throughout the night. It was now the wee hours of the night, or early morning, depending on which way you looked at it. He attempted to put on one of the condoms I had.

"This condom is way too small," he stated proudly.

"Well, that's all I have," I said. Phew, maybe we didn't need to have sex.

"I have a condom in my car," he said and waited for some response from me.

I hadn't decided if I did or didn't want to have sex. Yet I'm the one who handed him the initial condom. I did want to, if I knew that's all it would be. It had been so long since I'd last had sex with Jared. There hadn't been anyone since. But I knew that by having sex, I'd be digging myself deeper into something I was nervous about.

It's said that silence is consent. I was silent as I contemplated my answer.

"I'll go get it!" he said, leaping out of bed. He threw on his jeans and my fluffy pink robe, which stretched tight across his back, with the end of the sleeves cutting off at his elbow. Oh my god, please let all the neighbors be asleep and not looking out their windows!

I can still change my mind, I thought, but I hadn't even decided one way or another. Was this just going to be sex? Yes. *Then OK. I can emotionally handle that. Gosh, what's wrong with me? I'm overthinking this; I'm overthinking this.*

For a moment, I finally got what Jared was talking about

when he said he couldn't pinpoint what it was about me that didn't fit. It was indecisiveness, I firmly concluded. Right at the peak of expectation, I'm not sure which way I want to turn. I falter, I doubt. Or I simply need some form of inner convincing. Maybe because there's something I question about the other person. Or myself. I'm not an impulsive buyer, so why should I be an impulsive lover? Maybe because I am an impulsive lover, sometimes, and society tells women we aren't supposed to be. And I fully struggle with that.

I think if I learned of Jacob's past and present over time, rather than the first fifteen minutes after his coming through my door, I'd have thought nothing of it. But I hadn't had time to digest all that he said. If I had been the one to bombard him, in the first fifteen minutes, with all my failed relationships, my distrust, or my love for a married man, I would have been the one with whipping red flags. I chose to keep them hidden, for now, secure, tight, and neatly packed like little anchovies, hoping the can was never opened.

Jacob returned in a jiffy, Magnum condom in hand, and proud of that. And how was sex? Just that—sex. Not bad, but definitely no connection. Sex is sometimes just sex.

The next morning, he sprinted out of bed and said, "Gotta get to work. See you at the gym later?"

"Yeah."

***

I called Meena to kiss and tell. "Oh, Meena, he's practically homeless!"

"*What?*"

I explained how the night unfolded.

"Wow, I wasn't expecting that. Why does he live in a hotel?" She wanted to know how this might be a financial benefit or bust.

"He mentioned having really, really bad credit or something," I said, thinking this would be the least of my concerns.

"So did you have sex with him?" she asked excitedly.

"Yes, I'm a whore. I still had sex with him, a homeless man!" I laughed.

She laughed. "At least he's good for that! Don't go falling in love with him."

"I won't."

"So, how was it?"

"He's a freak," I said.

"Oh my god, tell me what happened!"

"So, during my non-massage, all of a sudden I felt something wet on my butt…hole. He tried to lick it!" I knew I was blushing recounting this event.

"Oh my god!" she said, followed by fits of laughter. "What did you do?"

"I flipped around and said that I wasn't open to that. So he didn't try it again."

Meena later told me that anal sex and stimulation is very common these days. In her *National Geographic* magazine—no, not that publication, but somewhere in some hopefully reputable magazine—she recalled reading a well-researched article about how young girls, especially Muslim virgin girls, now actively participate in anal sex. They do this to maintain their "true" virginity. Well, I'm not Muslim, and I'm not a virgin. So my answer would still be *no* to anal sex.

My other friend Zane said that it was "wonderful" that Jacob was so different from me. "Opposites attract," he said, "and that way you're always discovering and trying new things. People who have everything in common get bored right away. Give Jacob a chance. I think you're dismissing him way too soon." And his advice on the anal sex? "In due time, once you build trust, you'll be open to it," he said.

Zane is a man, a gay man. Did I want to take anal sex advice from a gay man? Is it better or worse to take advice about anal sex from a gay man? The opinion would be so biased, I presume. Regardless, my answer would still be no.

I thought about the other opinion he'd offered. Was I dismissing Jacob too soon? So much doubt inside of me.

I saw Jacob that afternoon at the gym. He had his iPod on, working out; he was all sweaty and smiley. He did a little dance as he made his way over to me. I specifically remember him smiling at me this time; it was the first of the three or four times I'd ever see him smile at me.

"Working tonight?" he asked.

"Yeah, at eleven."

"Well, text me or something."

"OK."

"Or I should be texting or calling you, because it's the first twenty-four hours after sex that are the most critical," he declared.

I laughed at how correct that statement was, or is. It's that first phone call post-sex that women wait for so they can judge or analyze what it meant and where it will all go. And when that phone call doesn't happen within twenty-four hours, it creates confusion, wonder, an empty feeling. It's like having a surgeon do an all-night, invasive surgery through your abdomen, only for him never to call postoperatively to tell you what was found or diagnosed or to ask, "How are you feeling now?"

I didn't hear from Jacob until late that evening. It was at 10:20 p.m., when I pulled out of my garage for work, that I received a text from him. The text said, "Nite!" That was it, not even a full, "Goodnight," text. His twenty-four-hour, most critical moment was fulfilled. In his mind, he made the effort: he texted, "Nite!" to me.

I tried to justify this by thinking that it was enough, it was OK; after all, we'd seen each other earlier at the gym and spoken briefly. Stop overthinking—and what did it matter? I knew he and I were too different to have a relationship.

Jacob started regularly coming over on my nights off from work. I whipped up dinners left and right after my own workouts with Sheila. I'd see Jacob at the gym, and we'd confirm whether he was or wasn't coming over after work. I didn't want Sheila to know I was seeing him. I was afraid to get her opinion, so I kept silent.

.

TOURETTE'S OR NOT TOURETTE'S

"What are you gonna make for dinner tonight?" he asked after my workout with Sheila.

Jacob was half Italian, half Irish, so I thought I'd make something Italian, as I hadn't learned anything Irish. I told him I'd make him homemade lasagna.

"I'll be over after work. Oh, I wanted to ask you if you knew of anything I can do about my eyes." Had he noticed that I noticed his frequent and hard blinking? He continued, "My eyes are all bloodshot because they're always so dry. I have to constantly blink to try and wet them. I don't know what's wrong with them, and it's getting worse. Do you know of anything I can take?"

So that's what it was, dry eye syndrome? All this time I believed he had Tourette's. I wasn't a doctor. I couldn't diagnose, but his eyes were dry; how difficult is that? He couldn't produce enough tears or maintain the watery layer over his eyes. It commonly occurs in people over age forty; Jacob was forty-four. *How does he release his emotional toxins?* was my real question, but instead I asked, "Have you gone to the doctor?"

"No, I don't have insurance."

"You need an ophthalmologist," I said. He stared blankly at me, blinked some more, and gave no other indication of a response or of understanding me. I grabbed a piece of paper and wrote "ophthalmologist" on it.

"I know what an ophthalmologist is," he said, quite offended. "My dad *was* a doctor!" His dad was a doctor? How should I have known? And just because his dad was a doctor didn't mean a thing. Later I learned his dad had been a gynecologist and cut off one of Jacob's hemorrhoids right in his office. His dad was now in his eighties, was at a board-and-care home, and had dementia. All I knew about Jacob was that he and I didn't know how to communicate, much less telecommunicate, with one another. I interpreted his blank stare as his not knowing what I was talking about. Later I learned he stared blankly just to stare blankly, and I shouldn't interpret such stares and lack of emotion as "stares" and "lack of emotion." Got it?

"Have you tried eye drops?" I asked.

"Yeah, they don't work. You don't know or have anything from work?" I hated that question. Trying to diagnose a problem with a slew of symptoms is always fun, and I'm up for the challenge with friends complaining of non-life-threatening ailments. But people asking if I "had anything from work," meaning medication or pain pills, drove me crazy. So many people think nurses house entire pharmacies in their cabinets. The only time we might is if we're prescribed those medications for our own health issues. I don't have Vicodin, Norco, Percocet, Dilaudid, anti-nausea or high blood pressure medication, or insulin at my home. I have Aspercreme, Motrin, and Visine, all purchased over the counter.

"I'll see what I can find at the pharmacy next time I go to the store," I said.

"Visine doesn't work, babe."

"There are other eye drops, like those fake tears. I'll look into it."

"I need health insurance. Can you research that for me, too, like what number to call?"

I suddenly felt that weight again, like his first night over. I felt I needed to somehow find the cure to his dry eyes. He was depending on me to do so. In the brief time I'd known him, I knew that if there was ever a man that needed to cry, it was Jacob.

He mentioned his mother on occasion, saying how she was abusive to both him and his father. His father worked long hours; he'd come home, and Jacob's mother would begin to verbally abuse him, throw things at him, and not allow him to sleep. His father had crashed three times from falling asleep at the wheel. I hated his mother for what Jacob claimed she did to him and his father, and I told him so.

"No, you have to forgive, babe," he'd say. "That's what the Bible says, to forgive." Jacob was Catholic. I was not. He would use his beliefs and throw them at me whenever it benefited his situation and forget them at other times. It was during those forty-five seconds of his opening up about his mom or dad that his eyes looked like they were prepping themselves to cry, but either he wouldn't, or he couldn't.

I wanted to give him my tears. I wanted to cry for him. I wanted him to be able to have punctal plug surgery. I wanted to lick his eyeballs moist, the way an animal would to her offspring. I wanted to weep over his open eyes and let my tears run over his bloodshot, dry, itchy eyes to soothe them. But human beings don't do any of that. Instead, they turn to what money can buy.

I looked up health plans for him and printed them out. I gave him the number to call and told him to ask for detailed information on copays, deductibles, and whether the plans included eye exams. I never called the number for him, and he never called for himself.

"Maybe this is what you need," I said, handing him a printout on punctal plugs.

"What is it?"

"They're tiny little plugs that are placed in your tear ducts," I explained as best as I could from the little I read. "When your eye makes tears, they drain down your tear duct and eventually your nose, like when people cry. So the plug blocks that duct, and the tears stay over your eyeball instead, keeping them nice and moist." I was excited that I found a possible solution for him.

"Yeah, I'll have to look into it," he said monotonically and placed the papers aside. No reaction. I couldn't see if his pupils dilated, which would have indicated that he really was excited. Remember, his blank stares didn't necessarily mean he wasn't excited.

I couldn't force him to read it. I couldn't force him to call and get health plan information. I couldn't make him want his eyes to feel some relief no matter what it took, although he complained incessantly about their dryness! The most I could do for him was to go to Walmart and purchase the best over-the-counter eye drops available.

I read the active ingredient on the back of every box. Ay-ay-ay, reading all the hard-to-pronounce, multisyllabic ingredients were making me cross-eyed. It was all so confusing. Did I want redness relief in addition to lubrication? What if his dry eyes indicated an allergy? Did I need antihistamine product? I purchased the one that sounded the most familiar and gave him the box when I went to the gym.

That night he came over and said, "I can't get those drops into my eyes, and there's hardly anything in the vial."

"There's one drop in each vial. You need to use a separate vial for each eye. That's what the directions say."

"Oh, I didn't read them. I was trying to use one vial for both eyes. I brought one so you can put it in my eyes." He pulled out the tiny plastic vial from his pocket like a child.

"Which eye do you want to lubricate? There's no way I can put half a drop into each eye." I sounded like a mother.

"Never mind. I'll do it tomorrow when I'm at home."

"Yeah, give them a try. They were expensive. Maybe they'll work."

No response then or ever and I never asked. I didn't need to inquire. I knew that either they weren't enough or he never learned to apply the one-drop dosage into each eye, as his frequent, heavy blinking twitch continued. There wasn't anything more I could do.

AN IGUANA IN THE MINEFIELD

Our relationship was carried out primarily in silence. I've tried to recall his laugh but can't. I've tried to recall if he made me laugh; he didn't. I can barely recall the sound of his voice at all. The nine months he was coming over, we ate great dinners in silence, we watched semi-decent movies with an occasional glance, and we could have had another full-grown adult sleep between us in bed.

Jacob's conversations were one-liners most of the time. "I'm tired. I need a massage, babe. I worked *all* day, babe. Got any food? Gotta wake up early. Can't stay tonight, hon; I'm stressed!"

The only time I saw his eyes light up and heard a sentence containing more than four words was when he was talking about CrossFit or his star-athlete client, Katie. But when he came alive, it was something to live for. I'd feel my heart jump-start on the very few occasions we had normal exchanges of dialogue. My heart was waiting for those moments, as it was dying from lack of attention, and circulation, in between these rare takes of interaction.

Phone conversations were rare. We texted—also one-liners of three or four words. "I'm on my way. Gonna cook tonight? Can you wash my clothes?" He only communicated his *needs*. One time, after learning Gold's hadn't paid him his full commission, he phoned me. He blabbed on and on about all his sales, how hard he worked, what they owed him, what they paid him, and what the labor board said about his case. He then said, "I'm sorry I'm going on and on like this."

I said, "No, you're talking!"

He seemed equally surprised, as there was a pause (he was thinking), and he said, "Yeah"—another pause—"I'm talking!" I remember he chuckled (although I can't recall the sound of it) and said, "Well, you keep saying you want me to talk. Pretty soon you'll be asking me to stop talking so much!" And that was probably the most normal relationship exchange we'd had up until that point.

Needless to say, we hadn't uttered the words, "I love you." Although it was only a three-word sentence and would have met his per-sentence word limit, we never said it. We never felt it. "I love you," is also less than the 140-character maximum allowed in a Twitter message. I imagine Jacob is now thriving in the Twitter world of one-liners. I know that I honestly never fell in love with him, yet my actions screamed otherwise. I never repeated a home-cooked meal, with the exception of my favorite, broiled salmon. I'd spend the days before he came over thinking of what to make, reviewing cookbooks and recipes, purchasing organic or grass-fed beef, his preference. I thought about the presentation and imagined what he'd say: "Gosh, babe, this is a great meal. Where did you get the recipe?" But no, it was usually, "Got any more?" and, "Thanks, babe. Got ice cream?"

And I didn't just scoop and serve ice cream. I'd get a nice deep bowl, swirl chocolate on the bottom, place perfectly rounded scoops of vanilla into a voluptuous mound, swirl more chocolate on top, and stab Japanese chocolate-covered Pocky sticks on top. It was beautiful. I'd serve this scrumptious creation to him as he gazed straight ahead into the television, mindlessly. The first time I ever served it to him, his eyes lit up like a five-year-old child's! Times thereafter, I think I heard, "It needs more chocolate," in a complaining tone. Actually, I know I heard, "It needs more chocolate." My kitchen's layout is wide open to the living room. I had a perfect view of, and aim at, the back of his head.

It took all my power not to throw the bottle of chocolate at the back of his unappreciative skull and scream with frustration, "It needs more fucking chocolate, Jacob? Well, here!" I imagined flinging the plastic chocolate bottle in resentment across the kitchen at the target of his big, fat head. I was becoming his mother. Instead of putting him to sleep with sips from a bottle of red wine, I'd knock him unconscious with a hard occipital blow with a chocolate syrup bottle. I was becoming increasingly violent in thought, and for a moment I sympathized with his mother.

By the time I finished cleaning up the kitchen, I'd hear him belch. That was my cue. He'd hand me the empty bowl. I'd sit next to him and finally—yes, finally—he'd rest his hand on my leg and finally—yes, finally—make eye contact with me. I yearned for this precise moment, a touch, and a slight connection with the man I was working so hard to please. And then he'd speak. "Will you massage me?" My heart would drop. If I gave a look of disinterest or irritation, he'd say, "Babe, I worked *all* day!" or, "I really need it tonight. I'm so sore." He'd name a CrossFit workout he did and his timing. For example, he'd say, "I did Fran in thirty seconds less than my previous time! Not bad for an old man, huh?" *Sure, I guess.* I'd always agree to the massage. He'd lie on the ground or couch butt naked. "Gonna use oil, babe?"

"Yeah." I could hear how monotonically, how softly I spoke. I was barely audible, and my voice cracked on that one syllable, that one consenting word with which I gave into him on many occasions. Joe was right. My voice went into a whisper when I was shy or afraid to say what I really wanted to say. Jacob never noticed. Goodness, I missed Joe.

I'd go get the oil and pour a few drops on his back. He'd squirm and say, "Warm it up in your hands first, babe!" Of course! What the hell was I thinking about that I didn't warm it up in my hands first? Joe. I was thinking about Joe. And this was Jacob. This was our nightly ritual, every single time we hung out. Dinner, movie, and a massage. But shame on me for not warming up the damn oil. How careless of me.

And yet I believed (and maybe I still do) in treating your man like a king, and I was more than practicing what I preached. I was only a whispered hint away from his asking me to feed him grapes and fan him alongside his other concubines. Oh, wrong man—that's Jared. Jacob didn't have a harem; he couldn't multitask like Jared. Jacob behaved more like a spoiled child than a noble king. Therefore, it was only a matter of time before I pulled out my tit to breastfeed him, and perhaps burp him, too. Side note, only treat a man like a king if he *deserves* to be treated like a king.

Jacob never complained about the meal or massages. That

would require talking and the possibility of an argument. However, he did make comments about things in my home that I knew he wanted me to change. He'd say things like, "That TV is way too small for that space." Translation: "Get a bigger TV."

"It's like a hotel TV." Translation: "I know, I live in a hotel and the TVs are small and suck, like yours."

"If you had a pool, I'd be here all the time." Translation: "Get a pool before summer, and *then* you'll really have me here visiting you. And my buddies and I can swim and BBQ during the day while you sleep!"

"Your bed's too hard. I can't sleep here." Translation: "Get a better bed for my back." Or, "I can always use your lousy bed as an excuse as to why I can't spend the night. Perfect!"

"That vegetable lasagna you made...gave me the shits!" Translation: "Don't use so many damn vegetables when you cook. It gives me the shits!"

"You're drunk. Night shift's made you crazy." Translation: "I fucking resent you." He once said this upon entering my house, and I hadn't taken one sip or spoken one word—yet. I guess I had that drunk and crazy look.

Perhaps I assumed or put too many words into Jacob's mouth, but I had to; I was getting nothing out of him. And, God, how I did try.

And why did I continue to try? I don't know. Actually, I do know; I just don't know how I was able to tolerate it so long. But I do know why I tried. I wanted to prove to myself that I could have a successful relationship, that someone *did* want to be with me, that I wasn't a failure, that I could reel in a man and keep him happy. Isn't that what society says women are to do? And if we can't do it, then something is terribly wrong with us. We have to be able to do it once, get married and then divorced, and then people will at least stop questioning why we don't have a man. A divorced woman has proven her ability at least once and ranks higher in judgment than a single, never-been-married woman. And I wanted to prove to Jacob that life could be good. I absolutely knew he had it in him to be a loving, considerate man. I knew it was deep down in there, and I wanted to dig it out of him. Couldn't he see through his twitches and dry, bloodshot eyes that I was worth having and loving?

I shared my woes with Zane: "I feel like I have lots to offer, and he doesn't want it, beside the massage and dinners."

"You do have a lot to offer."

"I feel torn between thinking so lowly of myself, like I can't get a guy who lives in a hotel to even like me, and thinking so highly of myself, like I'm his winning lottery ticket and he should consider himself lucky."

"You *are* like a winning lottery ticket for him, yet he's settling for the fifty-dollar Walmart gift card!"

"Exactly!"

"I know what you mean. I've had those relationships, too," Zane confessed.

I was babysitting my brother's iguana one night that Jacob came over for dinner. He strolled in, texting or looking at his cell phone, as usual, and turned on the television while I cooked. I served him and said, "You didn't even say, 'Hi,' to the houseguest," and motioned toward the pillows that Bruna the Iguana rested upon.

Jacob's eyes lit up; he put his plate down and went over to her. "Hi, baby," he said, caressing her green skin. "Can I pick her up?"

"Yeah, she's friendly."

He gently lifted her off her pillow and gave her light kisses and spoke baby talk to her. "I want her to play," he said like a child.

"She doesn't *play*. She's old. That's all she does: rest, sleep, eat, and sunbathe."

He put her down, disappointed, and returned to his dinner, still looking at her. "Wake her up!"

"She is awake. She's resting," I reiterated.

"Aww." Again disappointed.

After dinner he attempted once again to pet her, kiss her, talk to her, but she stared blankly at him. Maybe now Jacob would understand how it feels to beg for attention and get nothing in return. For that split second, Jacob and I would have something in common: disappointment from lack of acknowledgment.

I sat on my side of the couch.

"Massage, babe?" he asked.

"I'd love one," I said, knowing that's not what he meant.

"Babe! I worked *all* day!"

"So did I!"

"But that's different."

"How so? I lift patients, heavy ones. I turn them over and wipe their ass. I reach up high to hang things and grab things. I bend down to empty things or pick things up. I help the elderly, the ill, and the injured all night long. My back is always killing me."

"If you had a massage table, I'd give you a massage," he lied.

"I give you one all the time on the floor."

"Yeah, but you're little. It's different for me; I'm a lot taller."

Whatever.

He fell asleep during the massage. I woke him up and he followed me to bed. The sex was becoming nonexistent. And I wouldn't have complained if we at least had some other form of interaction, but we didn't. I kept my night-light on to do some reading; I wasn't tired yet.

"Turn out the light, babe," he didn't ask but told me.

"I'm reading."

"I can't sleep if there's light."

Reluctantly, the book went down, and the light went off. I snuggled up next to him; he didn't reciprocate. I waited several minutes until he fell asleep. Then I crept out of bed. *Who the fuck is this guy?* I thought. For the second time—yes, the second time (of only two times ever in my entire life)—I went through his wallet. The first time, while he was in the bathroom, I'd opened up his wallet to confirm his full name and age. I quickly glimpsed at his debit card and driver's license. Yep, it matched. This time, while he snored in my bed, I took the wallet to my kitchen and placed it in my utensil drawer. I figured I'd look through it with my hands in the drawer. If he were to walk in on me, I'd push the wallet further in, grab a spoon, close the drawer, and serve both of us some ice cream.

My heart was racing. Was this the type of psycho my friend Alicia said I should be? She'd tell me that I was "too normal" and that in order to really pique a man's interest, I should hide out in the backseat of his car and then, when he got into the car, pop my head up and be like, "Oh, hey, I was waiting for you." This complete invasion of wallet privacy was the most I could do without causing myself an anxiety attack. How do women do this shit? I considered snooping a total lack of respect on my part, yet I had to continue this investigation. I carefully looked at each card, and then I saw it, the same exact card I saw before, but this time I read it carefully. His name wasn't Jacob, it was Joshua. Why did I see the name Jacob before? Because we see what we want to see. There's even a word for it. It's called denial. My eyes had tricked me earlier on in this relationship to allow me to continue on this dreadful path. Why? Because that's the only way I *could* allow it, by a trick of the eye! I finished looking through the wallet: a haircutting business card, a GNC shopper card, a gas card linked to hotel stays (he must have endless points on that!), a Gold's Gym guest card, 140 dollars cash, and a photo of a very young-looking "Joshua" on his driver's license. I wrote down the address, a post-office box.

I put his wallet back into his pants, lying on the floor. I went back into bed as quietly as I could. I lay there in the darkness, no questions answered, but a more profound *Who the fuck is this guy?* swarmed about in my head. Now I really couldn't sleep. *I'll search him out on the Internet.* Again, I climbed out of bed and went to my laptop, which was on the opposite side of the house. I typed in his name, his real one, and the Google search immediately brought up his name followed by the words *serial killer*. No! Oh my god, what do I do if I click on this headline and I confirm it's the same man who is lying in my bed? Do I run, even though he's fast asleep like a baby? Or do I call the police and wait outside for them? Yeah, that's what I'll do: take my cell phone outside, around the corner, and call the local police. I thought about how he hated the show *Dexter*, a show about a serial killer. "That's so fake. I hate that show," he'd said to me once while I was watching it.

"It's great," I argued. "I love Dexter. He should be everyone's hero."

"There's no way he could commit those crimes with his build. It's not realistic."

This conversation streamed through my mind. Is this why he hated *Dexter*? How would he know what kind of build was needed to take down prey?

I clicked on the *Wikipedia* article; this serial killer was listed in freaking *Wikipedia*! There was a photo, *phew!* It wasn't him. It was some other crazy-ass person. I couldn't finish reading the article; I'd have nightmares. And besides, I needed to research the stranger lying in my bed, not the serial killer that's now locked up.

I ran a search with his full name and bought a background report for a mere fifty dollars. A steal. The report was instantly available for viewing. I perused the record: no marriage, no divorce, no property owned, nothing. Absolutely nothing that stood out. No criminal record. Nothing. What a waste! Or was it? It gave me a sense of relief knowing that the man in my bed, fast asleep, didn't have a criminal record, wasn't a serial killer…yet was still a mystery. Is finding nothing better than finding something?

It was 3:20 a.m. by the time I finished reading the report of nothing and attempting to get to know him via Google searches. I hated the Internet for its lack of privacy. I climbed back in bed and was now tired, ready to sleep. I thought, *He's safe enough. Relax, worried mind; you have nothing to fear but fear itself.* I scooted close to his body; he moved. He was awake. "Hold me," I whispered in the darkness.

An explosion! He angrily flew out of bed, screaming at me, "I NEED TO SLEEP, AND I CAN'T SLEEP WITH YOU ASKING ME TO DO STUFF! MY SLEEP IS IMPORTANT TO ME! DON'T YOU GET THAT? I'M GOING HOME!"

My eyes had had no time to see this red flag, this bomb, coming.

I was rattled. My legs wobbled with fear or shock or confusion as I tried to follow him.

He marched into the living room and started dressing. "What's wrong with you?" I asked. I was scared, but I wasn't backing down. "Let's talk it out."

"IT'S THREE IN THE FUCKING MORNING. I'M NOT GONNA TALK ABOUT ANYTHING RIGHT NOW!" he screamed.

"No! This isn't how you handle things, Jacob!" I tried to

reason, being the damn girl that I am.

"Well, this is the way I handle things!" he said and headed straight out the door.

Silence. I stood there and watched the headlights of his car as he drove away. Silence.

Wow. I'd never had a fight like that before with anyone. I'd never been walked out on before by anyone. I stood there, shaking, thinking I'd see the headlights of his car return. But I didn't. I saw his red brake lights stop at my corner, turn, and drive away. Did people really behave this way? I'd seen it in movies but not real life. I waited a few minutes at my door, confused, heavyhearted. I made my way back to the tension-filled bedroom, and although he was gone, I still felt heat, his red-flagged presence burning throughout my home. I'm surprised my fire alarms didn't sound. Bruna the Iguana remained innocently on her living room pillow. She probably wanted to bitch slap me for having let this toxic man into my home.

The wonderful thing about having friends that work the night shift is that they're available at half past three in the morning when your night goes unexpectedly haywire. I texted Meena a quick message saying that Jacob and I had fought and he had walked out on me. She quickly phoned me from the bathroom at work. "Are you kidding me? What exactly happened?"

I told her about the whole night, the Google searches, everything.

"Well, now you know how he'd handle any problems you may have. He'd walk out."

Yes. She was right, and I knew it. I didn't want to know it.

I replayed everything over in my head. Had I crossed the line by asking him to hold me? Was I that much of a nuisance? He seemed to have been sleeping fine, even snoring.

The words, *Let him go*, repeated in my head like a mantra.

I couldn't sleep. I'd been so tired but now was wide awake. I thought back to before I met Jacob and what my plan was: to have a baby. I'd still been actively looking at donor profiles and saving a few that I liked. But I hadn't purchased any sperm. I was secretly hoping that things would work out with Jacob and I could leave this sperm donor plan behind. But I knew that the sperm bank route, Plan A, was the better choice. I went back to my laptop at four thirty and went through profiles for a few hours. I'd found my donor. He was half Mexican and half German and was said to resemble Olivier Martinez, the actor from the movie *Unfaithful*. Fitting, don't you think? I loved the lover he portrayed in that movie. I loved his essay (the sperm donor's essay, not the actor Olivier Martinez's essay); he was right brain *and* left brain, analytical and intuitive, from what I read. He felt overwhelmingly like the right choice.

In a matter of a few hours, I'd gone from purchasing a background check for an asshole and stranger lying in my bed, to purchasing vials of a lovely sounding stranger's sperm, lying in wait at a sperm bank. I was ecstatic! I'd never felt this excited over a donor before. Anytime I did anything to progress my journey of having a baby, I felt a surge of positive energy. I knew this was the road from which I should never have strayed.

I returned to work the following night. I hadn't heard from Jacob, and even though I was back to my Plan A, I was still down that things hadn't worked out.

At work, I felt that I could hardly breathe. I placed the pulse oximeter on my finger to check my oxygen saturation. My heart was beating, according to the machine, at a slow, but within normal limits, heavy sixty-four beats per minute. My oxygen was 92 percent even with the deepest breaths I took. 92 percent? Anything above 90 percent is normal, but geez, my patients with chronic obstructive pulmonary disease (COPD) could maintain higher oxygenation than that! I wanted to lie down in the fetal position. Then I thought about the fetal heart and lungs, with holes and fluid. Maybe when we're hurt and want to revert to a cozy fetal position, our heart and lungs also revert back to how they were in utero. It was another long-shot theory, but I bought into it, as that's how it felt. Everything was going in the wrong direction, like my breech birth.

I recounted the story to Zane. I told him how the night started and finished. I needed a male perspective on the whole scenario. And this is what Zane's bottom line and response was: "So, basically your iguana got more loving attention from him than you did for the whole night, because he didn't touch you once."

Correct. I laughed. I had to. "At least one of us did."

Zane continued, "Are iguanas from Italy?"

"No."

"Hmm…because Jacob is like an iguana. He sits there on your couch, doesn't do much."

I'd seen the comparison, but no, my brother's iguana was much more loving. This iguana loved to cuddle *and* would make eye contact with me. She'd even stare at me at times. And she never exploded or ran off when I touched her. Jacob was proving to be lone as a hawk and much colder than a reptile.

A few days later, I had a workout session with Sheila. I put on my armor and horse blinders and headed into the gym. I'd stay focused only on Sheila's face and words. I wouldn't look around—I, too, would avoid eye contact with Jacob. His behavior had been unacceptable. That may sound motherly, but it was true.

Sheila had me run around the building a few times to warm up. When I entered the side door, there he was, hanging from a piece of equipment. "Hey," he said in a friendly tone.

I lifted my eyebrows in acknowledgment and continued on.

"I'm not mad or anything," he began his explanation. "My sleep is really important to me, as it probably is to you, working nights and all."

I didn't say anything. Now he wanted to talk it out, during my paid personal training session, in the middle of the open floor area of the gym? No. Now, his sorry-ass explanations would have to wait.

Sheila continued as if she were oblivious to all of this and had me sit on the floor for some floor exercises. I was concentrating on my core, or whatever, when a small marble hit me on the shoulder. Luckily, it didn't take out my left eye. I looked up in the direction it came from. Jacob was sitting at the personal trainers' desk. He pretended to be looking at the computer and had a boyish smile on his face.

And I felt that sadness I'd felt the first day he came over. Because I knew this was his pathetic way of apologizing, throwing a marble at me. This was the only way he knew how to do it. It was his way of saying, "Can we still play together? Be friends again? Please don't be mad. I'm not."

He looked up and said, "What? I'm not doing anything," and he smiled (smile number two or three, if you're keeping count) at me. *God, if you exist, please help me help myself right now!* Fuck. I really wanted to be angry; I really did. But it's not my nature. The most I could give myself credit for was ignoring him throughout the remainder of my workout.

He approached me later. "So can I still come over?"

"Don't ever do that again," I said.

"You're making a big deal out of it. Let me come over tonight."

I let him walk back in as easily as he'd walked out. I hated myself for this. Habit, or our core nature, is so hard to break. We always revert to what we know. We repeat our behavior, for better or worse.

THE RETURN OF JOE

It was mid-May. My frustration was growing and my relationship with Jacob was the same as it ever was. I never even mentioned him to my family. Why should I? There was no progress. I was a soup kitchen and masseuse to this man. The more my frustration mounted and I remained mute with Jacob, the more I was justified in reaching out to someone I did love and respect, Joe. But I contemplated this danger and instead sent a text to someone safer, Jared.

Jared and I planned to go out the following Saturday night, but that was still over a week away. I was so restless.

I looked up Joe's work number at his new place of employment as an accountant. I can't recall who told me where he now worked. I found his name in the directory, called after hours, and left him a message. I wished him a happy birthday and said that I simply had been thinking of him (constantly) and hoped he, and his family, were doing well (truly). *Innocent enough*, I thought. That was a Thursday night. He called Monday morning. It was a relief hearing a voice that was filled with excitement to speak with me. He quickly explained that he had Fridays off from work so he'd just received the message, that he missed me, that he thought about me often, that he always wanted to ask the coffee shop workers if I'd been by but was afraid to, that he was so happy that I called, that he wanted to see me as soon as possible. I took a deep breath. I knew my oxygen saturation was at 100 percent and my heart was at a serene sixty-four beats per minute. He asked if I was seeing anyone; I told him about Jacob and how lousy it was. He wasn't fazed by Jacob, as he shouldn't have been, because he knew he was the special one. He reiterated how he wanted to see me and asked me to e-mail him my address.

We planned for a Friday visit. His mom happened to live up the street from me. Imagine that! He would visit her and then me, or was it me and then her? All I knew was that after nearly two years, I'd see my Joe again. Hallelujah.

Friday finally came. I didn't tell anyone—not my cousin, not any of my friends—as I wasn't sure how things would go, or how far things would go. I made lunch, tri-tip and quinoa. I left my garage door open, and he called out my name as he walked in through the garage door. I jumped up from the couch and rushed my little legs to meet him in the hallway, my heart beating fast, my underarms starting to sweat. I was nervous. I was excited. I couldn't wait to see him. And there he was. Beautiful as ever, towering over my five-foot stature.

"Hey," was all I could say. I swear my eyes must have been sparkling and my words breathless.

"Hi, kid," he said. Joe always called me "kid." I liked it. I hoped he didn't call his wife that, too.

We hugged. I didn't have to ask. It was natural. It was nice. It was strong. It was wrong. It was too late. I could never have met him and *not* have done this time and again. He was irresistible. He was relaxed, or appeared to be. There were no holes in my heart, as it was melting, expanding, and collapsing onto itself with every beat. *This is where I belong, in this man's arms.*

"Show me your new house," he said.

I gave him the tour while holding his hand.

"I'm so happy for you," he said.

He and his wife had had a baby, a girl. He showed me photos of her on his cell phone. She looked exactly like him. He asked about my baby plans. I told him I finally bought donor sperm. He asked about the donor.

"He's eccentric, kind of like Johnny Depp," I said after describing him.

"He's gonna be a weirdo then?"

"Oh, all men are jealous of Johnny!"

We laughed. "I'm happy for you, Julie. I want you to have a baby because I know that's what you want. You deserve to be happy."

We sat on the couch two feet apart.

"Are you scared? You're sitting so far from me, like you're afraid to touch me," he said.

"No. I want to look at you. It's been so long. You know I always want to touch you."

"Then touch me," he encouraged.

I got close, laid my head on his chest, looked up at him, and caressed his face, outlining his eyebrows, cheekbones, and lips with my fingers, as I'd done in the past. He let me. We looked at each other without saying a word. Now, these are the types of nonverbal moments that I appreciated.

"I made lunch," I said.

We maneuvered our way to the kitchen. He took a seat on one of the stools as I got out plates and something to drink. We talked nonstop; I don't know what about. My lungs must have been filled with so much air—I felt I was floating. He grabbed me and had me sit on his lap.

"I've missed you," he said.

"I've missed you."

We kissed. We ate lunch. And then we had dessert. Yes, yes. Yes—we did.

Joe and I always had the most intense conversations before sex and highly emotional and honest conversations after sex. Always.

"We're no longer on the same playing field," he said.

"What do you mean?"

"Well, now you have someone. Before, it was just you and me. I didn't have to worry. I hope Jake the Snake doesn't give me anything."

"We've never been on the same playing field, because you've always had someone."

"No, it's different now." He repeated, "Jake the Snake, Jake the Snake." I thought it was funny.

"You'll always have her, though. I won't always be with Jacob."

Then somehow the conversation progressed to *if* he should

ever get caught, he knew that his wife would leave him.

"Then why do you do it?"

"This is who I am. I don't like it, but I accept it. I'd cheat on you, too, if we were together."

I knew that! Joe was like a beautiful exotic bird whose DNA necessitated his flying around for sheer mental survival. He couldn't be caged by marriage or a child. I knew that four years ago when I first met him.

"There are times when I'm about to do something bad, and I know I shouldn't be doing it," he explained.

"Is this one of those times?" I asked.

"No. It's different with you and me; you know that."

"Because you know I'm safe and won't tell?"

"No, because we're friends first."

"I don't understand why you'd cheat if you think she'd leave."

"I guess I'm willing to risk it. I'm stupid. No matter how much I hate my dad for doing it to my mom, I'm the same. It's the same cycle."

"If your wife finds out, she won't leave. I just know it. And you'll stay, too."

"It seems like you want me to get caught."

"No. I have to be careful because if I get pregnant, I know I'll be the one left all alone."

We'd have this conversation or something similar to it every time he visited. He looked like he felt bad about it every time. I felt like shit, too. I knew it was wrong. He explained himself and his situation so quietly and calmly, so remorsefully, every time. He said he could never leave; it would hurt her. She didn't deserve that. After all, she was the one who'd stood by his side when he had nothing, was lost; he owed it to her, staying with her.

"I want to see you every Friday that I have off," he said.

And because I could see myself doing this every day, and any given day for the rest of my life, it was no wonder that I then immediately had to lie to him, to say, "I no longer feel for you the way I used to." I had to lie to myself to save myself from *this* that couldn't be.

He gave a slight nod of his head to acknowledge what I said. "Can we ever get together without having these intense conversations?" he asked gently. Joe never raised his voice or sounded irritated. Everything was tranquil. Every discussion, every disagreement, everything was intense but composed.

I didn't know. I gave a slight nod of my head to acknowledge what he'd said.

"Let me hold you for a bit," he said and had no problem staring at me in long moments of silence. It was such a different type of silence. A lovely, welcomed one. Sometimes silence says everything.

I walked him to the door and wondered how long we could actually do this.

"Do you think when you're fifty years old and I'm…." I started calculating my age in my head, even though I knew I was seven years older than him.

"And you're seventy!" he said jokingly. I laughed.

"Yes, seventy. That you and I will still be—"

He cut me off before I could finish my sentence. "Probably," he said.

And that's what I was afraid of, that we would continue this relationship for a lifetime. And what I was really afraid of was that we wouldn't. Could I possibly ever be over him?

I don't know.

KOKO

Jacob's stress level was mounting. He no longer ran around the gym to harass me during workouts; he'd make comments about how at least my job as a nurse was secure, because his wasn't. He was attempting to start CrossFit at the gym. Gold's was a typical gym and didn't want change. Why fix what wasn't broken? People signed up, paid their monthly dues, and didn't use the equipment. Why rattle things? And that's exactly what Jacob wanted to do, introduce CrossFit, make something his own. But management or the owners were on his back. All they wanted him to do was sell personal training, not bring in big, heavy tires and endless, strange lifting equipment that shook the ground when dropped during training. He worked night and day on the implementation of CrossFit into the gym. He rarely came over in May and June. And considering my reunion with Joe, I didn't bug him or even want him coming over.

It was Saturday, the night Jared and I'd planned to do something. He was at a charity event. I was at home drinking. Knowing Jared, I figured he'd meet someone there and forget about our date. So I thought it best to make the most of my own night. But then at midnight he asked if I wanted to go out with him and another friend of his, a good female friend of his. I didn't. I couldn't believe—or rather, I *could* believe—he waited until midnight to ask me this. I wasn't in the mood to go out. I couldn't drive. I was halfway to being drunk. I'd need to sober up, shower and get ready all over again. I felt down. I'd slept with Joe the day before, Jacob was too busy for me, and I was waiting on Jared. My self-made trinity of a mess: Joe, Jared, and Jacob.

I texted him back, "You suck."

He said he'd be right over. Well, that was easy. That's what I wanted!

By the time Jared arrived, I'd nearly finished the decoupage of a wood hope chest, and I'd certainly finished off an entire bottle of Pinot Noir. I was feeling weepy, emotional. I was an emotional drunk. I grilled some meat and laid out some cheese for Jared upon his arrival.

"You're such a Latina," he stated.

"What do you mean?"

"The moment I walk in, you're in the kitchen prepping to feed me. That's a Latin woman thing."

I opened the second bottle of Pinot Noir and we began, or continued, to drink.

He told me about how he'd nearly slept with his first black girl.

"Tell me about her. Why *didn't* you sleep with her?" I asked.

"She didn't smell right."

Oh, here we go again. Jared and his fucking nose smelling the wrong, right, or absent pheromones from potential one-night stands or future relationships.

"What do you mean?" Did I really want to know?

"Well, we were dancing really close, and she said she'd never been with a white guy. I told her I'd never been with a black girl. She basically indicated she was open to having sex with me, and I found her attractive. So while we were dancing, I placed my fingers down her and then I gave it a taste."

Poker-faced, I stood staring at Jared in silence. I finally spoke. "You did this in public?"

Laughter. Jared nodded yes. Laughter.

"OK, then what?" Did I want to know?

"Well, she didn't smell or taste right, like something bad was happening down there. My finger smelled bad. Something wasn't right, and I got turned off."

"Something like chlamydia?" I asked laughing.

"Possibly."

"That's gross, but funny. How can you do that?"

"Do what?"

"Taste girls like that. That's disgusting. The vagina is like an open wound, oozing and stuff."

"That must be your upbringing, because I remember you didn't like oral sex."

How can the preference for oral sex be based on upbringing? I don't know one family that encourages, discourages, or talks about oral sex and how to be open to or reject the idea of it.

"I'd rather just have sex," I said.

"But you did let me once."

"I remember. Your facial hair was growing out and it was a very scruffy feeling. I actually liked it. It felt like an exfoliation," I complimented.

"Like a spa treatment!" he said.

"Did I smell or taste bad?"

"No. I don't remember. But I'm guessing not. I only remember the bad-smelling ones."

Relief. "It's gross," I reiterated, "but I know women who say they lock their boyfriend's head down there. It's a requirement for them! They aren't to come up for air until they're finished."

"Are you self-conscious?"

"I guess. It's so different from male genitals. It's not an open wound, it's more like a finger."

"Or an arm," he said, referring to his manhood.

"Actually, I think it's because I get irritated and bored!"

"Bored?"

"Yeah, it feels like this to me." I demonstrated by taking my index finger and poking at his rib repeatedly. "It's irritating!" I said. "And I feel like they're down there and not paying attention to me. I get bored. I just like sex."

"Then they're not doing it right."

"If I said I don't like vanilla ice cream and tried several different vanilla ice creams, then we would conclude that I don't like vanilla ice cream, right?"

"Maybe." He wasn't ready to give in.

"Yet with oral sex, everyone thinks I gotta keep trying it. I don't like it." No, I'm not a fan of the cunnilingus. Even talking about it bored me. I moved on to what was really bothering me. "I think Jacob's too sexually advanced for me."

"How so?"

"I think he likes anal stuff, and I'm not open to that."

Jared laughed. "Why, what happened?"

"Well, he went for my butthole one night with his tongue. I screamed and turned around. It was him trying to lick it!"

"Yeah, I remember you didn't like any of that."

"What? What do you mean?" What the hell was he referring to?

"I tried that once on you."

What? Jared? *What?* My clean-cut, silly, naïve boy tried that on me? He, too, was into that? "No, you didn't. You must be confusing me with some other girl."

"No, I specifically remember it was you. You said, 'What was that?' I could tell you wouldn't be open to it, so I pretended it was an accident."

I was mortified by his words! Not rejected, for once, but mortified! "Are you sure it was me? Because I don't remember any of this."

"Yeah, it was you."

Oh my gosh, was I that behind the times? I didn't have a Facebook account, I never tried Internet dating, I didn't have an iPhone or iPad, I hated text messaging, I still believed in the handwritten letter and old forms of communication—like the telephone (landline preferably)—and I didn't have any desire to experience any form of anal manipulation. I have an occasional pesky hemorrhoid! And he's a doctor. Had he forgotten about *Clostridium difficile* infections (*C. DIFF!*) and the endless stinking diarrhea that comes out of our patients

I lost my appetite.

I always tell my girlfriends to forget about prostitution and strip joints; I have a business idea that would for sure rake in the cash, and that business would be...butt sniffing! If Jared could build a relationship based on smell, then I could build a business based on it. Men are disgusting and are like dogs in that they love to sniff ass. This business venture would be set up like the old-fashioned money-slot peep shows, but we would take cold, hard cash or credit cards. Once their money was inserted into a pay machine, the curtain would rise, a woman would press her ass up against a Plexiglas window that had precut, strategically placed air holes on it. The paying, nostril-flaring man could take a couple whiffs and views for the allotted prepaid time. We would make millions! And the man could have his choice of the type of asshole he wanted to view or sniff—freshly washed, three-hour musk, a hairy hole, a bleached hole, a shaven hole, a where-the-hell-is-the-hole—the options would be endless. There would never be any penetration of any kind, and yet we could make millions with this fetish! There's gotta be a state in this great America of ours that would allow such a business. Calm down, PTA moms; we wouldn't only pay taxes, but we would be located on some lonely industrial road—the kind of road your husband takes home from work. We needed a catchy name, like Stop-n-Sniff. Or Holey Scents! Or Order An Odor or Freaky Fragrance. For those men who are more middle-of-the-road in level of freakiness, like Jared, we'd also offer cleavage sniffing. Hey, Jared was right: there might be something to this whole pheromone attraction thing.

I needed another glass of wine. "Yeah, one night, Jacob and I were having sex, and right when I was about to orgasm, he shoved his finger up my butt!"

"Didn't you like it?" he teased.

I hadn't told a soul about this embarrassing incident. But once I did start telling a few close friends, they were like, "Oh yeah, me and my boyfriend do that to each other, too. It's like a special treat every now and then." Who was the freak, they or I?

"I read it's to make your orgasm last longer." I ignored Jared's question.

Jared flashed the boyish smile that all men show whenever talking about sex. "And did it? How did you like it?"

"Strange, not bad," I admitted. "I was caught off guard, then it was too late, it was done! We never mentioned a word about it. And it never happened again."

"I think it's a control thing with you," he said, analyzing why I hadn't let a man in my back door.

A trust thing? A control thing? Probably. I figured I'd had enough ass manipulation in my life. After all, I'd been born butt first. All I knew was that if I ever were to have anal fondling or sex, it would be (a) with my husband that I completely trusted, (b) if I were kidnapped by aliens and anally probed out of my control, or (c) if I got reincarnated as a virgin Muslim girl who desperately wanted to maintain her virginity to avoid a stoning. And since I didn't see a husband or alien invasion in my future, it was only option *c* that I had to worry about, since I do believe in reincarnation.

"So do you think Jacob and I will work out?" I was feeling more depressed by the minute.

"No," Jared stated simply and continued to eat the last of the grilled meat.

"He was severely abused as a child by his mother," I said, trying to explain or make excuses for Jacob.

"How do you know?"

"Because he told me."

"But does he have fractured bones or any scarring?"

"No scars. I don't know if he has fractured bones."

"Well, you said he was *severely* beaten." Ugh! Leave it to a doctor to ask whether there's conclusive evidence, such as X rays, showing his *severe* beating. There's what's said and then there's scientific proof!

"Well, that's what he says." I guess it's all relative. I'd categorize the way Jacob treated me as mental abuse, but compared to a woman who is constantly belittled and beaten by her man, my treatment was really nothing. Damn it. Jared was right again! How did I know Jacob was severely abused by his mother? Just based on the fact that he was an emotionally fucked-up man? That he couldn't cry and was now toxic? Perhaps his mom yelled and once *did* throw something at him, and it was forever etched into his memory as something she *always* did to him.

"So you don't think it's gonna work out with us?" I wanted another confirmation.

"No. It's all a numbers game, Julie."

"What do you mean?"

"Well, you have to go through a lot of people to find one that you're compatible with. That's why the dating sites work, because there's an endless supply of people. Someone you get along with is bound to fall under the bell curve."

"Bell curve?" My head was spinning.

"Yeah, if you date enough people under the bell curve, you'll meet someone. But see, you're probably one deviation point outside of the curve."

"I'm lost." *And I'm buzzed.*

Jared grabbed a piece of paper and pen and drew a bell curve. "You see, most people fall under this part of the curve. Let's say the majority of people do. And everyone under this curve is similar. So if you date the people from this area, you will eventually find someone looking for the same thing as you. But you're out here to the side somewhere." He drew a dot representing me to the left of the bell curve. I was out in left field.

"Why am I outside of the bell curve?"

"Because you're different and want different things."

Like no anal sex? Like a normal conversation?

"You see," he continued, "there are fewer people to choose from out here, so it's harder for you to come across people who are like you or want the same thing. You'll find someone. It'll just take a whole lot longer." This was his way of making me feel better? He added some random dots out to the left, near my dot, to represent that potential person that I might one day meet. There were so few dots out there.

Was this true? Was I outside the bell curve? Was I only one standard deviation point away, or was I two, or three, or twenty? Was this a good thing or a bad thing? I thought I wanted what everyone else wanted: someone to share my life with, to be a team, to love and be loved.

I knew that Jared's bell-curve theory had validity because, come to think of it, I rarely wanted the same things my girlfriends wanted, which was a rich man to support their materialistic desires. I wanted a smart man that I could learn from and have deep, provoking conversations with. I also realized that I learned more about myself not from my girlfriends but from Koko, a caged gorilla.

My friend Alicia joked that once I finished the linguistics class I was in, *then* perhaps I'd have the lexicon required to express myself to these men and they would finally understand me. And it was in linguistics that I first learned about Koko. And it was she, an orphaned gorilla that had been raised by human beings and taught sign language since the 1970s, who shed light on my behavior with men. Koko was only one year younger than I was. She was a Cancer, too, born July 4, 1971.

Koko knew over a thousand signs, and as soon as she was able to express herself, she let it be known that she deeply wanted to have a baby. With no male suitors in sight, her human caregivers bought Koko what they thought every single, non-child-bearing female wanted, a kitty. And Koko was open to this idea, unlike myself. Koko loved the kitty, held and caressed it, and it seemed to fulfill her motherly needs. But one day the kitty escaped into the woods of Oakland, California, and was tragically killed by loggers (true story). Koko's caregivers broke the news to Koko, who was devastated.

To console Koko, they compiled some videotapes of other gorillas at various zoos, kind of like an animal kingdom version of Match.com. Koko watched the videos and dismissed some gorillas at first sight but expressed an excited interest in one particular gorilla named Ndume. She signed that she "loved" Ndume and kissed the television screen on which he appeared. Ndume was brought to Koko's facility. A wire gate was placed between them so that they could smell one another (I hoped Koko's breast smelled of honeysuckle so Ndume would want her).

After some sniffing, the caregivers decided to open the gates for a union of these two mighty gorillas. Koko was ecstatic and could barely contain herself. She demanded in sign language that the human caregiver "hurry" and open the damn gate. The gatekeeper told Koko to be good and basically slow down; don't ambush Ndume. "Koko good! Hurry!" Koko signed. "Hurry! Hurry!" The gate was opened and Koko, never having been around other gorillas, not knowing the rules of her society, ran aggressively toward Ndume. Naturally, he was confused, caught off guard, and became frightened. He tried to run and hide but Koko chased him, threw a ball at him, and waved a flag. Meanwhile, Ndume was running as far and as fast as he could away from Koko.

I understood Koko. She knew what she wanted, and she didn't need to go through all the formalities. She was ready to lay it all out on the line. Why waste time? I watched the video a few times, and each time I whispered to Koko, "Slow down!" But I knew exactly how she felt. Although I had all aspects of my financial, family, career, and educational life in perfect order, I behaved this way with most men and scared them, the way Koko scared Ndume. Too fast, too soon, too much. I was Koko. Nearly forty years old, never had a baby, and impatient as hell when I *finally* found someone I liked. I behaved like a caged gorilla, unnatural. But this *was* my natural way of being, and like Koko, it didn't fit into the rules or guidelines of how a lady should behave to get a man. No matter what she expressed, her desire for a baby or her love for Ndume, nobody could help her. Boy, I could relate. It didn't take a refined lexicon; it took fewer than a thousand signs or words for both Koko and me to ruin things with our fellow primates.

"You behaved that way?" my friend Kim asked when I told her about Koko.

"Well, yeah, I know what I want."

"Julie! You can't do that; you need to *slow down*. I'm going to call you Koko from here on out." But what did Kim know about being me? Kim, like 99 percent of the population, knew and followed the rules of society, and society had responded with approval. Therefore, her view on how to behave was correct, and mine was not.

Again, this is who I am, how I am. Give me a man that has no fear, is what I say. And I don't *seek out* men the way most women did. It isn't my priority to find a man, not even on my top five lists of things to do. But if one walks into my life that I actually like, I usually go full throttle. The only reason I could think of for going full throttle with Jacob was because I was trying to please my society. I knew I didn't love him.

I started crying, and I couldn't hold it back. I knew it was the wine and the quick lesson of probability theory and Koko and her fucked-up caged life that made me cry. "I've dated some really shitty guys," I said, restarting the conversation with Jared.

"Hey, thanks a lot. I'm here. I am one of them."

"You're probably the best one, and we can't even say we dated it was so short. You never gave me a chance." I tried to think of the guys I'd dated and blurted out, "God, my dad would have been so disappointed with the guys I've liked." I could barely talk; my eyes were brimming with tears.

"Go ahead; you can cry."

So I did, like a single drunk woman, all slobbery and ugly. All that was missing was a pet cat to jump on my lap to console me.

But I'd dated. OK, maybe not dated, but I'd at least gone out on a date or two. During the height of Joe, my cousin had set me up with a nurse named Matthew. Another Diana setup. I needed to learn my lesson! She'd said Matthew was a hard worker, had green eyes, and was very responsible. He and his friend would meet up with us for Japanese food. He arrived a half hour late and drunk. He said he'd left a party where he'd been drinking all day and had sped the entire way to Stockton to meet up with us. Great, a drunk driver. Real responsible, just like Diana said. He never made eye contact with me, and he ordered only a soda for dinner. He closed his eyes, hummed along with the overhead techno music, and made flailing, groovy-like motions with his arms. When he got up to use the bathroom, I looked across the table at Diana and said, "Are you kidding me?"

"He's behaving weird," she said.

You think?

I can't even remember how the night ended. Did we say good-bye? When it *was* over, I turned to Diana and yelled, "He showed up drunk, and he doesn't even have green eyes!"

"I swear to God he had green eyes at work!"

"Well, he doesn't. Did you see how he was dancing all strange-like in his seat?"

"He must wear green contacts at work. Wow, they looked so natural."

"He's on drugs," I added.

"No, he's usually not like that."

"*He's on drugs!*"

That was my only date ever with Matthew. I never asked about him; he never asked about me. He probably didn't even remember meeting me in his inebriated state. Several months later, my other cousin, Marie, went out on a party bus and stated Matthew had been there. I told her my thoughts about him. She confirmed what I believed; he did do drugs! She said he'd asked to "put something" in her purse. Later that night she'd reached into her purse to get lipstick and found a small bag of cocaine. "Can you believe that?" she exclaimed.

"Yep, I was right; he does do drugs!"

"No, that he didn't even offer to share. How rude!"

Then there was my forced date with Ronald. He'd sold me my Toyota Camry. It was a repossessed car, only ten thousand miles and in pristine condition. He took my mom and me out to lunch the day I bought the car. He went on about how he purchased his Land Cruiser with cash because he felt the car salesman thought he had no money. He wanted to prove that salesman wrong. I couldn't have cared less. But he seemed very proud of that fact, so I smiled and said, "That's great," while I tried to calculate the depreciation of a Land Cruiser as you drive it off the lot. Why am I this way? I try not to be. Is this the deviation point Jared was talking about? I think it's great if you can pay for anything with cash, but do you really need to brag about it? And even though I was only there to purchase my vehicle and leave, he insisted on buying us lunch.

When I got home, I realized that the car floor mats he promised me were not in the car. I left him a message asking if I could pick them up. He called a few days later and said that he'd get me a set of new car mats, but we'd have to go to lunch. I asked if I could pick them up at the dealership. He stated that I could not, as he had to "strike a deal to get you new mats and I can't have my coworkers see me give them to you."

"What's the big deal? When you sold me the car, you said you had the mats for me."

"Well, those were used mats, and I got you new mats. That's like a two-hundred-dollar value."

I wasn't sure what his point was. We'd talked about the car mats prior to my purchasing the car; he said he had them. I thought he'd forgotten to give them to me and that I could pick them up. Was he stealing these mats?

"So do you want me to pay for new mats even though you said you had the mats the car came with?"

"No, I have new mats for you. I pulled some strings. So if you want the mats, meet me tomorrow at one at the sushi restaurant by 24 Hour Fitness, and I'll give them to you."

Fuck. I hung up.

"He won't give me the mats," I complained to Diana.

"So what? Use him. Get your mats and get a free lunch out of it. Then change your phone number," she laughed. "He obviously wants a date out of it. What's he look like?"

"He's Filipino. He's older and he has ptosis. Right eye."

"Oh hell no!" she shrieked.

Ptosis is the drooping of an eyelid. Ronald's right eyelid was completely drooping—well, fully closed. His left eye was wide open, showed expression, the pupil was round and would be reactive to light if I were to perform a neuro check, but the right eye was closed. And not due to Bell's palsy, which would be temporary. He couldn't get it up, much less keep it up. The right eyelid, that is.

I met him for sushi. I wanted my mats.

The beauty of nursing is that not only are you able to look at every strange growth, cut, abscess, rash, deformation, or malformation, but you're expected and required to do so. In a patient's room, you turn on the brightest light, take off the hospital gown, and inspect the malady from every angle. You can put on a glove and touch it, ask if it's tender, test it for edema and pitting, measure the area, rewrap it, and pretend like it's no big deal. But out in the real world, it's not polite to stare at a malfunctioning body part. You pretend you don't notice Aunt Candy's lazy eye drifting far to the left or Cousin Maria's hairy patch of bearlike rug growing on her left shoulder. So there we were at the sushi bar. Where were my mats? They better be in his cash-paid Land Cruiser.

Ronald told me again how he'd gone fishing, shown up in flip-flops at a Toyota dealership, been treated rudely by the car salesman, who thought Ronald had no money to buy a car, and then how he really showed that salesman when he said he'd take that Land Cruiser and pay straight-up cash for it! "Oh, you really should have seen the look on his face when I said that," Ronald boasted.

"That's a great story," I lied.

I kept trying not to stare at his right-eye ptosis. But gosh, I really wanted to grab a toothpick and prop it open. I bet he looked different with both eyes open.

I made it through lunch, staring primarily at the left side of his face. Was that obvious, too? I should have been looking at his face as a whole, not avoiding the right and only looking at the left. After lunch, we walked out to his cash-paid Land Cruiser, and he gave me my car mats. "Thank you so much for the mats. I really appreciate it. Thanks for lunch, too."

I got my mats, and I never saw him again. I felt like a bad person. That was what I deserved. Here this guy had only one good eye but probably could see, better than Jacob with his dry, blinking eyes, that I was worth chasing.

Ronald, right-eye-ptosis guy, was the only guy I went out with in 2008. Was I being too picky? I have mentioned that I dated a guy that worked in the plumbing department of Lowe's and had only one testicle, have I not? I'm not picky! And dating Jacob was becoming the lowest of the lows in dating. I wish I were picky!

A coworker of mine set me up with a fireman. I thought of Jon, the LA fireman I'd dated, and agreed to meet my coworker's friend. This new fireman's name was Edgar. He didn't text me but called me (brownie points). We spoke for over an hour about our families and about the homes we'd each purchased. He did seem to have it all together, and we hit it off over the phone. We agreed to meet the next day for coffee in Roseville. It was a Friday afternoon, and I'd drive the forty-five minutes there to meet him.

He bought me coffee and a cookie. We sat outside. He kept his dark sunglasses on the entire time. Did he have a ptosis eyelid? Did he have fake green eyes? Did he have dry, bloodshot-red, blinking eyes? Not sure. He did have a large nose, but that didn't bother me, unless of course it was picking up my unscented pheromones. Edgar loved being a fireman. He spoke about how he'd been a fireman for only five years, was the youngest at his station, and was being primed for captain. He had his life planned out: what year he'd make captain, when he'd get married, how many children he'd have, and how he'd never visit El Salvador or any Latin country due to the drug cartel and violence against tourists, and that he'd vacation in Hawaii every year where it was safe. Boring. He seemed appalled that I wasn't considering moving up to management at the hospital and that I loved vacationing in Thailand or Brazil.

"So what do you plan on doing, if you don't want to move up at the hospital?" he asked.

I hadn't given it much thought. "Well, I'm still such a new nurse. I feel I have so much to learn still."

He stated that he'd want his wife to reach for the highest position possible in whatever career she'd chosen. I respected that. I don't think I fit into his carefully etched, fully thought-out life plan. Nonetheless, I thought we could have another date. He said he'd drive out to Elk Grove on the next date and that he'd call me soon. I never heard from him again. And I fully respected that.

But back to Jared. There I was with him, more than a year after our whirlwind, hot, one-second first date. I enjoyed him. I did. But I enjoyed him alone, not with his friends. He *was* easy to talk to, but maybe because there wasn't that expectation anymore of whether he would or wouldn't like me. I knew I didn't wow him.

"You always say there's something you can't pinpoint in me. Just tell me what it is. I won't get mad. Help me out," I cried.

"No, there's nothing. Don't change; be who you are," he said.

"I thought you said—"

"No, you have to be who you are."

I calmed down, and Jared excused himself to the bathroom.

"OK, time to go to bed; it's three o'clock!" Jared said upon his return.

"OK," I said while cleaning the kitchen island.

He came over and kissed me on the lips.

"What's that for?" I asked.

"Mmm, I just wanted to kiss you."

Jared *loved* to kiss; it didn't matter with whom. He loved the act of kissing, as did I. I love it more than sex, but most times I didn't love kissing more than I loved a back massage. I was, or I am, the biggest back-massage whore there is. Back massages are a ticket into my own personal red-light district.

Jared and I showered together. It had been a long time since I'd seen him naked. He was so thin, so narrow, compared to Joe and Jacob. But I'm sure I was much plumper than most of his lovely ladies.

"I forgot about your penis," I said.

He laughed.

"I forgot that it was big."

"So I've been told. And I remember you telling me that before."

And I remember the first time I told him his penis was big, he said, "Tell your cousin how big it is so she can tell everyone in the

ER about it." Being a young, handsome, social doctor wasn't enough. Having a big penis and knowing your coworkers knew about it was *everything*. I refrained from telling him that I'd been with bigger, and smaller, and better.

"Yeah, for some reason with you, it's always a surprise, but a nice surprise," I said, complimenting him.

I remember my cousin Marie telling me that skinny white men were always the most well-endowed men. "And sometimes it's so long, it's crooked, like the letter L," she explained.

"L?"

"Yes, L, like in *love*." She broke it down for me and drew an L with her finger in the air.

"Eww!" I made a grossed-out face.

"Oh, but those are good ones, too! I once had boyfriend with an L-shaped dick. He was ugly as fuck, so I'd ride his L-shaped dick backward. That way I didn't have to look at him!" she reminisced. Her eyes lit up, and she giggled like a schoolgirl. I knew she was telling the truth.

Jared was skinny and had a good-sized organ, but it wasn't shaped like the letter L as in *love*. It was straight, like a thick, long ruler or demi-baguette. He would love the French-associated demi-baguette compliment. I kept the thought to myself; I'd already complimented him enough. I didn't want him to think he wowed me, because he didn't, and it takes more than a big dick to wow me! I'm not that kind of girl. I was becoming more of a *sapiosexual* kind of girl. *Sapiosexual*: a person who finds the intelligence in others sexually appealing. It was my latest favorite word. So what the fuck was I doing with muscle-head Jacob?

I told Jared I'd massage him first. I knew he'd reciprocate; he always did, so I wanted my massage last. I wanted to fall asleep while he worked away. I was willing to do half an hour, which was a drop in the bucket compared to the one-to-two-hour massages Jacob received. After ten minutes of massaging Jared, he said, "OK, your turn."

"Already?" I was just getting warmed up.

"Yes, I can't last thirty minutes massaging your back in return, so I better just take ten minutes."

"OK." Beggars can't be choosers. And this was far more than what Jacob would ever give.

All massages lead to sex. Remember, it's the red-light district. It's one of the unwritten laws of the universe. Unless the massage is for Jacob—then it's me giving a massage with nothing in return. And that's because something is wrong with him, not the law. Jacob was the anomaly. Otherwise, under normal circumstances, all massages lead to sex. Don't try to argue with it, fight it, deny it; it's just so. And that's *OK!* Especially after a few bottles of wine, crying, showering with the opposite sex, massaging naked in a bed, and basically being an emotional wreck at three in the morning! Sex is the wrap-up and shut-up of the entire event.

However, in the past, Jared had proven to be as wishy-washy as I was when it came to sex. So I was quite surprised when he entered me.

"Mmm…that initial thrust in is better than the actual orgasm," he said.

Yes, he'd told me this before, many times. Jared was like an old man with dementia. He repeated his stories, his one-liners, his observations and analyses many, times over, either because he couldn't remember who he told or because he liked hearing his brilliant thoughts.

He tried to recreate the initial thrust in. But the initial thrust is the initial thrust; it can't be repeated. Another unwritten law of the universe.

And all I could think was, *I had sex with Joe yesterday! I'm such a whore. Such a lost and lonely whore.*

***

The end of May and all of June were a hazy blur. I twisted my ankle at the gym trying to jump in and out of a tire. And no, Jacob didn't rush over with his strong, muscled physique to sweep me up and carry me to my car. I limped out by myself with an ice bag in hand, and he muttered that I should file an incident report.

I spent time on my couch with my swollen ankle propped up (doing RICE—rest, ice, compression, and elevation—that's Orthopedics 101!) and exchanging either e-mails with Joe or time in bed with Joe, at least on his Fridays off. Definitely not as much time as either one of us would have liked. I had to play it safe, whatever that means. But the e-mails were as follows:

Date: May 26, 2010

Subject: Hi

What's up?!?

I would call you but never know when you're available. Anyway, just wanted to let you know that I really enjoyed hanging out with you. You always make for interesting conversation. I hope all is going well for you. It is for me. I will be visiting my mom on Friday. Let me know if you want me to stop by. I'd love to see you. Just to say hi, you know?! Anyway, take care. I'll talk to you soon.

XO

Joe

And he did visit. And we did have another one of those in-depth conversations about all the what-ifs of our affair. The following e-mail came to my inbox:

Date: June 11, 2010

Subject: Hey there!

Hi Julie,

How's it going? I'm in our coffee shop. If you thought it was bad before, don't ever come back. My family relinquished their share and now it's owned only by the other people. Andre still works here. But he's depressed.

Work is crazy right now. I'm covering another lady's desk for a month. So much work. But whatever, I'm gaining experience. Besides that, it's the same ol' shit.

I gave a lot of thought to our talk. But the end remains the same. I'm selfish and will not change. But I'm ok with that. I've accepted me. LMAO!! Anyway, I was thinking about you and wanted to drop a line. Hope it finds you in good health. Hope your ankle is better. You need to invite me over, I miss ya.

Take care friend,

Joe

I liked how he referred to the coffee shop as "our" coffee shop. Good male lovers do that. They label things in the "our" form, so you feel you have something special with them—like this affair wasn't *his* secret, it was *our* secret. The only reason I kept it secret was for his sake. I didn't care who knew. Anyway, I did like the "our coffee shop" reference; I thought it was a sweet gesture. That's what made him a good lover.

I responded in an emotional-woman sort of way:

Date: June 11, 2010
Re: Hey there!

How are you? Sad to hear about the coffee shop. It's probably good that your family got out now, I guess. Andre needs to get angry and get out. Change is good. And forced change is sometimes even better, no?

Well, I really don't know how or if I am to respond to what you wrote. At least you know your demons and acknowledge them. Maybe? I don't know. We all have our flaws. A part of me is sad for you, also because things DO change in one way or another. You already know what the consequences will be should all this ever come to the forefront. The real Joe "revealed." I really don't know what to say and I'm in a sad mood today. Just as you make choices that are "not good," I wonder why I make such choices, too. I must admit, once it starts, I want more. Don't worry, not going psycho on you. I truly care about you as a friend and want only wonderful things for you, but my "love" for you is gone (finally). So you are safe! Hehehehe. When I say I want more, it's not from you. Just from life in general. I'm going to be 38, and never to have had someone want to truly be with me is quite devastating on the ego. It makes me wonder what my character flaws are that I'm not aware of. I'm REALLY TIRED of trying, in everything. I have very high standards, and I always fall so short of them. I'm tired of being a secret whenever I am with a guy. I want a companion, someone not afraid or embarrassed or whatever to be in public with me. I feel like a failure as a woman. And it's a very difficult feeling to have. Why am I telling you all this? I don't know, but we do have good communication, and if you were here, I would be saying the same thing in person. I think because I'm typing it, it seems more serious than our normal conversation. And I'm talking in circles now. Don't even know what my point is, so let me move on.

    Deep breath. I'm just having one of those days.

    Gypsy Jacob...is probably a no-go. Surprised? He's very nice to me, but the situation is dead in the water. Sometimes I feel like he's searching my face for an answer (to what, I don't know), and I'm searching his face for something, anything, and everything is just very sad and empty.

    Mi casa es tu casa. You can come over anytime, Joe. You don't *need an invitation.*

I love you (as a friend), my friend.

—JaG

P.S: If I don't hear from you…have a Happy Father's Day. :)

I had to lie to Joe about two things: that I no longer loved him and that Jacob was very nice to me. A good female mistress does that; she denies being in love so that her lover feels safe. And she mentions the other man in her life so her lover feels super safe that she will keep *their* secret. After I sent the e-mail, I wanted to buffer the situation. I was confused; I wanted him, and yet I knew I shouldn't want him. I e-mailed him a few days later:

Date: June 15, 2010

Subject: Hey

Hey…. Did my last e-mail scare you off? Sorry. I was just having a frustrating day. I hope you are well and not working too hard.

Everything is the same old thing here. Working lots, too, but I'm not gonna complain (this time).

Hope all is fabulous.

—JaG

And as good male lovers always do, he eased my troubled mind with the following e-mail:

Date: June 16, 2010

Re: Hey

You're hilarious! No, not scared. We're cool. It's true I didn't know how to respond. I mean, it sounds like you want to continue hanging out. But at the same time, you are regretful of the situation. At any rate, it truly is up to you. It's fine if you want to be pen-pal friends, and not "friends." I am at peace with either situation. Of course, I would prefer to be "friends." Always a great time. Thanks for waiving the invite clause. I want to stop by next Friday if you're not working. Let me know.

Have a great day!

Joe

And as good mistresses always do, I eased his monotonous married life. We went through the motions again, and after, we spilled our emotions again. It was all getting so intense.

Date: July 20, 2010
Subject: Been a while
Julie,

How's it going? It's been a few weeks since we last spoke. I've been super busy. Year-end closing at work. Total pain in the ass. But that's probably not the only reason I haven't contacted you. Last time we saw each other was a bit much. Even for me. It kinda weirded me out. We seem to always enter a strange cycle of conversation, sex w/ potential to go wrong, and then another conversation that has some remorseful tones. It really is unhealthy, don't you think? I feel that part of it is that

you're not the same. What I mean is you're more cynical now that you're trying to make it sex w/o feelings attached. It is not a natural fit for you. The other part is I'm very comfortable with you. Maybe too comfortable. I tell you my thoughts when I shouldn't. I don't know, maybe I'm crazy or just overthinking the whole thing. However, you know my feelings, my vulnerability, and you make comments that don't help. They are definitely truths, but not really what I need from a buddy while we're still naked. I know that I just want to have my cake and to eat it and to be cleaned up after. But we used to be in that situation and that's what I long for. I want to see you. I'll always want to see you. I just don't think you get what you need from "us." I don't want to waste your time or feelings messing around with me. I know this whole e-mail is bizarre. I just need to get my feelings out. I'm surprised I'm even sending this. Usually I would just disappear. But I care about your feelings and value your friendship. I hope you understand. At any rate, I hope this finds you in good health. This is not a good-bye. I'll come see you any time you want.
Talk to you soon,
Joe

He was right; I wasn't the same anymore. I was vying for the attention of Jacob, a man I was starting to despise, and suppressing my love for Joe. I was simply in complete misery and confusion.

Date: July 20, 2010
Re: Been a while

My Mr. Joe,

First, let me start by saying I am so sorry. I apologize for having made remarks (at any time, in or out of bed) that offended you. I never meant to make jabs at you, if that's how you took it. You know that you have a very special place in my heart and head, and I have no intention of hurting you. You're right; I have changed and my feelings for you have changed. It took me a very long time to accept that you would never be in my life as I had initially hoped. Once I accepted that—you can call it cynical, but I call it realistic, and I finally found peace with it. At times when you are here, I feel that you want me to be crazy about you. I'm not sure if it's that I have my guard up or my feelings are just truly gone. Sex with you isn't even the same anymore, as I think I'm more connected and "into it" when I'm crazy over someone. It's that whole emotional thing women feel. I'm not saying I don't enjoy it, I do. I love our interaction and comfort and conversations (even when they go sour). And why do we always end it badly? I don't know. Maybe we both have frustration within ourselves, and we escape for a minute only to be angry at the reality of it all once it's over.

Yes, you do want to have your cake and eat it, too. I feel I have more than provided that. Yes, I make sarcastic remarks, but I ask nothing from you, and you know very well that I would never even think about trying to impede on your marriage or home life. You ask a lot—basically to give you what you want, feel nothing, remark on nothing, and smile as you leave. I too have a lot at stake. The reality of having unprotected sex could lead to disease, pregnancy, or me liking you once again. Although I do think I have a strong position on the last. And should any of those things happen, who would I turn to? I would only have myself. I'm tired of only having myself. Despite your marriage "situation," you have her, she would be there for you. I have nobody to turn to. I wouldn't ever even dream of texting your cell, as I know my position with you, and it's not very high on your list.

Perhaps this feeling of "unhealthy" or it not being the right fit for me is because what we are doing is NOT right. What we are doing is selfish on both parts. I'm selfish, too. Maybe it was very naïve of me to think I could contact you, have you over, and just be friends. It seems we cannot be alone together. I would love to have you in my life in some way. I am glad you feel comfortable with me to tell me your vulnerabilities. If we didn't share that, then it would be you basically just having sex with me and leaving, all within an hour and a half. And isn't that something you can have with any girl? I'd like to think I'm different from the rest. I want to hear about your worries, dreams, and even about your baby or wife. If I had zero connection with you, I wouldn't ever invite you over.

So it seems like we are taking turns being emotional about all this and sending each other e-mails. I really don't know what more to say. Do you want to say good-bye and this is your way of doing it? I'm hoping we can find a common ground, and it may not include sex, where we can be friends and in each other's life in some capacity. If that's what you would like…. Are you disappointed that I didn't contact you or invite you over last week?

How do I end this e-mail? I don't know, so don't be surprised if I send you another and another. I was very taken aback by your e-

mail. I feel bad if I hurt you. I apologize.

  You say you "long for" that situation we used to have. Things change, and I don't know if I can give you what you want. You may have felt it was perfect back then, but it was torture for me every time you would leave. It seems like someone will always suffer in this situation. Tell me exactly what you want and how you want it, both physically and emotionally. Let's be honest with one another as we always have. I don't want there to be resentment on either side.

  Ok, I'm signing off, but don't know if I resolved anything. So for now, I send you a big apology and hug, until I can work out my thoughts.

—Julie

When Joe didn't respond within twenty-four hours, I panicked. I was so incredibly torn between knowing that the right thing to do was to end it and wanting to take advantage of every possible moment with him. I sent him an e-mail with the heading "So are you mad at me?" and the following question:

> Date: July 22, 2010
> Subject: So are you mad at me?
>   Do you not accept my apology and rambling e-mail?
> —me

> Date: July 22, 2010
> Re: So are you mad at me?

Hi friend,

No, I am not mad at you. I couldn't respond to you yesterday because we were all home all day. I don't think I was really hurt either. I can't really explain how I felt. Maybe it's like you want me to learn a lesson. If I got something or got another woman pregnant or just got caught, there would be zero tolerance or sympathy. I would get fired from my marriage. Period. It's a risk I am stupid enough to take. I've always said I am selfish, so there is no new news there. Basically, I'm just trying to be happy. I want to spend time with other people who gain happiness from my company. It is true that you don't ask for anything in return. I do not know how to express what I want physically or emotionally. It's just sometimes your comments make me feel awkward. Like "You are going to get caught." It makes me almost feel you want that for me. Hell, I guess if I was you, I would share a slight feeling toward that, too. Not to say you do want that for me. It's an "in the moment" perception I have. I don't want to say good-bye at all. However, this time around is just different. Maybe I am too selfish. Or maybe I do just want you to appease me. But mostly I think I want to feel guilty and worry after I leave, not when I am there. If you can't smile on your own when I leave, then why have me over? Julie, you ARE my friend. I would never want to hurt your feelings. I got to get back to work, so I'm going to wrap it up. Just know that sex is just that. Your friendship is more important than sex to me. Write me back and we can work this out.

Always,

Joe

Date: July 22, 2010

Re: So are you mad at me?

Hello my Joe,

I felt really bad after sending that e-mail, as it just talked in circles. And this e-mail has the potential of heading the same direction. Your e-mail of today makes me see your perspective better. And I am sorry for those comments that I do tend to make. It's the passive-aggressive person in me…and I guess also the "bitter" woman in me. Hehehe. No, I don't want you to learn your lesson or get caught—it would serve me no purpose. I want you to be careful, that's what I want. I'm not worried about you being careful with me, as I'm not a threat. Even if anything "bad" should ever happen, I would deal with it on my own, so there isn't anything I could gain by wishing something negative on you. It's not my nature and you know that. I think I make those comments out of my own frustration with men and the very bad luck, or non-progressive luck, that I have had with each and every one of them. It's sad for me to say that you say you care about me (or my feelings anyways) as you are the only man who has ever told me that. And that is the most or closest I've ever gotten to an "I love you." God, this e-mail is getting cheesier by the minute, sorry! But I'm trying to psychoanalyze myself here. I guess I just don't get it. I don't understand why these little rendezvous are all I ever get from anyone. Most times I do want more, other times I am so happy with where my life is, alone and planning the baby. It's simpler alone. But it also can be very lonely and difficult to understand, "Why am I alone?" when I see others doing the natural progression in life: career, relationship, marriage, family…. Many times

I think you too just want me to "appease" you. That's when I think, "And what am I getting out of it?" Which leads me to...if we are to continue with sex, then I have to truly be a friend and/or responsible willing party and accept the situation for what it is and not make judgments or comments along the way. I'm a grown, smart woman and know what I'm getting into. You have not forced me to do this, so I, too, either own up to it or I let it go.

If you really are honest and do want us to be friends, then I accept that and look forward to having you come by. But please don't say that you do if you really intend to just fall off the face of the earth. At this point in time, I am not sure I can give you more than a genuine friendship, for a few reasons. One, it seems like we (or I) don't know what type of interaction/relationship we really want. You said you can't express what you want physically/emotionally from me. Until we both know, I think we would continue hurting one another as no boundaries are set. Maybe that's the reason this whole conversation is now happening. Second, I don't want to resent you. Knowing you go home to someone that loves you and that you love, and I go on to a hope for Jacob...I guess I feel the playing field is not even. You're right, sex is just that. What I really love about "us" is our conversations. And I want a friend that's genuine, too, and not gonna bail on me because they get tired of hearing about Jacob or my plans to have a baby in February! And of course, I'd return a listening ear!

I know this isn't the end of this conversation as this e-mail rambled. But know that I was your friend in the past and I am your friend now. And if you can be a friend to me...? Let's start there for now, as we have always just jumped ahead to the "benefits." What do you think?

Tu amiga,

Julie

P.S: You missed my birthday :)

Date: July 27, 2010

Re: So are you mad at me?

Hi there!

    Sorry I missed your birthday. :(I hope you had a blast! As for me, I think I'm getting strep. My throat is all bad and I have a history. Anyway, we can and should be friends. However, I don't think we should hang out for a while, as we will just be back to where we were. Feel free to write me and tell me all about whatever you have going on. I don't mind listening. I do miss our conversations about anything. Especially when you would enlighten me. I think that I am in a strange place right now. And it pains me to know that the "real" me can be a disappointment to all who interact with that person. They deserve better and you deserve better. You are my friend and I want you to continue to be. I have to go now. Just know I am not sad and this is not meant to be a downer. I just need to meditate on it. ;)

Always,

Joe

Date: July 27, 2010

Re: So are you mad at me?

My heart feels really sad, as a friend, to read this. I'm not sad that we aren't going to continue "as is." I KNOW that is the right thing to do, because eventually something will change or break and it will be out of our control. This is better, we're putting things in check now. I'm sad that you think you're a disappointment to those you interact with. Isn't this the whole problem, that people do enjoy you? It's just the situation doesn't lend itself to where we or I can fully and openly "enjoy" you. That's what makes it hard. I love seeing you, talking with you, but both of us are in strange places right now. I truly hope we keep in touch. I know I'll bug you with e-mails. You are a good person, Joe, and I wish you could have the full happiness that you, too, deserve. Only you can provide that from within yourself, not me, not her, nor the next girl can provide that. It's like with me; in reality no man can give me happiness or self-worth or whatever. I have to just find it and be it from within me.

Let's not be complete strangers. I already miss you. And I, too, want to hear about what's going on with your—work, family, friends, ANYTHING. I ALWAYS have an ear or two for you.
Hope your throat feels better.
I send you many hugs,
Julie

***

Fourth of July weekend, Jacob was fired from Gold's. First they told him he couldn't do the CrossFit program. He said he didn't want to do sales anymore and would just be a personal trainer. They said that was fine. Then they fired him right before the weekend.

According to him, he was fired because of his "attitude." Surprised? I knew it was coming, even though he and I had rarely spoken since I twisted my ankle. He texted me; he was down. He came over that night.

And if I thought he'd had emptiness across his face before, now there was truly nothing. "I love that job, but fuck, I hated the boss. Did you see how out of shape he is? And in the Gold's contract, it states all employees must keep up good physical appearances."

"What are you going to do?"

"I don't know. I have about three months of savings to live off of. I don't want to work for a big gym anymore. I want to do CrossFit. That's my life."

"Then you need your own gym."

"Yeah, but that takes funds."

"Get a business loan."

"I have bad credit."

"You need to look into it. You haven't even tried. You can do it; I know you can."

"I don't know, babe." He looked remote, stranded.

"I'm here to support you."

"I can always up and leave. I have to go where I can get work."

Jacob may have been an emotionally fucked-up man or a douchebag, but he was a hard worker. He was a great personal trainer—he was a different person when training. He laughed, he *spoke*, he smiled, he encouraged, and he got excited seeing someone do well. I could envision him with a little gym of his own. I knew he could do it! I wanted him to do it.

By the end of the week, he'd struck a deal with a smaller gym to train clients in CrossFit. In addition, he could pocket the majority of the money earned from his personal clientele. His first client, Katie, signed a one-year contract with him worth seven thousand dollars. She'd pay five hundred and some-odd dollars a month to be trained. He was ecstatic. I'd never seen him in such a great mood. She was athletic, she swam to Alcatraz once, she had a "big smile," Jacob would always say, and she was a nurse where I worked. I didn't know her; she worked on a different floor and on a different shift.

Was I jealous? Yes, but not in the sense that I thought he liked her. I was envious of people who were athletic and could push themselves physically. I could only wish to have such a competitive nature within myself. I wanted to be athletic and impress Jacob, but I could never stick with it, and I didn't know how to push myself in a sporty way, unless he gave me step-by-step instructions. Again, that fucking Yakima car rack came to mind! I bet she had one on top of her car. I bet she even knew Jared and competed against him in mini-triathlons.

Jacob said she and I should meet and be friends because we had so much in common, both being nurses and all. From what he gathered, she wasn't happy in her marriage; she seemed sad and "probably could use another girl to talk to," he said. As a trainer, he could spot every sadness and insecurity in his clients and provide support and resolutions, like, "Let's put all those feelings into your workout. I know just the CrossFit workout you need to feel better!" As a boyfriend, he may have been able to spot every sadness and insecurity in me, but he chose to ignore it. If he couldn't solve it with a CrossFit workout, then he couldn't solve it, nor did he even want to try.

But when his CrossFit program was doing well, he and I were doing well. And so things did get relatively better. July was the highlight of our relationship. He had more time to visit, since he was starting at the new gym. He had great ideas for how to promote himself. He was training a high school soccer team, and he loved being a positive influence on the kids. I'm sure he loved the attention. This was his realm—what he knew, what he loved—and finally he was training others that were excited about it, too.

He wanted to buy equipment, a rower. I offered to help him get equipment. He didn't ask; I offered. I have to remind myself of this: He didn't ask; I offered. He had zero credit. I told him I'd look into getting him a charge card, even if I had to cosign for him. We made our first—yes, first—public outing together…to Bank of America.

He needed a credit card for business purchases. The bank declined him a credit card; his credit was that bad. The banker told me I had great credit and offered me a credit card with a limit of fifteen thousand dollars.

"Then I could make payments toward the card," Jacob suggested.

It was better than any loan interest rate. I saw something in Jacob's eyes for once: "Yes, please, we can do this! Please help me!" I felt an uneasy feeling in my gut. Either it went away, or I ignored it. Or maybe I felt like part of a team, a couple. So, I went with it.

I gave the banker my personal information to process the application. He said it would take five to seven business days to receive the card. I left feeling okay with the decision I had made.

We walked out to our vehicles, as we'd driven separately.

"Thank you for helping me, babe," he said.

"You're welcome."

"I really need to stop living at the hotel. I can't take it anymore. It's so depressing. There's this one dude that walks around in a robe all day long, smoking. Maybe you could cosign for me to get an apartment."

That uneasy gut feeling returned. I'd just applied for a fifteen-thousand-dollar credit card for his sake. One thing at a time, please! "You need to try on your own first, Jacob. See what they say first."

"OK, I will. So I'll see you Monday night?"

"Yes, it's my birthday Monday. I'll pick us up some steaks, and we'll watch a movie."

"Yeah, that sounds awesome."

He called a few days later to say he got an apartment all on his own. I had my doubts, but considering the housing market and everyone's poor credit, maybe he had. He said his *friend* told him about the apartment. He was excited. He asked if he could charge a few things on the credit card, like a bed and television. "To get me on my feet again," he said. "I'll pay you back, babe. I can't sleep on the floor. It'll mess up my back."

"Sure," I said.

And charge he did. At Bed Bath & Beyond, Walmart, a website for a television, W Hotels for an expensive queen-size mattress, and here and there for miscellaneous charges.

"I need you to pay me every month, Jacob," I said sternly.

"I will, babe. I've never burned anybody in my life, and I'm not gonna start."

It was my birthday; I was thirty-eight years old. With each year approaching forty, I was reminded of how I didn't have a baby and how time was running out! I had my purchased sperm, I was working to save a nice nest egg, and I had my plan to begin artificial insemination come February 2011. And then there I was, dating Jacob, helping Jacob, knowing full well that he wouldn't be a part of my plan. Not for a lack of physical ability but for a lack of effort, a lack of wanting.

My birthday was like every other day. Jacob showed up and asked why I was all dressed up. I'd gone out to lunch with my family and still had on a summer dress. Clearly, he'd forgotten it was my birthday, or he wasn't going to acknowledge it. "It's my birthday," I said flatly.

"Oh, babe, I forgot! I'm so bad with stuff like that. I'm sure I'm going to get Alzheimer's because my dad has it. Is Alzheimer's hereditary?"

"I think so," I said in a flat, I-don't-give-a-shit tone.

"You see, I probably already have the beginning stages of it. I have the worse memory, like my dad. He has Alzheimer's." *Oh, but you recalled the exact brand of expensive mattress to purchase for your back.*

He was starting to sound like Joe, blaming all the bad aspects of himself on his father and forefathers. Was this a male trait?

I wasn't in the mood to argue. Would I have liked him to simply have remembered and said, "Happy birthday"? Absolutely. I knew I was right in keeping the doctor's appointment that I'd scheduled for the next day at the reproductive center.

SUICIDE & CONSENSUAL ROBBERY

I went to the infertility appointment to get information on the process of artificial insemination and go over the results of the initial work-up. I looked up my results online—FSH (follicle stimulating hormone), estradiol, prolactin, and CMV (cytomegalovirus). From what I gathered, I looked to be in pretty good hormonal shape for having a baby.

I met the nurse practitioner. The first words out of her mouth were, "So you and your partner are considering having a baby?" She assumed I was lesbian.

"I don't have a partner. I'm not gay." I explained.

"Oh, OK. So are you doing this by yourself?"

"Yes, I wanted to get some information on what needs to be done beforehand."

"Are you sexually active?"

"Yes."

"Well, that's going to get real complicated when the time comes. You won't even know who the father is." Was she insinuating I'd end up like the women on *The Maury Show* being asked, "Who's your baby's daddy?"

"There will be no confusion when the time comes because by then I'll have either stopped seeing him or chosen him to be the father and not be doing this," I snapped back. I didn't know that my information session was going to be accompanied by such assumptions and judgment.

"Oh, I see," she said. What did she see? I could see judgment reeling in her brain; she was thinking I'd come here on a whim. What did she know about how many years of planning it had taken to get to this point?

"The goal is to get pregnant, is it not?" I asked sternly.

"Well, yes," she replied in a matronly schoolteacher tone.

"So if the person and I don't work out, then I'll be doing artificial insemination. As you can see, my age and time are my concern."

"Yes, and why are you waiting until February to start trying?"

"Financially I'll be where I want to be in February. Since I'll be doing this alone, I want to have some sense of security."

"That sounds like a responsible plan," she said in a now-surprised tone.

"I already purchased sperm. Do I need any lab work done?"

"Taking into account your age, you may want to redo you blood work as you get closer."

"Will it change that much in six months?"

"Possibly. And you're CMV negative, so make sure your donor sperm is also CMV negative."

"I don't know if he is." I hadn't given that any consideration.

"You don't want to use CMV-positive sperm. You'll end up with a child with neurological defects."

Huh? What?

"Isn't CMV a common virus?" I asked, trying to recall

anything from nursing school and patients at the hospital with CMV.

"Yes, but if you were to get CMV from the donor sperm, that would be dangerous for the baby."

"What if the sperm is CMV positive?"

"Then you need to exchange it," she said, with a distinct "Duh!" tone.

I rushed home and pulled up my beloved donor's profile. Damn it, he was CMV positive. No! Now what? I read quickly on the sperm bank website that I should speak to my physician about the risks involved in CMV-positive sperm and CMV-negative mothers.

It's rare to be CMV negative. Most people have this simple virus and don't even know it. The real danger comes when you're either immunocompromised or happen to catch the virus for the first time while pregnant. If a woman gets CMV during pregnancy there's a chance the mother will pass it to her unborn baby. Then there's a risk that the baby will develop a lousy functioning liver, seizures, sight and/or hearing loss, among other ailments. So, injecting sperm that was CMV positive into me, a CMV negative woman, could *possibly* cause me to become CMV positive at the most inopportune time.

I decided to wait until I spoke to the main doctor at the reproductive center. I made an appointment to see him in November. It was four months away. I had time to contemplate my decision, do research on CMV, ask around at work, and if possible, become infected with CMV so that I could keep my donor! Since you can get CMV from bodily fluids, like saliva, after family BBQs I drank the remnants out of everyone's glasses before placing them in the sink for washing. Someone in the family must have CMV, and I was determined to get it *prior* to pregnancy.

Jacob and I were seeing each other regularly and uneventfully. One night he told me that his young friend got knocked up by some guy who abandoned her.

"He didn't even stick around. Can you believe he did that?" he asked. Was this dismay at another man's behavior a flash of his own potential to be a responsible father?

"Of course I can. Men do that all the time. How old is she?"

"I don't know, maybe twenty-five."

Then he asked which hospital I worked at. Had this man not listened to a damn thing I ever said?

"Oh, because I took my friend, the pregnant one, to have an abortion, but it wasn't where you work."

"You went with her to have an abortion?" I asked. This is the man who wouldn't go to the grocery store with me, only to the bank, yet he went with this *friend* to have an abortion? Who is this man?

"Yeah, it was embarrassing. The doctor was telling her all about birth control for the future. Like she didn't know. She decided not to have the abortion, though."

"Is it your baby?" I ask.

"No! She's just a friend who needs support because that dude left her after finding out. Isn't that horrible?"

No, fucker, what's horrible is that you have never once supported me!

I was tempted to say, "If she doesn't want the baby, I'll adopt it. Tell her I'll adopt it." But I didn't. Instead I thought it was a good segue into telling him how I wanted a baby. "I want to have a baby," I said.

"How?" he asked.

"I don't know. Do you want to give me a baby?" Might as well throw it out there.

"I've never gotten any girl pregnant. I think my stuff is all messed up from the years of steroid use."

"Then I guess through donor sperm," I said. I was going to have a baby, with or without him.

"That's disgusting," he said.

"Why?"

"Because it's against the Bible, against how God intended it to happen!"

"I don't recall reading the part about artificial insemination in the Bible," I said sarcastically.

"You know what I mean. It's supposed to happen between a man and a woman."

I couldn't deal with this contradictory man. Did he just not say he'd driven his friend to have an abortion? I guess terminating a pregnancy is acceptable in his version of the Good Book, yet creating a life through donor sperm, one that was truly planned and wanted, was, in his words, "disgusting."

His narrow-minded views irritated me. And I knew my liberal views irritated him. I remained silent. *I need to move on and out of this relationship,* was my only thought. He joined me in bed later that night. Surprisingly, he wanted to have sex.

Jacob wore a gold chain with a cross on it. I can't remember if it was a simple cross or if it had Jesus painfully nailed to it. Regardless, he never took it off. During sex, the cross started off hanging dead center between my eyes, attempting to hypnotize me or poke my eyes out. I felt sickened by the whole idea of having him on top of me. All this time I thought it was Jacob with the twitching eye problem, but in reality it was I who had the eye problems. I'd been blind, by crucifix poking or not. It was as if I'd been enucleated all along. If a medical diagnosis were given to me, it would read, "Enucleation, removal of the eyeball, possibly done by crucifix"!

When he moved on top of me, the cross floated across my mouth, sometimes into my mouth, attempting to choke me. Was this motherfucker trying to choke me? Jacob was creating my autopsy report: asphyxiation by crucifix! I felt like I was being blinded, being shut up. I wanted to reel the crucifix and chain in with my tongue, place the chain tightly between my teeth, and rip it off with a werewolf-ish, primitive grunt. King Henry VIII would have sent me to the Tower for such a thought: "Blasphemy! Heretic! To the Tower for beheading!"

Other times the cross swayed across my large forehead in a rhythmic manner, attempting to perform an exorcism on me. I was sure of it. It was Jacob's remedy: remove my demons through fornication. The bottom of the cross poked me, taunted me, or, when he stopped moving, rested flatly on my forehead. Heavy, like ashes thumb printed on my forehead for Ash Wednesday, marking me, burning me. He was burning me at the stake in my very own bed. But it was no longer a past-religion imposed guilt that I felt, but frustration and anger. I'd placed a laughing Buddha on his side of the bed with an art print that said, "Buddhists always welcome." I did feel guilty about that. He didn't seem to notice, or at least he never acknowledged, the Buddha, the sign, or the ugly person I was turning into. I really hated and didn't recognize this person I was, or was becoming, and this person that silently cried herself to sleep. I was so good at keeping silent with my words, thoughts, and tears. Most nights I cried right next to him, and he never even noticed. A cold war had started between us.

And yet I continued, he continued, we continued, in an uneventful, mainly mute sort of way.

Work for him at the new gym was slow.

He said, "I think I'm gonna have to start stripping again, until business picks up."

"Do what you have to do," I said, feeling completely disconnected from what he'd said.

"I think I look pretty good for a forty-four-year-old. What do you think?"

"Yeah, you do look good," I agreed. And he did. Aside from his dry eyes and blinking, he was a very good-looking man. Not a Joe. Ahh, Joe. Nobody was a Joe. But Jacob was handsome.

"I might do these videos where they film me jacking off. They pay two thousand dollars," he said.

"With another person?" Goodness, why is it that when this man did decide to talk and share, it was about things I really didn't want to hear?

"No, alone. I've done one before. It was called *Morning Wake-Up Call* or something like that. It took me forever to ejaculate with so many people watching and videotaping. But so worth the money."

"So is it a video to buy?" Now I was curious. Stripping is one thing, being filmed jacking off is another.

"You can download it. It's for fags."

"Don't use that word. Just say 'gay men.'"

"Oh, yeah I forgot your buddy is *gay*. So disgusting."

"Just a different preference, Jacob."

"It's wrong. It's against the Bible. But if your friend wants me to train him in CrossFit, I would. I'd charge him more since he likes men."

"Oh, here we go again. But I bet you don't mind two women getting it on."

"Hell no! I don't like watching two women. That's wrong, too. It says so in the Bible."

At least this once he was consistent, even if for the sake of this argument.

"So I already placed a call for stripping, and I have a show next weekend. Pays a hundred bucks."

"Good luck," I said.

I didn't care anymore. I wanted him to make money. He was making endless charges on the card, and I wanted him to make payments as needed. He needed new brakes; those got charged. He needed stripper advertising; that got charged, too, I later found out.

His work at the gym was now a no-go. A new manager or owner was taking over and Jacob was out. He had a few clients. He was in a panic about where to train them.

He came over, sullen. "I don't know what I'm going to do," he said.

"You need to train privately on your own," I said.

"I'd need a place, equipment, funds," he said.

"Apply for a business loan," I suggested again. But, again, I knew his credit was bad.

"For the first time, I really thought about ending it all," he said.

"What do you mean?" I felt scared.

"I have nothing to live for. I thought about killing myself." A *red flag*—that he nailed to my forehead!

"Stop it!" I yelled. I was scared. "That's not going to solve anything. You have to get back on your feet and fight."

He stared off into the distance. I rambled on about how he needed to get clients, how he had to find another way, not suicide. He left to go home to "take care of something." I begged him to promise me he wouldn't do anything, to text me as soon as he was home, to call me if he needed anything, to please not kill himself. And if I'd thought his crucifix felt heavy, like asphyxiation, the pressure I felt now didn't compare. Lesson Number Three: *Learn to breathe.* But nothing in my physiology could compensate for that drowning feeling. I tossed and turned all night until it was a decent early-morning hour to text him, to get a response that he hadn't done anything stupid.

The next night he came over, he acted like nothing had happened. Had he been calling my bluff? Was he deceiving me with these threats?

Somehow we rolled into hot August. Jacob was doing one to two shows a week stripping and body modeling for fancy art photography. I remember one photo in particular. He was naked in the photo and positioned in an artistic dance form that hid his family jewels and his face. He was crouched down and slightly twisting. On his back was a naked ballerina, posing elegantly. Every muscle from his tiny toe up perfectly shadowed the next muscle, all the way to his jugular. God, I loved those photos. He promised to get me one. He never did. I guess that's for the best, or else I'd have it hanging in my entryway and would have to explain to every guest that came and went who that man was. It would turn a beautiful photograph into a complete downer, leaving my guest feeling uncomfortable for ever asking who that was in the photograph.

It was a rare August night. Jacob was in a good mood. The soccer team he trained at the little gym where he no longer worked still wanted him as their trainer. In addition, the coach knew other teams that might be interested in having CrossFit workouts.

"I'm starting to think I can have my own thing, babe. I'm going to buy as much equipment as I can with the credit card, OK? I'll have it shipped here," he said.

"You can have your own thing," I confirmed.

"But I may need more funds," he said.

I let the hot air suck up that last comment and said nothing.

I was working nonstop at the hospital, picking up extra shifts and doing sixteen-hour shifts. I was well on my way to meeting my baby fund, but I looked like a zombie. I was tired.

"You're always in your pajamas when I come over," he said.

"I'm tired, and you always come over so late," I said.

"Why are you working so much?"

"Because I have a goal," I said. *And because I need to start paying what you're charging on my credit card*, I thought. "Come February, I'm going to try to have a baby," I said, in case he'd forgotten.

"Why don't you have my baby?" he asked. I looked at him in disbelief. He was in a *really* good mood. "Yeah, why not?" he asked himself more than me. "You know me, and it would be cheaper, too."

"Because if things didn't work out between us and I wanted to up and leave, I wouldn't be able to," I said, as it was the only excuse I could come up with on the spot.

"I wouldn't care if you left with the baby," he said.

Of course he wouldn't. And that's *exactly* why I didn't want to have a baby with him. I may as well have the baby on my own, using donor sperm, if he didn't give a shit if I got up and left. Why deal with all his drama for the rest of my life if I could do it on my own?

"Yeah, we should have a baby!" he exclaimed, like a light bulb had brightly lit up in his head. I could see a million thoughts running through it.

Was he serious?

"Some things just need to happen, Julie. Stop all the planning," he advised. Because he'd done so well in his own life by not planning?

"I agree with that to a certain extent. Some things do just need to happen, but if I end up alone, I need to be prepared," I said.

"Why wouldn't you have my baby? You know me; you know what you'll be getting." Dear God! "And I'd want my baby to have a good mom, and I can't think of any better person than you." It was the only, and the best, compliment he ever gave me, besides liking my massaging and cooking. But of course, I'd been a great *mother* to him.

"We'll see where we are come February," I said. It was six months away. A lot could change in six months.

I went to bed after he fell asleep. He must have been exhausted after so much excitement and *planning* in one evening. I didn't know what to think, besides, *Is he serious?* If I had a baby with Jacob, I wanted it to be because we loved each other, not because in the middle of his unusually good mood, he came up with this crazy notion to become the father of my/our child and because I was desperate. I wanted him to care, to really care. He'd have to step up to the plate and be a great partner and even better father. It couldn't happen in the condition we were currently in. I wanted him to prove me wrong. I desperately did. My heart hung on to the hope that maybe he'd begin making more of an effort. I fell asleep with those hopes.

He woke me at two, his usual time to join me in bed. "I'm

gonna go home," he said softly. So much for making an effort to be the father of our baby.

He rubbed his hand over the roundness of my stomach.

"Come February, a baby," he said sweetly. I'd never heard his voice sound so beautiful and peaceful. It was a first and only moment.

"But we don't even have sex," I said quietly.

"You have to have faith," he said.

In what, immaculate conception? Jacob and I were going to have the second Jesus? I couldn't remember the last time he *knew me*, biblically speaking. Blue moons were more frequent than our sexual encounters. And when we did have sex, we always used condoms. I did need faith, as we needed a miracle! I went back to sleep after Jacob left, hoping Angel Gabriel would come whisper about the birth of our baby in my ear and tell me not to worry and not to plan so much! No such dream.

I shared with Zane how I did wish Jacob would somehow see the light and be a better boyfriend to me. If he was, then I'd be open to having his baby. Zane and I went to lunch and then walked over to an empty building across from where we were.

"See, this is what I imagine for Jacob. A gym this size to do CrossFit," I told Zane.

"He doesn't realize he could have a stable life and his own little gym if he was with you, but he has to want it," he said.

I allowed myself to fantasize even further. "And we could put a little crib or play area over in that corner," I said.

Zane laughed, probably at how farfetched the idea of Jacob being a better person to me and an awesome dad sounded.

I told Jacob about the empty spaces I'd seen and that he should consider them. We drove around town looking through dusty windows of previous businesses that had resided there and ultimately failed.

"This is a perfect place, babe, especially with that back alley. Clients could do sprints there or work with the big tire." He was fantasizing about the possibilities the way I fantasized about having a baby.

"It would be very nice. And it would be your own," I said.

"So you'll help me, babe?"

"I told you I support you one hundred percent," I said. What that meant I wasn't sure, but I knew I'd *encourage* him 100 percent.

"I'll call tomorrow on a few of the places."

I was running out of recipes for Jacob. The more depressed he became, the more he came over, and the harder I tried. Why? I guess I was still trying to prove to myself that I *could* make this work, regardless of what it took out of me. Although I wasn't sure if I even *liked* him. I was sure I couldn't stand him most moments. He was over almost every night I had off work. The topic of our miracle February baby was never mentioned again. We usually slept apart, he on the couch or guest bedroom, and I in my room alone. If he did go home, it was after his meal, massage, and catnap. He was on the verge of a nervous breakdown, and I was on edge as well. On that level, we were in perfect sync.

Most nights he appeared glued to my couch, cemented in his own depression, staring at my "too small" television. I, on the other hand, would be on the phone, hiding in my closet, complaining about him to friends or e-mailing Joe, trying to salvage something, anything, of my life. I was a mess!

I wrote Joe:

Date: August 9, 2010
Subject: Friend

I miss my friend, or maybe I miss not knowing if he is angry, sad, happy, overworked, feeling better.... Or maybe I still feel unsettled from the last e-mails, which we don't need to get into again. So I write to share some Hafiz with you. You don't know Hafiz? A 14th century poet, probably one of my favorite poets. Here's your introduction and weekly installment of Hafiz from me to you, since I could only wish to write so eloquently.

I sent him "The Sun Never Says" and "The Gift."

Date: August 10, 2010
Re: Friend
Hello my friend,

I am not mad or sad. I have meditated or thought very deeply about the whole situation. It is funny that you contacted me, as I had just thought about you earlier in the day. I have been checking my mail to see if you would contact me. It is a pleasant surprise! I am well, mentally and emotionally, even though I haven't changed at all. I like the last poem a lot. The past can be either a foundation to something grand or an anchor to a longing for what was. I like to look at my past as the first. The conclusion I've come to is this: No matter what, I cannot lie to myself. I know who I really am. And I accept me. There will be consequences and repercussions. But this is the nature of life. I am not good or evil. For I do not drive myself to be either. I do not want to be a perfect "self." However, I do not want to be totally undisciplined either. I feel that life is just one big high-stakes gamble. We all want to hit it big, but in reality, sometimes you just have to be satisfied with breaking even. Or willing to accept the bust. I appreciate your poetry and look forward to more. I hope this finds you in good health. I hope that you are progressing wonderfully on your journey. Have faith that all will work out in the end. You will have your jackpot soon enough! Don't work too hard.

Talk to you soon.

Always,

Joe

PS: I start grad school on the 23rd and I'm super excited. Oh and my baby girl has two teeth. Too cute!

A few weeks later, I sent him Hafiz's "We Have Not Come to Take Prisoners." He responded:

Date: September 2, 2010

Subject: One more thing

Hi there!

I am doing just fine. I started grad school two Mondays ago. I am super busy. My classes are interesting and challenging. I will make it though…I think. ;) Anyway, the rest of my life is running on schedule. My son turned eleven on Monday. My daughter is crawling all over and will be walking any day now. She is highly intelligent, which is extremely frightening. Work is just work. I look forward to doing something for a living that is more fulfilling.

I'm glad to hear that you and him are trying to work it out. It's weird to me though because it seems as if you are settling. I mean, from my understanding, he has already made you feel pretty shitty. Why go back to that? But people and situations change. So I hope this time has a better outcome. Just don't discount yourself. i.e., get what you deserve! This is just my assessment of the situation, so don't put anything into it. I care about you and only want the best in life for you.

Well, thank you for your poetry and still thinking about me. It's a crazy life that we lead. I look forward to hearing how your life is progressing. February is right around the corner.…

Always,

Joe

Was it that obvious? I was settling? I *was* settling. Lesson Number One: *The head and the heart are the most demanding of organs. To settle for less would put this precious life at a high risk for demise.* No wonder I felt like I was dying. Why couldn't I break away? Instead, I allowed him to suck me into his undertow. When would I finally drown, allow my corpse to fill with water and float? But it wasn't the lesson of demanding or breathing that I needed. It was Lesson Number Two: *Rid yourself of toxins*. I logically knew that was the answer yet couldn't make the break.

Jacob brought over all his sales figures from Gold's to prove to me that he knew if he got his own gym, he could sell one-on-one training. He then gave me a CrossFit workout in my backyard. The pavement was hot; he loomed over me, calling out my lousy time and how many repetitions of this or that jump I still needed. I had my first Spanish paella in the final baking stages, sitting in my oven, waiting for us. If he was attempting to impress me with this killer workout, I'd impress him equally when I whipped the saffron paella out of the oven. Even if it wasn't truly authentic paella, I could smell that we were going to enjoy it. He was in a bad mood. I could sense it. I was walking on eggshells. I could feel them prickling under my feet.

"I'm gonna get going," he said immediately after the workout.

"Why?" I asked out of confusion. For God's sake, he'd never left *before* dinner.

"Because I have things to do," he said curtly.

"Stay and eat first. I spent all afternoon making this dinner." I wasn't walking on eggshells; I was standing as light as possible on them, trying not to blink. But no matter how still I stood and no matter how quiet or shallow I breathed, the heaviness in the room grew, and they started cracking.

"Well, I don't feel like it. I want to go home." His voice was sharp, edgy, no hint of an attempt to sound relaxed and in control.

"What's wrong with you?" I asked timidly and held my breath. Too late. It was the straw that broke the camel's back, the point of no return—I'd crushed all the eggshells to dust.

"YOU KNOW I DON'T HAVE TO PUT UP WITH ALL THIS QUESTIONING! YOU'RE SO NEEDY! I CAN'T TAKE IT!"

I? Needy? This cash cow was running dry, and I was emotionally drained from *his* needs!

In true classic Jacob fashion, as I'd witnessed before, his explosion was immediately followed by a quick bolt out the front door to his car and back home.

"OK. There, it's over, truly over," I said to myself. The oven heat, the August heat, or the heat from Jacob tightened around my throat. *Fucking breathe!*

I took a deep breath and held back my tears. In true June Cleaver fashion, unfazed that a toxic bomb had blown up in my face, I whipped out my lovely paella, enough to feed an army, and texted Jared asking if he'd like to come try my first paella. I didn't hear back from Jared until the following day, but by then I'd eaten four servings all by myself and taken the remainder to work.

However, I did hear from Jacob within hours of his dramatic departure. He texted me a novel about how it was wrong of him to have stormed out, that he was under a lot of stress, not knowing what he was gonna do for work, that he really did care about me, how hard he really was trying, and that I hadn't given him *any* credit for the changes he had made.

He'd made changes?

He texted again about how he'd been trying to spend quality time with me during the day and not just at night. Oh yes, I do remember one day-trip besides the bank. I asked him to go with me to a new organic grocery store to pick out vitamins. He agreed but said we had to hurry, as he needed to go visit his dad in the Bay Area. In the parking lot, I stumbled ever so slightly on my flip-flop. Yet I was nowhere near falling. He turned to me and said, "You're so embarrassing to be with in public." He kept a good five-foot distance from me there on out. I stood in line alone as I watched him fiddle with his cell phone outside of the entrance. I was embarrassed that I cared for such a person. But *did* I care for him? I simply hated myself for putting up with any of this. He then walked ahead of me to my car and said, "Let me drive!" He drove like a bat out of hell from the parking lot to his apartment.

I remember that when my first boyfriend dumped me, converted from Catholicism to Islam, and decided to marry another Muslim, I went to speak with the priest at the university I attended. I was still a Catholic at that time. After I gave the priest a rundown of my relationship and what was said and done, he looked me right in the eye and said, "Julie, you have an incredibly high tolerance for pain from another."

Here I was, nearly twenty years later, having not learned a damn thing, only increasing my tolerance. My tolerance for bullshit.

Now back to paella night. Jacob's texts continued that night, saying that no matter what he did, it was never enough for me. Was I that way? Was I the one that wasn't behaving appropriately? Was his perception of me the same as my perception of him? I was already at work with paella in hand. I simply said we'd talk about it later; I had myself to compose and patients to tend to. After placing the hot dish in the pantry, I grabbed a pulse oximeter to get a read on my oxygen level, as I felt like the summer heat was swallowing me whole. My oxygen was 88 percent. Not surprised. *Wonder what my heart's doing. Deep slow breath.* My oxygen raised to 91 percent. *Good thoughts, nice slow breath.* 94 percent. *Close your eyes. No need to cry, Julie. One more deep breath.* 97 percent. *Good enough. Now put that happy or serious nurse face on and get to work! Patients have far worse problems than you!*

The very next day, I received a text from Jacob stating he'd gone to the bank and looked into loans. He couldn't get approved for anything, needed a cosigner to secure the loan, and could we meet there? I called him, as I didn't know what the hell he was thinking.

"After walking out on me, you want me to go take money out for you?"

"Oh, so you helping me is conditional?" he asked, flabbergasted by the absurdity of my question.

Silence on both ends. I really didn't know how to scream, how to say, "I hate the way you treat me! Why should I help you?" I really wanted to know how to vocalize that exact sentence at that exact moment, but I was mute. Deaf, dumb, and mute? No, just dumb and mute. I heard his request, his *needs*, clearly.

"Are you going to help me or not? God! Please...." I heard

his voice rise and crack. It was the most desperate plea I'd ever heard. "I feel like just ending it all." There, again, was that threat. I knew he was crying, with or without the production of tears. And inside, I was crying, too. "Are you going to help me or not?" he asked again in a broken-down-man tone.

I'd have liked to blame someone or something for tolerating this, for my next decision, for this behavior of myself that I did not recognize. Perhaps it was in my upbringing, a deep-rooted teaching that I learned long ago that didn't allow me to walk away. I'd seen (and participated in) my mother constantly helping Neil with the obstacles of his life, hoping for change with him and the dynamic of their relationship. But that was her being a mother and my being a sister to Neil. This was Jacob, some random turd I met at the gym. I could only blame myself. I had no excuse, and, for whatever reason, I felt I had no choice.

"Yeah," I said feebly.

If only I'd called one friend, or stopped a stranger in the street, they probably would have said, "Are you insane? Don't do it! I'm going to shackle your legs to this fence so you can't go help him!"

The last time I spoke to Meena about Jacob, she flat-out said, "I'm not in the mood to hear about Jacob anymore," and she hung up to go take a nap before the night shift, leaving me hanging on the line to deal with my downward spiral. There wasn't one single person I felt I could call. I knew I could never tell a soul of my pure stupidity. I was getting into this mess all by myself. The weight of it all. I was sinking, sinking, sinking, but had yet to drown. My heart was a hustler, hustling to survive, like Jacob.

We hung up, and I felt and saw myself going through the motions, like an out-of-body experience. I saw myself getting dressed, getting in my car, heading to the bank to meet him. I knew this was wrong, but I couldn't stop. My actions were working independently of my true thoughts. I could not, I did not, say *no*. I don't know why. Where the hell is Suze Orman when you need her to say, "Girlfriend!" and slap financial sense across your face? I actually prayed that I'd get into a car accident on the way to the bank so that it would divert me from my stupidity of helping him. Unfortunately, I got to the bank alive and well.

When I got there, I couldn't even look him in the eye. I was so ashamed of myself and repulsed by him. I was helping someone who last night had screamed at me and walked out. We sat side by side in front of the loan officer, to whom Jacob gave a very animated sales pitch about CrossFit and how he'd give her a good deal. When she walked away to make a copy of something, he whispered, "She's out of shape and could really use a workout."

His credit was even worse than I imagined. A cosigner wasn't enough. He needed a *secured* loan—which required my placing ten thousand dollars in the bank in case he defaulted on payments. Am I kidding? I wish I were. I felt like I was consenting to his robbing me. And I was.

We made the necessary transactions, and I signed what felt like my firstborn away. The check was handed to him. He smiled at the check and not at me. "Woo-hoo!" he exclaimed. "I'm gonna skip town and have a great time," he joked. "I'm kidding," he said when he saw my stern, unhappy look. "Babe, it's gonna be all right. It's gonna be hard with only ten thousand, but I can make it work." *Only* ten thousand dollars? Had he forgotten about the fifteen-thousand-dollar limit on the credit card?

"I hope so," I said. I'd put my money where my mouth was, and I was counting on him to make it work. I really did want him to have his dream, but I wanted mine, too. Which was…? Well, his treating me better and, of course, a baby. But not his baby.

"I'm not *giving* you this money, Jacob. It's a loan. I *need* that money back. So you need to pay off this loan ASAP so that I can withdraw my money." It was the strongest thing I'd said in months!

"*I know!* You don't need to keep reminding me! I plan to pay a thousand a month at first, then pay you off as soon as possible. Is that OK?" he asked, irritated.

At that moment, everything changed. Jacob no longer merely had nothing to offer me; now he *owed* me. I imagine there's nothing worse than owing someone, someone you don't even care for. Resentment was bound to grow. We left the bank parking lot in two separate vehicles. He went one way; I went another. I left as I arrived, alone. In addition to another ten thousand dollars, I lost a little more of my soul that day.

I'd become one of those women that gives money to men—something I thought I'd never, ever do or tolerate. I work with women whose boyfriends don't work; they buy their men the latest in electronic gadgets, take them on vacations, and dress them nicely over a period of many, many years. I could no longer and would no longer judge these women. I was now one of them. Instead of having Jacob move in and giving him the money little by little, year after year, I handed him the whole chunk at once. And in return, I took his abuse and ingratitude with open arms.

If you're going to support your man, it has to be the right man. Take, for example, Hillary and Bill Clinton. She teamed up with him, supported his political career, and a whole slew of other crap…but he became president of the United States. *El Presidente*, ladies and gentlemen, Mr. President! Any time you support a man when he's starting out, it's a high-risk gamble, and you hope you come out ahead, not looking like a total fool. If he's a success and stays in the relationship, other women will say, "She was smart to stick by him!" If he's a success and leaves the relationship, other women say, "After all she did for him!" If he isn't a success, they say, "She was so stupid!"

I knew then, driving home, that Jacob and I were not going to be business partners, or lovers, or even friends. It was all a matter of time before people said, "She was so stupid!"

Two days later he texted me that he'd found a spot for the gym and was on his way to get the keys. I called him to get more details. "I'm at the bank right now," he said, irritated.

"OK. I just wanted to hear about it."

"I'll call you back." He hung up.

One hour later he called in a cheery mood. "I got the keys,

babe!"

"Now you're happy?" I inquired.

"I think I'm bipolar," he said.

"You said it, not me," I agreed.

"Hey, now, not nice!" he said happily. "I was stressed, but once I got the keys and saw the place, I felt it, babe. It's gonna be OK!"

"I want to see it."

"Of course, you can come to work out any time!"

Within a week he'd moved all the equipment that he'd ordered on my credit card into the gym. He had a small office with a window facing the side street. He had a couple clients lined up. He was excited.

"It's great, Jacob," I said when I finally visited. "Why do you look sad?"

"It wouldn't have been possible without you," he said. "I'm up all night thinking how I'm going to pay you back." A glimmer, a speck, of hope.

"You said you had that all figured out. It'll take time, but it'll get up and running." I was worried. What about all his bullshit sales figures and the endless list of people he knew, that he was going to market to, and what about his CrossFit "community" that he always referred to? Let me reiterate: I was worried. But it was too late. I couldn't hold his hand any longer. He had to prove to himself that he could do this. He resented me. I could feel it. The more I tried, the worse it would get. I had to take a step back.

I worked out on occasion with him. He was very inconsistent. At first he encouraged me to come, then he'd compare me to the other nurse he trained. There was *no* comparison. Need I remind him, she was an athlete who happened to be a nurse, not the other way around? He, again, reminded me she'd swum to Alcatraz once! I hated the comparison. I never compared his inability to cry to Joe's ability to make misty-eyed eye contact with me in bed. I felt so worthless in the workouts. He was such a good trainer when I first met him; now I could tell I was a nuisance, and he made every attempt to make me feel as such. Mentally, and now physically, he made me feel worthless.

"Can you come for your workouts at, like, ten in the morning?" he asked.

"No. I get off work at seven thirty. I'll be too tired to work out right after work," I said.

He let out a long sigh. "Well, this five o'clock time really doesn't work for me."

I could tell only one person, my best friend, Dahlia. I told her, and only her, every detail. She listened silently, no, "Hmm," or, "Uh-huh," or, "Oh," or, "What the fuck?" comments. After I told her about the money, the workouts, the tantrums, the no sex in God-knows-how-long, she concluded with the following: "His job is to train people so they can feel good about themselves and what they accomplish. Yet he's doing the opposite with you. You have never sounded or felt so low being with someone."

"I don't know what to do."

"Stop beating yourself up, first of all. Do you know how many women lend men money? Nearly all of my girlfriends have done it at one time or another."

"I don't know what to do," I repeated.

As it turned out, I didn't have to do anything. Jacob slowly started to distance himself. I'd experienced distancing from other men before. It was only a matter of time before the final breakup. He then made it clear that I was to set up an appointment in advance to work out, not to drop by. Ever.

I looked up his gym website, and lo and behold, there was a huge error. His stripper and male escort information displayed on the page. I knew about the stripping, but not the male escort aspect of his secretive life! He'd obviously uploaded the wrong information to the wrong web address. I looked through it. He was advertising himself as a male escort. Interested women could purchase different "levels" of him, should I say. He had it broken down like a meal. He called the lower purchases "Starters," like salads, then there was the "Entrée," or hell, if you wanted it all, he listed what he called "The Feast." I wish I were kidding. His euphemisms didn't mean shit! His description of what he could give included, "What women deserve, nice back rubs, candlelight, great conversation." I'm paraphrasing. Yeah, right! A back rub? Great conversation? All for a nice price. In very tiny fine print, he adamantly reassured visitors to the website that he was in no way a prostitute. Maybe not, but he was sure as hell a hustler, and I'd been hustled and sucked right into his toxic vortex.

I felt nauseated. Jacob indeed was like a meal, a very bad meal that not only didn't satisfy but left me feeling completely ill. I started dry heaving. That's what toxins do to you. After I'd read every word and looked at every ten-years-younger-than-now picture he'd posted—in a tight shirt or undies outlining his erection—I texted him that his gym website had all his "porno" stuff posted instead of CrossFit gym information. Within minutes it was corrected.

I wrote Joe, just to write Joe:

Date: October 11, 2010
Subject: Happy October
Hey my Joe!

How's work? I've been working like crazy. I've thrown myself completely and totally into work, doing 80 to 104 hours a pay period. Which may not seem like a lot, but doing a 16-hour shift on your feet…is exhausting! At the same time I think it's my escape. After my last e-mail with you…I realize I'm happier keeping a distance from Jacob. He provides nothing, not even good companionship. We haven't even had sex in over 2 months, and I don't even care. I just feel like I'm finally happy with myself and know I don't need or want him. I'm happy with my February baby plan, and I'd rather be alone than around negative or moody people. I've even come to this conclusion with my girlfriends. In life you can really only count on yourself, and I think I've been managing fine. Don't get me wrong, I do miss having dinner with my girlfriends or having some interaction with a man…but at the end of the day, I'm OK. I have my health and a great job, what more could I ask for. Well…a little baby boy, maybe :)

Well, just wanted to keep in touch. I do miss you. Wish you were here to serve me a great cup of coffee with an equally great conversation. Maybe the best friendships are those that are at a distance? I don't know. You know me and MY moods.

I hope you and the family are well. And hope you're learning LOTS in school.

I send you big hugs, xoxoxo

—*me*

Date: October 11, 2010
Re: Happy October
Hi my friend,

All is well. The family is great. My little girl will be 1 this Friday. Time sure does fly!

I'm glad you've come to terms with the Jacob situation. I don't know him, but he sounds like a real scumbag. You don't need that in your life at all! I'm glad work is keeping you occupied. However, you do need other things, too. It's human nature. I wish I could still provide that for you.

Julie, I miss you, too. I try to tell myself it's not a big deal. But it kinda is. I miss all facets of our friendship we have developed. I wondered if you were going to write me again. It had been a while. Like any typical male, I wouldn't have written you first. The way I figured is if you really wanted to talk to me, you would. I'm happy you did.

Anyway, keep doing what you're doing. Stay positive. And keep finding new and exciting things to become interested in. I truly do admire your curious spirit. Take care, sweetheart.

XO

Dante aka Joe

I was planning an engagement dinner party for my friend Liliana. She lived in Los Angeles now but had worked for the majority of her career in Sacramento. The engagement party would be for all her Northern California friends, whom I'd never met. I told Jacob about it. "I don't feel comfortable around people I don't know," he said. He wasn't coming.

"I don't know them either," I said.

"My best friend Tony is coming to town next week. I told him all about you. He says I'm lucky."

"You are lucky," I said.

"I told him how you cook all the time, have your own house. Hard worker."

"Glad he sees it. Doesn't seem good enough for others." I was making my passive-aggressive jabs at him.

"*Nobody* deserves to be with you. You got your shit together." Was this a compliment? I wasn't sure.

"That's a bullshit excuse. If you wanted it, you would be a part of it, be involved."

"Like going to your friend's engagement party?"

"Yes, like going to my friend's engagement party. That's what people do; they make an effort."

"I'll think about it. But can you make dinner for Tony and me when he's here?"

I was curious. I hadn't met any of his friends. What would a friend of Jacob's be like?

A week later they arrived for dinner. Jacob had been drinking. He was elated. His friend was the complete opposite of him. Tony was normal. He didn't work out, hadn't lifted a weight in years. He smiled. He was polite and talkative. He was also very good looking and charming.

Jacob's mood was nearly euphoric. I'd never seen this side of him. He offered Tony something to drink. He went to the kitchen, grabbed glasses, poured drinks, wrapped his arms around my waist, kissed my cheeks, said everything smelled delicious, opened cabinets, helped me set the table. Who the hell was this man? He'd never been on the other side of the kitchen island, as I'd always tended to him, and now he navigated my kitchen confidently, taking ownership, like he'd built and stocked the kitchen himself. He laughed, he smiled, he talked nonstop, and he kept grabbing me, trying to give me loving affection.

"What are you doing?" I asked, shocked at his out-of-the-ordinary behavior.

"Give me a kiss," he said. I could smell liquor on his breath. I turned my head away from him.

"What? You don't like me like that anymore?" he asked.

I turned to Tony and said, "He never behaves like this. He rarely ever touches me and now he's trying to be all loving in front of you." I was angry.

"I've been stressed, Tony. With the gym…you know how it is

when you're stressed. You don't feel like doing anything."

Tony agreed. Jacob grabbed me and tried to pull me tight to him. It was all a show for his friend.

"I can't remember the last time he touched me, actually, and I always massage him," I said.

"Guys don't massage girls, number one rule," Tony said.

"What?" I asked.

"Right, Jacob?"

Jacob laughed, "That's right, buddy!"

Tony explained, "Once you start massaging a girl's back, then they expect it and it never ends. So you never do it, not once; then it's never expected."

Well, he was like Jacob in that manner. And that's why Jacob never once massaged me. Now I knew.

Jacob grabbed me to squeeze me tight.

"Stop it. I'm not used to you behaving like this," I said sternly and motherly.

He chuckled. Nothing was bringing him down tonight.

"You have a nice house. The floor plan is so open," Tony said, unfazed by Jacob's behavior.

"Yeah, it's been great for entertaining. I'm throwing a party in a few weeks for my friend," I said.

"Isn't that the party I'm coming to?" Jacob asked.

"Oh, you're coming?" I asked.

"Um, yeah! You keep telling me about it. I told you that I would."

"Yeah, we'll see if you show up."

He laughed and said, "She's always throwing these parties."

I spent the entire dinner staring at Jacob. So this was what Jacob was like when he was comfortable. This was how our relationship would have been if he could have been this open with me. Why were he and I so awkward and dysfunctional in our relationship? Did I need to keep him this drunk and move Tony into my house for him to acknowledge me? His animated ways continued throughout the night. He told Tony about the gym, his plans, and after every sentence, he'd look at me (he'd look at me!) and say, "Right, babe?" I nodded and smiled. I was beside myself, angry that he saved this behavior to demonstrate who-knows-what to Tony.

I didn't hear from Jacob over the weekend, and I didn't interfere with his BFF time. Monday, after Tony had left, I presume, I received the following text from Jacob:

"Sorry for my behavior the other night. I'd been drinking and was horny. Not a good combination."

His elated mood was now deflated. He came over and sat on my couch, staring straight at the television.

My friend's engagement dinner was a few days later. Couples arrived hand in hand. Men showed their respect and love to their ladies, and this was before they started drinking. *This is normal*, I repeated to myself. *This is what a normal relationship looks like.* I hosted fifteen couples. I smiled, I laughed, I carried on like I didn't have a care in the world, and I didn't. I was determined to become a living example of "Fake it till you make it!" I knew Jacob wouldn't show up, and it proved he'd *never* make any effort in our relationship. As if all the other things he'd done and said weren't enough!

The *only* thing that held me to him was the idiotic fact that I'd lent him money. This is when keeping your friends close, but your enemies closer, is crucial. If I ended things horribly, I was guaranteed to never receive a penny of it back. I had to end it on friendly terms somehow to hopefully get some of my money back. Why had I been such a fucking idiot? I was stuck. And more than anything, I hated that all this came down to money. But I felt like he'd taken an emotional toll on me, and I refused to let him finish it with a financial blow.

The day after the dinner party, I sorted through bills. The payment for the credit card was due, and I went through the list of charges Jacob had made: 140 dollars to a website called Party Pop. I researched the website. It was everything you needed for a party, including available strippers in the area. There he was, his stripping profile and information. I was livid. The card was to be used to establish his gym and get him on his feet again, not to advance his fucking stripping career. Was this ever going to end?

I grabbed the credit card statement and drove like a madwoman to his apartment. My hair uncombed, wild, and unruly, I jumped out of my car, statement in hand. I'd been to his apartment only once, to take him to the airport. I'd never been invited otherwise. I figured this would piss him off royally, and in a way, I wanted it to. I imagined I'd find another girl there when I knocked on the door. I didn't even care if I did. But things never go as planned. When I was about to climb the stairs to his second-floor apartment, he opened his door. He came down the stairs and said, "Hey!" when he saw me. He was nicely dressed, clean shaven, hair perfectly gelled, and he had a small carry-on suitcase in hand.

"What are you doing here?" he asked nicely.

"Going out of town?" I asked motioning to the suitcase.

"No. I have a stripping job right now and will change once I'm there."

Then I laid into him about the credit card statement, the ridiculous charges, that I wasn't going to be paying for his stripping advertisements, when was he going to focus on the gym, and did he think I could afford all this shit?

He turned it around on me and said, "I care about you. I don't know what I have to do to prove that, but I don't appreciate you coming over here and accusing me of all this! I'm going to pay you back. I have a job right now, and I'll give you the money to cover it! I'm trying my best!"

Why did I always feel like shit one way or the other? "I know you're trying, but I told you before not to go over the limit or else it's an added charge, and you never discuss any of this with me!"

"I'm forty-four years old! Do you think I like having to go strip at age forty-four to make money? You never think about me and how I feel. I'll come over tonight and we'll talk about it then!" He threw his suitcase in the trunk, got into his car, and sped away, leaving me standing there, watching him blaze away in his car—which had brakes he'd purchased with my credit card. From a spoiled child to a rebellious teenager was the only growth I'd seen in this man.

Four hours later he came over. He was drunk. But unlike the happy drunk state he was in with Tony, he was now cold. Where was Tony when you needed him?

Jacob sat there in the dimly lit room, staring at the television. Without turning his head, he said, "There's only one thing I'll ask of you. Don't you *ever* come to my place uninvited ever again." It was a threat, not a request.

"Excuse me?" I asked in amazement.

"It's the only thing that I have that's truly mine, my space. I don't want anyone coming over uninvited."

"What are you hiding?"

"Nothing! Don't you get it? You're not to arrive at my house or my workplace uninvited!" The workplace I paid for—I wasn't to go there uninvited?

He got up to run to the door.

"Go, that's what you do best," I said.

He faltered and walked in circles in the middle of my living room.

Leave, I thought. I was scared of him.

"I don't need your attitude. Don't *ever* do it again. Understood? And you're pissed because I didn't attend your stupid dinner party. So don't try to pull an attitude with me," he lectured.

I said nothing and rolled up tight in the corner of my couch. He sat back down and I kept my eyes focused on the television.

Within two minutes of his lecturing me, I heard him snoring. He'd passed out. Maybe he'd had some wine prior to coming over.

I went to bed and left him there. In the middle of the night, he got in bed and on top of me. I held my breath, tried to pretend I was sleeping. He wanted to have post-fight sex. I was afraid to fight, to speak, to move. *Get it over with*, I thought. And he did.

The next day he said, "I'll come over on your next day off."

I called in sick to work the following night. I was sick of myself and all that I was tolerating. Pure human poison. I didn't tell Jacob I called in sick.

I needed a night alone. Or so I planned. But my entryway had become a revolving door for Joe, Jared, and Jacob in no random order or reason.

Thank God not Jacob, and unfortunately not Joe, this time Jared texted to ask if I was at work. It was midnight. I was enjoying my night of solitude, but was open to having him over. He must have been looking for something or *someone* to do. "Come over," I said. He did.

I opened the door and said, "Wow, you must be really lonely to be coming over at this hour." He was dressed nicely. Obviously, another event ended early.

"Well, that doesn't speak much for your confidence," he said jokingly, or not. If he only knew the whole truth.

He'd just gotten back from the Bahamas with his kids the previous night. I told him about my dinner party. "And you didn't invite me?" he asked. This is what I loved about Jared. He would happily have attended my dinner party and hit on every woman there. He would have entertained every table and been the food critic to the Moroccan cuisine I prepared. He would have been the life of the party even though he didn't know a soul in the room.

I told him about Jacob. He nodded his head up and down, perhaps wondering why I was putting up with the bastard. I had the same question in my mind. When you tell friends about your asshole boyfriend and they just nod, or remain silent on the phone, it's because they're busy thinking, "Are you fucking stupid?" When no advice or comments are offered, *that's* the best indicator that you're in a really bad situation.

"Let's go to bed now; it's late," Jared stated.

He was so comfortable with himself, with everything.

I wanted to be with him for this one night. It was a choice, my choice. I wanted to wash away my last sexual encounter with Jacob. I wanted to share this—sex—with someone who took the time to have a conversation with me, who didn't yell at me or make me feel so worthless. Even though I knew that I could never wow Jared, I felt at least like a human being when I was with him. I wondered if his nose could detect not only pheromones but a woman who desperately needed to be tended to in times of trouble. He always seemed to show up or be available at the most opportune time.

Jacob showed up the following night for his meal and massage. "Gotta go to bed now," he said afterward, as he made his way to my bedroom. It was ten, and he had to be up at four thirty to work out with a client at five.

"Good night," I said, dragging out my laundry folding as much as possible.

"Aren't you coming?" he asked.

"No. It's too early," I said.

"*Babe*! Just come lie down," he demanded.

Why couldn't he leave? Why did he even come over if he needs to be up so early? Is this man trying to sabotage my night off? Does he know that I called in sick last night and that Jared was here? Would he even care? Probably not.

"I'm not tired," I said.

"Just lie down next to me until I fall asleep," he commanded.

Really? Should I sing you a lullaby as well?

We got into bed, and I turned my back to him. He snuggled up close behind and started to kiss me. "Do you have a condom?" I asked before he made any further attempt. If he didn't, I'd lie and say I didn't either. If he did have a condom, I'd lie and say I started my period. I had absolutely no desire to be fast asleep next to him, much less have sex with him. I was revolted by the thought.

"I do, but it's in the living room. I'm too lazy to go get it," he said.

"OK." I didn't offer to go get it, and I didn't have to lie. I wanted out of this mess.

"Turn out the light, say your prayers…oh, I forgot you don't believe in God," he said sarcastically.

I wasn't going to argue with him how I did believe in a higher power but not the way he did. "Believe me, I think about God every single day, you asshole," was what I wanted to say. I wanted to tell him that I'd had a relationship with Jesus once. Of course I had. Jesus was, after all, a man whose name started with the letter J. And like all the others, of course, it, too, was a long-drawn-out, tumultuous relationship, thanks to the church. But that's another book entirely—a book beyond the book of Revelation. I didn't say anything.

Jacob was wrong. It wasn't that I didn't believe in God or some higher power; I didn't believe in love. And I was giving up—giving up on trying to love, to be in love, to be lovely, to be loving, to know love, to be loved, to believe in love. It was the last night he stayed over.

In five years and three men, I'd gone from being overly infatuated with Joe, to really liking Jared, to truly hating *myself* with Jacob.

NOVEMBER'S END

By November I was seeing Jacob once a week. He'd give me a workout, and I'd cook him dinner. He said it was an equal exchange, but I never agreed with him on that. He had yet to make a payment, aside from the twenty dollars he'd given me over the summer. The workouts were the only quality time we spent together. He would actually speak to me: "Give me fifteen burpees. A full push-up, Julie! I said *run*, not *jog*; do it again. Hold that plank another twenty seconds." OK, so he wasn't asking about me or my day or telling me about his. There rarely was a verbal exchange between us once the workout was over.

The year was quickly coming to an end, and I knew I had to make some heavy decisions: one, ask him about where, if anywhere, our relationship was going; two, remind him that February was now only weeks away; three, break completely away from this septic situation. Deep down I knew the answers—the relationship was dead in the water, and come February, I'd be trying to have a baby by myself. I was still fighting myself on how to detach completely from him. Who would have thought that detaching from a completely detached human being would be so difficult?

Jacob had made zero effort to get to know me as a person, much less meet my friends or family. The only friend he ever met was Zane, and that was because Zane had briefly thought of hiring him as a trainer. The subject of the baby had never been mentioned again after that one brief moment of his being in a good mood. Since July, we'd had sex once. Protected. Subconsciously, I knew that I didn't want his toxic DNA to swarm in me with the possibility of conception. Lesson Number Two: *Rid yourself of toxins.*

I had an appointment with the main doctor at the reproductive center to get a more in-depth answer about my donor's CMV status. He got straight to the point.

"You're CMV negative. If you become CMV positive from the insemination and you have a baby with neurological defects, you'll never forgive yourself. You need to exchange your donor sperm."

"But from the research I've done, the odds of becoming CMV positive from IUI sperm is incredibly low," I argued. I wasn't ready to give up on my dream donor.

"But why risk that chance?" the doctor countered.

"But if I met this man on the street, fell in love, and got pregnant, wouldn't I still be in this position? Nobody is checking her husband's CMV status."

"That's different. They're having a child as a couple. You're not in love with the man that's donating this sperm. You're a single woman who's actually in a better position than someone having a child with the man she's in love with. You're in a position to choose the best sperm, genetically. You want the healthiest child possible, and you have the choice to pick the highest chance for that."

"But I do love my sperm donor. I'm attached to him."

"You love the qualities that he wrote down on that profile. You need to go back and do a search on CMV-negative donors." His response sounded final. He wasn't going to argue with me anymore. "I know you'll make the right decision and exchange donors," he concluded.

I was hitting road bumps, and I hadn't even had my first insemination. So I wasn't going to have a baby from this Mexican-German man that sounded sincere, smart, and eccentric? I had to exchange him for a new donor? The doctors made it sound like exchanging a shirt for a different color. "Oh, that color doesn't bring out your eyes. Exchange it!"

"But I love this shirt. It took me months to pick it out," I'd argue.

"But you have the chance to buy a shirt that brings out the dazzle, the glory in your eyes. Why would you settle for less? I'm telling you, exchange it. That shirt's threads have the possibility of coming loose and falling apart! And you're a single woman; how would you handle caring for a shirt that's not 100 percent perfect? Exchange it now, or I will not medically treat you wearing that shirt!"

Of course I wanted a 100 percent healthy, intelligent, genetically strong baby. I knew I had to exchange the donor. Even though I'd love my baby, no matter how he or she came out, I knew the doctor was right. I couldn't take the chance when I knew there could be consequences using this sperm.

After the appointment, I met Jacob for our scheduled

workout. I was emotional. I was sad. I was weepy.

"Why are you crying?" he asked, annoyed.

"I had a bad day." *I can't use the donor sperm I purchased!* I thought.

"Are you lonely?" he asked in a mocking tone with a smug half smile on his face.

I looked at him, his feet solid on the gym floor that I'd helped him establish. He looked full of himself. He was back on his feet, figuratively and literally speaking, and he was ready to make a mean break from me.

"No, I'm not lonely," I said firmly.

"Hmm," he said, not convinced.

Something had changed. He'd been with someone. I could tell.

We started the workout, and he had me run across the lot with a sandbag. I looked back at him. He was texting; he wasn't paying any heed to me. Yes, he was confident and exploring new women.

"No workout Thursday, since it's Thanksgiving," he said as we finished the workout.

"What are you doing for Thanksgiving?"

"Nothing. I don't do good with holidays. Bad memories. That's when my mom would drink and throw stuff at me. So I like being alone. Hope you understand." This was a very long dialogue from Jacob that really meant, "Don't invite me to your family's get-together, because I won't go."

"OK. Want me to bring you food after? I can make you a pot pie," I suggested, still trying.

"Yeah, pot pies! OK!"

"OK, see you then." I walked away and distinctively remember looking back at him. It was a very gray night, cold. Even after a sweaty workout, the wind sent a cold chill through me. He was locking the door to the gym. He never looked up at me.

All secrets have life-spans of their own. Then comes a specific day or night, a specific hour, usually a dreaded moment, in which the secret expires. And once the secret is no longer an assumption but a known fact, it causes a domino effect that abruptly ends certain things, fixes important things, covers up remnants, and begs one person while denying another.

It was days before Thanksgiving, a little before three in the morning. I had the night off and was sleeping comfortably, alone in my bed. My cell phone went off. I had a new text message from Joe. My first thought was that he must be in the neighborhood and wanted to come over. Yay! Instead, everything I'd predicted had occurred, and he was scurrying to hide or fix what he could. The text message said, "My wife found your e-mail. She knows that I have been to your house, but not the rest. I'm sorry. I can no longer be friends with you. I can't talk to you anymore. Have a nice life."

BREATHING THROUGH THE NIGHT

I texted, "What happened? I am so sorry."

He replied, "It's not your fault. It's just that she doesn't deserve this."

I didn't respond. I wanted to call him, text him, find out the details, but I didn't have the energy to go through it, for myself or him. And what could I say? "I told you so!"? I knew this day would come, and as my heart had always known, he'd beg her, choose to stay (and she would, too), and he'd deny me. It was over between us. I breathed lightly and quietly; my heart didn't beat fast out of fear or desperation to fix the situation. It simply resigned itself to a truth that had existed all along. I had lost. I lost my love, my lover, but more importantly, my friend. I lost my friend Joe. I'd never been in the running to win.

I literally felt my heart, not breaking, not beating, but quietly moving back, retreating, and shrinking to shelter itself from further damage. There's a song I love that talks about a *broken* hallelujah; *this* must be it, as nobody was rejoicing. I closed my eyes to concentrate on my breathing. It was all I could do. Lesson Number Three: *Learn to breathe.*

When he texted me that she didn't deserve this, it was as if he wanted me to have some compassion for her. He was right; she *didn't* deserve this. But I felt *I* didn't deserve this either. Many would argue that I did, that this was my karma. After all, I knew he was married. I *knew* I deserved this. Though it was wrong to be involved with him, my feelings for him were genuine, as genuine as hers. That's something she and I had in common: we both loved him. She just happened to meet him years before me, had the ability to get pregnant and have him marry her…and now have him beg her and possibly, just *possibly*, be faithful to her.

I was deeply saddened but not surprised. I'd predicted this would be our end. And it was. This was the consequence of loving a married man. I remained in bed all night, awake, alone, quietly breathing, and imagining how it must have all gone down on his end. To help me cope, I created the entire following scenario in my mind:

He probably ran off to his side job, bartending, in such a hurry that he never noticed that his e-mail session was still open on the computer. He kissed his wife and his baby girl, sitting in the kitchen high chair, with a quick sweep of his full lips across both their cheeks. His wife said, "Love you," to him and meant it.

He responded, "Love you, too." He answered automatically, a response that had no thought or feeling to it. Her face searched his for something more and hoped he'd see that she yearned for it.

She finished cleaning the kitchen and bathed her little girl, who looked exactly like Joe. There was an eerie quietness to all her tasks. She could hear her own heavy sighs, the sounds of water being wrung out from the washrag, and the sound of that little voice, the woman's instinct, nagging in her head, saying, *He's up to no good.* She really needed to stop worrying so much about whether her husband's infidelity would be a constant suspicion in their relationship. She placed the baby in the crib and thought to kill some time on the Internet before heading to bed. And that's when she found it: his open e-mail account and a slew of e-mails exchanged between us.

She read his words as if she didn't even know this person. He'd never spoken like this before. She reread them, trying to capture a glimpse of the man she was married to. She didn't recognize this man. It must be a mistake. But it wasn't, and she knew it. And here was the proof. She breathed heavily, and tears ran down her face. Her lips trembled.

She read the Hafiz poems this girl sent him; they made no sense. This interaction between them made no sense! She read her husband's reply, stating that he liked the poems and that he'd been meditating. *Meditating? When? Where? Who is this man I'm married to? Who has he been fooling, me or her?* She truly felt she didn't know him. She didn't realize all her actions and uneasy feelings were because she *did* know him. Instinctually she knew he was capable of having secret affairs; that's why she constantly called him, texted him throughout the day, in an attempt to know his whereabouts and his daily interactions with others.

She cried loudly, sobbed. And she waited. She got the baby out of the crib and held her for her own comfort. She had to approach this right. She wanted to see how much he'd come clean on his own. She didn't want their marriage to end. But she had to make him believe it would be ending, as she'd always threatened—actually, promised—him that she'd leave if he ever cheated. But what if he wanted it to end? Dare she play that card? If she played her cards right, she could gain the upper hand in this marriage; he'd never cheat again, and she'd finally live in peace, knowing he'd be at her beck and call. She could, and she would come out ahead in all of this. She'd be damned if she lost her husband, her marriage, to this fucking whore, after all the years she'd put into Dante. Not Joe, Dante. *And why the fuck did this whore address him as Joe?* she wondered.

The minutes ticked by slowly, intensely. It was after two in the morning when she heard him park his truck in the driveway.

He was surprised that she was still awake. The flicker of light from the television gave him a quick but recognizable glimpse of the deep-creviced pain on her face. Fear rushed through him. Something was terribly wrong, and whatever it was, he knew he was to blame.

"What's wrong?" he asked, not really wanting to know.

Finally, she turned her head to look at him, a penetrating stare into the face of a man she thought she knew. She calmly turned her stern look back to the television.

Fuck, he thought. *She knows.* A series of possibilities ran through his head. He thought about all the flirts and fucks he'd managed in the past year. Which one of these girls had he not assessed properly and now had gone off the deep end by telling his wife?

"So you gonna talk to me? You're obviously upset about something." He approached the couch but didn't sit.

She raised her eyes to look up at him. "Who's Julie

Guardado?"

The question, the name mentioned, caught him off guard. He hadn't thought about me in his list of flirts and fucks. Julie. *Fuck, Julie?* She *told?* He'd never thought of me as a threat. Things had wrapped up nicely; she hadn't even cried at the end. *We're friends, she's not a mistress...any longer.* How was he going to get out of this one? What did she know?

"An old friend," he said cautiously.

"From where?"

"I've known her a long time. From the coffee shop. Just a friend." He figured he better start emphasizing the *friend* part.

"Why is she sending you e-mails?"

"Because we're *friends*, babe. It's no big deal." *Oh God, what e-mails did she read? Hopefully, just the very last one where she wished me and the family a happy Thanksgiving.*

"How come I don't know about her?"

"I guess I never thought about it. She's just a friend."

"You're lying! Who the fuck is she?"

"She's no big deal. She's just a friend, but this is exactly why I never told you. I knew you'd assume the worst," he said. He was backpedaling now.

"So what is it, Dante? You never thought about telling me, or you didn't tell me because you knew I'd question you?"

"I...I...I don't know," he stuttered and attempted to pick up the baby from his wife's arms. He needed the comfort now. She pulled the baby tighter to her. Punctuating every word, she said,

"You. Are. Lying! I know you've been to her house! Stop your lying now!"

She knows I've been to her house? So I can't deny that one. What else does she know?

And as if she were reading his mind, she said, "I know everything."

A mélange of emotions came over him. The first, surprisingly, was relief. Relief that this day, which was bound to come, had finally arrived. *I've been caught. All the hiding is now over. I can breathe now.* The second, anger. *I've been caught. How could I have let this happen?* The third, guilt. *I've been caught. My wife is devastated. I've caused this. How can I fix this now?* The fourth, resignation. *I've been caught. I'll say and do whatever it takes to move past this as quickly as possible. I don't want to deal with this. I'll be stuck in this marriage forever. This is what I deserve. I'm ready to pay my sentence.*

"I can explain," he started, even though he didn't know how he could explain. *How does one begin to explain or justify years of infidelity? Is Julie the only one she knows about? And did she really know everything? The timeline, the years, the back-and-forth with Julie? Had Julie contacted her? That's where I'll start, blaming this on Julie.*

"What exactly did Julie tell you?" He felt like a fraud. He knew *I'd never approach his wife*, but he had to get the whole story and somehow flip it around as *his wife explained* what happened between him and me. This way, if she didn't know everything, he wouldn't be the one to give away any extra details that would sink him deeper into this shithole.

"She didn't tell me anything—"

He cut her off. "Because if she's saying there was something more between us, she's lying. I haven't even seen her in months. We're just friends."

"She didn't tell me anything!" she screamed as she rose from the couch.

"You're gonna wake the baby," he said, trying to diffuse her building anger and stop the tears running nonstop down her face. But there was no calming her. She went into the baby's room and locked herself inside. He could hear her weeping. It was a sound he couldn't bear.

"Open the door. Please, open the door," he begged. It was something he wasn't used to doing, begging. He repeated himself over and over, as he didn't know what else to say. He wanted to hold her close, kiss the top of her head, and somehow speak as little as possible but still get himself out of this.

She was crying. The baby was crying. He was on the verge of crying because he didn't know what to do. *Think*, he thought *What can I do? Better cut it off completely with Julie, ASAP!* He pulled out his cell phone. He knew this was risky, as his crying wife was merely on the other side of the door and could catch him texting me. He scrambled his fingers across the keys and texted me.

He quickly deleted the text messages and my number after his final text to me. He turned off his phone and placed it in his front pocket, as it felt safer to have it in the front pocket rather than the back. He would need to check first thing in the morning whether I'd sent him any further texts and make it clear that I wasn't to text him ever again, as he had a marriage and family to save, for crying out loud! He knew that it was finally all over between us, as much of the intrigue, the passion, and the want were contained in the possibility of being caught. And now that he had been, the excitement he lived for had been extinguished. Now the new challenge was whether he could make his marriage work and regain his wife's trust.

He knocked again on the baby's bedroom door. His wife opened it. The baby was in her crib; the wife looked like hell. *I've aged her*, he thought. *I'm no better than what my father was to my mother. This is who I am, and it's not good.*

He started again, attempting to hug her, "I love you and the baby so much—"

She pushed him away. "You don't care about the baby! You don't care about me! You fucked her! You fucked her!"

"Is that what she said?" He attempted again to turn my words into lies. It was his only way to get more information on how all this had unraveled in the six hours he'd been gone.

"She didn't tell me! Your e-mails to her did!"

He lowered his head. He was scum, and he knew it. *She got into my e-mail account. I'm fucked*, he thought.

"Babe"—he started crying now—"*you're* the most important thing in my life. This family is the most important thing."

"I want you out of this house by tomorrow." She decided to bluff. She was scared, shaking, but she had to get the upper hand. She'd threaten him with divorce, although never really wanting or meaning it.

"What? No. I'm not leaving you or my baby."

"You don't deserve to even be around our baby!" There, she did it. She'd use the baby to her advantage. The child card is the highest card in the family deck. It's the ace *and* the wild card. It always works, but she'd played the ace sooner than she expected. She'd seen the child card played many times by her own family and the women she worked with, and she hoped for an equally positive outcome.

"No! We can work this out. Let's talk about it. After all we've been through…no! We have a baby, this house—I'm working on my master's so we can get ahead. I love you; you know that. We have family coming over for Thanksgiving. I work this extra bartending job to have extra for us, but I'll quit it. I was actually thinking how I wanted to be home with you more…" He was rambling, grasping. She loved it. It was working.

"I don't believe you," she said, but a tiny part of her did believe him. She had to, or else there would be no point in staying. For now, she had to continue with her scam of wanting nothing to do with him. She had to stand her ground and frighten him to his core.

"I'm so sorry." His first hint toward confession.

"Do you love her?" she asked.

He didn't respond.

"Do you love her?"

"God, no, not at all. She's nothing. She means nothing. She's really nothing...nothing."

"You fucked her!" she screamed.

God, how many times is she going to say this? I know, I know, I know I fucked her! But come on; let's move on! Let's make up now.

"Why?" she demanded to know.

"Because I'm stupid, babe. I'm stupid. She was just a friend, and—I don't know...things got out of hand. I didn't plan it."

She didn't know how to respond. He admitted it. He'd had an affair. Even though she'd read it in his e-mails, hearing him admit it was different. It was absolute.

"I'll never trust you ever again. I don't want anything to do with you," she lied. She loved this man. He was the father not only to their daughter but also to her son from a previous relationship.

"You deserve better; I know," he said weakly.

Oh God, does this mean he's letting me go? She panicked. "You should be the one giving me better!" she screamed.

"I know. I will. I promise. Please don't leave me. Please. I'll change. It'll never happen again. Never."

Phew, he wasn't giving up on us, she thought.

"I don't know what I want anymore," she lied again. She knew exactly what she wanted. She wanted him—right in the palm of her little hand, once and for all, for happily ever after.

The night ended with their falling asleep in separate rooms and going through the next morning in awkward silence. He pretended to be packing his things to be out of the house as she requested. She felt so lonely. She knew she had to let him leave; that way he'd really know what he ruined and would be missing. He lingered. He couldn't leave, because then people would know their business. He knew he screwed up; it all caught up to him, as I had said it would. He had to make things right.

In the evening, after a full day of silence, he was the first to speak. "I was thinking that maybe we could go to counseling," he suggested.

She didn't respond. She didn't even acknowledge his presence, but she loved the idea of counseling. It also reassured her that he wasn't going to give up.

"That is if you'll give me a second chance. I'll do whatever you ask," he added. He knew this would be a hefty price tag. The price? His freedom, the rest of his days, his DNA, so to speak. No more running around alone; no more late-night jobs; no more hiding texts, phone numbers, or e-mails; no more telling her to stop assuming or accusing him or keeping tabs on him. No more, no more, no more. She'd earned a lifetime all-access pass to question his every move. The glorious gemstones inside his kaleidoscope shifted, destroyed, and would be forced to work with a new method of operation in order to survive this.

She didn't respond to his statement of, "I'll do whatever you ask," but a loud victory cheer resounded in her heart.

Night approached; he stopped his pretend packing. When he entered the kitchen, she kept her eyes on a magazine that she pretended to be reading. He opened the refrigerator and looked around.

"There's food on the stove if you're hungry," she said, extending an olive branch.

"Smells good," he said quietly and served himself.

She got up from the table and poured him some iced tea.

"Thank you," he said. She sat down and opened the magazine from the beginning and pretended to read it all over again. They sat across from each other, both of them relieved, knowing, thinking, *It's gonna be OK. It'll all work out.* Both pretending. *It'll all work out.*

Of course, this is only how I imagined it all unfolded. This is how I had to imagine it happened to accept that he was leaving me behind. Oddly enough, I, too, was relieved that the day had finally arrived—not to say, "I told you so," but to finally force me to change. I, too, needed a new method of operation. Second, I did feel guilty, knowing that she must have been devastated. But they would work together at this marriage that he called "a job." I knew that they'd survive this.

If I could bet on one part of my imaginary scenario, it would be the part where he said that I was nothing, that I meant nothing. I knew when it came down to the wire that (a) she'd stay, (b) he'd beg, and (c) he'd deny me. I guess that's what hurts the most: that he denied me. I predicted his denial the way Jesus predicted Peter's. Denial of any sort should be considered a sin—it could take the place of "Thou shall not covet thy neighbor's wife." If you're going to have an affair, live up to it, own it, the day that it all comes to the surface!

When I imagined those words, "She means nothing," coming out of his mouth, it melted his striking beauty, our endless conversations, our intimate moments, and our supposed friendship into nothing. Absolutely. Nothing. The perfectly angled mirrors I looked at to view his kaleidoscope beauty had been shattered. The gems that I held precious in my mind were but an illusion. None of it mattered. All those years and all that emotion boiled down to nothing. This dismissal, rejection, disregard was indicative of how easily he could write me off.

Everything was coming to an end, and it was now Thanksgiving.

The evening of Thanksgiving, after spending the day with family, I texted Jacob that I was on my way. He said, "Thanks, but my friends brought me food and are visiting right now." There was no invite over to his place; there were no further phone calls or text messages. This was his breakup. I no longer had to try. I was free from trying, and a deep relief swept through me, and yet a huge sense of failure lingered. I wanted to write a letter to that 99 percent of society that constantly pressured me that I *should* be married, or at least be sharing my life with someone. If I had, it would have gone something like this:

Dear Society,

After thirty-eight years of being told that I should be married, or at least be sharing my life with a man, I thought that I'd attempt to please you by doing just that. Although I have never once in my life wanted to be married, I thought that you must be pressuring me because marriage has some validity I was overlooking. The pressure was so great I thought that perhaps my brain was small, that it couldn't think for itself, and that you were simply showing me the way, like a big brother would. So my first step was finding a man.

I found one at the gym. He lived in the hotel next door to the gym. He was tall, strong, and good looking, and he was an available man. If you'd just looked at him, you would have been proud! And I know that you put great importance on how things look and not so much how they really are, so let's remain focused on how he looked and not how he really was. Most of you carry on behind a façade of happiness, and I'm sure you thought I could, too.

You also convinced me that the way to a man's heart is through his stomach. So I cooked endless meals that pleased his six-pack abs, but those meals never seemed to travel to his heart. Nonetheless, I kept cooking, slaving away over a heated stove. It must be my fault. Perhaps I hadn't cooked the right recipe. I know that behind every good, successful man is a good woman, or at least that's what I've heard from you, Society. So not only did I encourage and support this man, but I also helped him begin to manifest his dream of having a CrossFit gym. I put up the money for him to pay for everything from a measuring tape to his rent.

In summary, I tried, I tried, I tried. I also know men love sex. I had sex whenever he wanted and offered myself even more times when I didn't want to. I know men don't like pushy women, so I denied my own urges to be held on cold nights so he could fulfill his sleep requirements. I was the Little Engine that Could, or so I thought, as this Little Engine ended up in one big train wreck!

Society, let me say, some women are fine alone. And after much heartache, mucho dinero, and even more heartache, I realize I was really good before attempting to please you. So I kindly request that you no longer question me about why I'm not dating and why I'm not married. The answer will always be the same: It's truly none of your business, and more importantly, I'm strong and happy as I am—alone. I know you can't understand this and don't want to give up on me. And I thank you for your concern, but your vision and belief of how I should be is skewed. This is because you've been brainwashed by those among you who say that you're not complete without a man or drama in your life. The way you feel sorry for me for not having a man, I feel sorry for you for having succumbed to the pressure and illusions.

And because you, Society, can't keep a secret, I've heard that you truly are unhappy in your marriages but choose to continue your days pretending, or complaining without changing, or simply being in a robotic, emotionless state of mind, instead of working on your vows. But that's none of my business. I'll never begin harassing you to no end about why you remain as such or why you're scurrying to get divorced, if you'll finally stop harassing me about my own marital status.

And again, because habits are hard to break and brainwashing is even harder to change, I repeat: I kindly request that you never again ask me why I'm single. Should things change on my side (e.g., I get married or have a boyfriend I love and want to shout it from a rooftop, as some of you do), you will be the first to know. Until then, believe me when I say: I tried it your way, and I like it much better my way.
—Julie

***

As December came and went, I didn't miss Jacob, but I did wonder what I hadn't done right. I knew he was dating a young, blond girl. I'd seen his Facebook profile photo with her sitting tightly on his lap. She was a cutie, and she was Russian, or so I figured by her name. He was having a so-called grand opening at his gym and would be serving Russian shish kebabs, per his website. Jacob wasn't that creative; she must have come up with that! And I hoped she had. I hoped she had some business sense, as I wanted my money back. I wasn't jealous that he found someone, nor was I surprised; I had suspected and expected it to be the case.

The only sorrow I had was Joe. I'd never again be with the man that I loved. I had to move forward, on to my true dream, my true love. I had a baby to make, Joaquin, and I was thrilled!

JOAQUIN AMADEUS

DONOR #12362, LET'S MAKE A BABY!

I started looking at CMV-negative donors. There were so few. None of the donors were Hispanic, not that it was my priority to have a Hispanic donor. I had babies named, as everyone knew. If it was a boy, I'd name him Joaquin Amadeus, and if a girl, she'd be named Isis Siddhartha.

All my friends referred to my baby as *Joaquin*. "That's Joaquin's room. Is that for Joaquin? Will you teach Joaquin French? Are you going to be strict with Joaquin?" Joaquin existed in my mind, in my heart, in my gut, and all my friends and family were convinced of his existence as well, long before his conception. He existed; he just happened not to be here among us yet.

When asked what I wanted for Christmas, I told my mom and my brother Neil to write a letter to Joaquin or Isis. That was all I wanted, Christmas or not.

I was fortunate to have a family that supported my insemination decision. They had seen that no man had made an effort to be with me, and they knew my deepest desire was to have a baby, not so much a husband. If they had doubts, they didn't express them in front of me. My mom gave me a little stuffed monkey that held a handmade card and a letter that she'd written:

December 25, 2010
Dear Baby,

> *We have been waiting a long time for your arrival!*
>
> *Your mom has been wanting you and planning to have you for years and years. First, it took her a lot of hard work to prepare a nice home for you. Then lots and lots of research to find just the perfect donor. She had to be so careful in her selection because she wanted you to have the best possible chance of a healthy and happy life.*
>
> *I know your mom will be the best mother you could ever wish for. Thank you for making her wish come true and for all of us that will be part of your life.*
>
> *We are so excited to finally have you!*
> *With as much love as a grandmother can hold for you,*
> *Grandma Yolie*

My brother, Neil, wrote the following letter, also on December 25, 2010:

> *This is 4 Isis or Joaquin,*
>
> *You're probably wondering why you don't have a dad like most other kids do. Well this life we live can sometimes be complicated. Especially if you're a young lady who wants a baby of her own but hasn't found "Mr. Right."*
>
> *This is the situation your mother found herself in. And with time against her, because ladies can only have a baby safely between the ages of 17–35. After 35 it becomes more of a risk that you may not come out healthy and strong. So with no luck as to who would be the lucky guy 2 start a family with, she began looking into "other ways" to conceive (I'll let her explain that part). So she went back to school and studied very hard so that she could get a good job. Because if you're going*

2 have a baby by yourself you need to make a decent amount of money so that she can afford all that you will need and still have extra for stuff you and her don't need.

Well she finished her nursing school and got that good job. Your mom is the type who says, "This is what I want and will work hard to get it." And she does! She also bought a big house, and all the while she had you on her mind. Well by this time she was getting close to that age to where it would be unsafe if she were to wait any longer for that significant other, so here you are! She went ahead and had you now that she could give you all the love and guidance you would need. Not only that but she also knew that your grandma and grandpa would be there wanting 2 help out in any way they could!

As for me, being your uncle, I was excited, too! I want you to know that you can ask me anything, and if I know the answer I'll tell you the truth. Also, if I can help you with anything, whatever it may be, I'll try my best to make it happen (but remember Mom has the final say). Your birth is filling in the void to our lives and making your mom's biggest, best wish she could make come true.

You've been alive before you were even born, alive in our minds as your mom told us of you and how she would conceive you. So don't be angry or confused that you haven't a dad. It's OK. Many have had even less. It doesn't make you any less of a person than one with a dad, so when that day comes that you ask, "Why don't I have a dad?" I hope this letter helps you understand as to why your mom made the choices she made.

Love your Uncle,

Neil

Yes, he couldn't have said it more perfectly. This baby was alive before he or she was ever born, alive in our minds.

In January I kept busy. I started acrylic painting. I wasn't good at it, but I enjoyed it. I painted a whimsical tree for Joaquin's room. I envisioned the baby's room as *artsy*, not cutesy. I was inspired. I was going to be a mommy to Joaquin Amadeus. I made no pretense about how much I wanted a boy. I could barely deal with myself as a girl, so I wasn't sure how I'd deal with a baby girl.

By late January I decided on a donor. I kept returning to his profile over and over. I listened to his audio interview several times. I reread his essay. He had been to Africa and enjoyed West African music. I was a huge West African–music lover (props to artists like Ismaël Lô and Henri Dikongué—remember, I was in the music industry at one point), and it was a rare quality to have in common. Not that I was going to date this man, but I liked his openness to different cultures, which I wanted my baby to have and hoped would be embedded in his DNA.

His profile didn't stress to impress; it was normal. He was Italian, Irish, and Lithuanian. Lithuania? Where's that? My baby would be part Lithuanian? I'd have to research that later. I was confident he was the one and placed my exchange request for seven vials of donor #12362. I was only weeks away from my first insemination!

In February, I started my period. As soon as it was tapering off, I started taking home ovulation tests. On day nine, I got a positive for ovulation. I made an appointment for the next day, as ovulation should occur twenty-four to thirty-six hours after a positive test result.

The next day, at the reproductive center, I confirmed my donor number, I gave my menstrual cycle date and ovulation date, and I waited, impatiently, for the hour it takes to defrost the frozen sperm. I was called in and would be inseminated by a nurse practitioner.

"You're on day nine of your cycle?" she asked.

"Yes," I responded.

"And that's on Clomid?"

"I'm not on Clomid." Had she not read my file? I was doing this *au naturel*, *organico*, as-is. I wasn't on any drugs, including Clomid, a fertility drug that helps stimulate egg production.

"Day nine naturally, then?"

"Yes."

"We don't even look at women before day twelve," she said quite annoyed.

"What?"

"Your eggs aren't even mature enough for conception at day nine," she said in a you-should-already-know-this tone.

"Why didn't anyone tell me that when I came months ago for all the prep info?"

"I don't know," she said with an I-couldn't-care-less attitude.

"Well, I'm still going to have you do it, since you already defrosted my sperm; otherwise it truly is a waste. We can't refreeze the vial."

"I'll go ahead and do it, but I'd suggest you get on Clomid for the next insemination."

I was livid! It was seven hundred dollars down the tubes, my tubes. A month now wasted because no doctor had the forethought to tell me that ovulation had to occur at day twelve or later or else they didn't think I'd get pregnant!

The nurse practitioner then proceeded to struggle with my cervix. "I can't find the opening," she said, as if it were my fault. "Your cervix is tilted!" She huffed and puffed and placed a light between my legs that would have illuminated every ant tunnel in the Grand Canyon.

Twenty minutes passed. Her eyes narrowed. Her forehead frowned. I counted the passing minutes and wondered how many sperm had thawed out, swum around briefly, and died in the intensity of this room air. I thought I'd read that frozen sperm could live only one hour at room temperature. They're like frozen fish; they must be used promptly once thawed.

"Ah, there it is," she said.

She took a long, thin pipette and threaded my cervix. It felt like...being threaded with a needle. I took a deep breath, and it was over before I exhaled.

"OK, lie here for ten minutes. On day one of your next cycle, make an appointment to get on Clomid," she said with a fake smile.

I knew I wasn't pregnant. My body and I wanted this baby so badly that I knew I'd feel the moment of conception occurring within me. I felt nothing but impatience. I'd have to wait another month.

In March my period came, and I made the appointment to get on Clomid. Again, I was seen by a nurse practitioner, a different one—a nice, happy one!

She explained that she'd perform an ultrasound and count how many eggs I had waiting in each ovary. Exciting! She explained that Clomid would plump up those eggs and I'd ovulate closer to a preferred time, day twelve or later. I'd then come in on a day following a positive ovulation home test, and I'd be inseminated, and we would wait the two weeks to see if I conceived and an embryo had successfully implanted in the uterine wall. So exciting!

She gelled up the ultrasound wand, which looked like a long vibrator with a condom on it, and began her search of my insides. I looked at the monitor, too. Black, white, blurry. I couldn't make out a thing.

"There's your left ovary," she said. "One, two, three, four, five. Yes, five eggs on the left. You see? Very good."

"Is it?" I asked.

"Hmm…," she said, never answering me. She continued to explore. "Oh, what a shame!" she exclaimed.

"What?"

"See this?" She motioned to a dark spot on the monitor.

"Yes."

"It's a cyst, a transitory one, but a cyst. You can't get on Clomid this month. We'll need to wait for that cyst to pass."

"What?"

"Sometimes cysts form during your cycle and then they're gone the following month. That's why we need to do a sonogram every month while you're on your cycle to determine whether you can take Clomid. Clomid would feed the cyst and not your eggs, so we'll have to skip a month. Oh, that is a shame!"

Another month? My goodness! When will this baby come to fruition? Patience, I needed some. I'd waited nearly thirty-nine years. I could wait another month.

On day seven of my cycle, or about three days after my period had ended, I was taking a late lunch at work. I was the break relief nurse that night and hadn't taken lunch until five in the morning. I had shredded raw carrots and beets tossed with lemon juice and salt. I ate in a hurry to get back on the floor, as we were having a hectic night with the patients, and I knew help was needed. As soon as I stood up, I had a sharp pain in my right side. I doubled over and took a deep breath. It was hard to stand up straight. I figured I'd eaten way too fast. Gas pains from beets and carrots?

The pain subsided enough for me to finish my shift. I was home by eight. I tossed and turned; there was no position I could lie in to feel better. I showered twice to try to let the hot water relax my lower right side. The pain increased. I took an 800-milligram Motrin. The pain continued to become worse. I texted Diana, who happened to be working in the emergency room that morning. I told her I couldn't stand the pain and was coming in. I drove myself back to the hospital where I worked. It was March 13, 2011, a gloomy Sunday.

A creature of habit, I parked in employee parking rather than in the emergency drop-off area. I slowly made my way to the emergency room entrance. *Do I hope that Jared is my doctor or not?* I thought. He'd seen all the goods, but did I want his witty comments at a serious time like this? I knew something was wrong with my right ovary.

"Oh my god, you're sweating through your sweatshirt," Diana said when she saw me approaching, bent over, guarding my stomach.

"It hurts like hell," I said.

"Get in the wheelchair," she said.

"Hell no."

"Get in. I'll push you in!"

"No! I refuse. I can still walk," I said stubbornly.

She led me to a room where I waited, sweating, in the fetal position for a doctor to see me. My heart rate was between 117 and 124 beats a minute. My blood pressure was way above its normal 102/64. I can't remember what it was, but it was beyond hypertension, and that worried me more. One cute blond nurse started an IV on me—and yes, I did wonder if Jared had ever had sex with her—and another, older nurse reviewed my chart.

The doctor came in after about an hour. It wasn't Jared. The doctor apologized profusely for having me wait. She performed a vaginal exam. She asked me questions about the pain, when it started, what I was doing, when the last time I'd had sex was. I knew she thought I might have PID, pelvic inflammatory disease, usually brought on by an untreated sexually transmitted disease. I wanted to tell her that the last time I'd had unprotected sex was with her colleague Jared, and therefore, if I had a sexually transmitted disease, it was from him, and would she call him and tell him my results if that was that case? But I was in too much pain to reveal such details. I never dreamed that Joe could possibly have given me anything. Isn't denial great? I assured her that I thought it was my ovary, possibly ovarian torsion. She'd read my chart and knew I'd been inseminated in February but hadn't taken any hormones to date.

"If I can find your cervix…It's tilted," she said as she examined me.

"So I've heard," I said.

"That's very common, nothing to worry about. Does it hurt here?" She pressed on my left side, then my right.

"Only the right. It's always the right side that hurts when I ovulate, but this pain is far worse than any pain I have ever had," I told her. But it was only day seven of the cycle; I shouldn't be ovulating.

She ordered an ultrasound and pain medication, intravenous Dilaudid. I'm allergic to morphine (*yeah!*), and so I was finally going to get the chance to experience Dilaudid. Most patients at the hospital *always* wanted their Dilaudid; they loved it. I figured it must be good stuff, as they would get mad if we suggested pain pills. The older nurse brought me one milligram of Dilaudid. The pain dissipated, and I floated high. It *was* good stuff. My heartbeat returned to a normal pace, and I knew my blood pressure had relaxed.

After the sonogram, the doctor came in and said I had a hemorrhagic cyst. She said it had grown substantially from a few days ago when I had the previous ultrasound, and that's why it was hurting. My ovaries and fallopian tubes were OK; they hadn't twisted into a pretzel or exploded, as I thought. The cyst would pass, she said. However, if the pain came back with the same intensity or more, I was to come back into the emergency room, and they would get a surgery consult, as surgery might be needed. I got another dose of Dilaudid and tried not to worry. What more could possibly go wrong with these eggs, these ovaries, this attempt to have a baby?

MALIGNANCY

If malignancy can possibly be created from one moment, situation, discovery, or incident, then mine, without a doubt, developed on March 15, 2011. If I don't have cancer growing, spreading in me at this very moment, and it blossoms years down the road, I'll know that the seed was planted on March 15, 2011. It will have been lying dormant until it wanted to remind me of that specific day, in case I have forgotten by then.

On Monday, March 14, 2011, the day after my ovary episode, I happened to drive past Jacob's gym. I did this every now then; after all, I was financially vested in it, whether it succeeded or not. It was quiet; his car wasn't there. Instinctively, I knew something big was up. I thought perhaps he was hurt or his father had passed. He never missed work. The next day, I saw he was back, but something nagged me. I perused his website and clicked on the logo of the volleyball team he trained. Why? I clicked it because instinct told me to. I saw their CrossFit schedule and read the announcement: "CrossFit still a go on Wednesday, March 16." I wondered why it wouldn't have been a go.

Then I read the following line: "Jacob and Oksana had their baby!"

I read it again. "Jacob and Oksana had their baby!" And

again. And again.

Jacob and Oksana had their baby!

Jacob aka Joshua?

Jacob and *Oksana* had their baby!

Oksana, the blonde? The pregnant "friend," the new girl? Who?

Jacob and Oksana had *their* baby!

"Their?" As in they created this together? They *owned* this together? He did something with another girl to call it "their"? His sperm worked? Unaffected by years of steroids?

Jacob and Oksana had their *baby*!

Baby? A baby? As in a newborn? A baby, like what I wanted and was trying to create? Like what he said he'd give me? That kind of baby?

Yes, Julie, a baby, what you want and have not yet gotten. What he promised and didn't deliver. A precious baby.

My core shook, yet I didn't move. I was paralyzed by the words: Jacob. Oksana. Their. Baby. I gasped, yet I couldn't breathe. Those holes in the fetal heart I mentioned must have been wide open right about then. And my lungs. I could feel my lungs collapsing, like thin sheets of ruined origami paper.

Not Jacob. No, please. Our last encounter was four months ago. A baby takes nine months. It doesn't take a rocket scientist to figure out the math on that! Jacob—I'd fault him for many things but not a betrayal of this nature. But hadn't I lived this before? Another girl pregnant, capturing the man I wanted, birthing the baby I dreamed of? So why was this one different? And I knew it instantly: this time it *is* different. Something in me changed forever. I was damaged. It came down to this: I felt like he didn't deserve a baby.

Here I was struggling with cysts and eggs and ovaries, and he waltzed right into having a baby that he hadn't planned. The shock, resentment, and anger within me had taken root right in my core. Was the experience of Joe and his wife having a baby a foreshadow to Jacob and Oksana having a baby?

We all have malignancy hiding somewhere within us, and it may activate at one time or another. That's my personal belief. It's simply a consequence of living in a toxic world and not removing toxic people from your life, just as hitting your thigh against the corner of a table results in a bruise. Again, like times before with Jacob, I felt nauseated; I began dry heaving. Why? Because I had yet to fully remove Jacob the Toxin from my system. I felt a tight, murky, dark ball roaming throughout my being. I couldn't expel it. I shoved my finger down my throat and buckled to the bathroom floor. Nothing. It was rooted in me; it wouldn't come out.

I thought of the La Brea Tar Pits in Los Angeles, a collection of black, deep tar pits that I could smell from my office on Wilshire Boulevard when I worked for EMI Music. The heavy oil, bubbling up from time to time, and belching out of the earth, relieving itself…. But I couldn't belch this toxin out. I've never seen it but have read that animals get trapped in the tar pits, the oil sinking them, suffocating them, drowning them. Instead of my falling into the oil abyss and becoming trapped, the repugnant, dark oil was trapped inside of me. Some things are one and the same.

The thought of his hustling me, belittling me, and rejecting me to run off and have this baby tormented me. *No, Jacob, anything but this. Run away, never pay me the money you owe me, never speak to me again, but please, not this. This can't possibly be true.*

So while my hemorrhagic cyst was, well, hemorrhaging, denying me a chance to get on Clomid and possibly get pregnant, in the very same hospital probably, on or near the same day, my ex-boyfriend was coaching his new girlfriend through childbirth. I tried not to take these coincidences personally, but I did. I couldn't help it. A baby is all I wanted. Ever. And obviously, people all around me were having them, even when they didn't plan or want them. Jacob was becoming a dad? I sank into the tar pit of self-pity.

Was this the friend that he took to have an abortion? Was it his baby? I didn't know what I found to be worse, his cheating on me, creating this baby, or his dumping me to hook up with an already-pregnant woman. He *could* step up to plate and be responsible, but not with me? I didn't even want him or his steroid sperm and skanky personality. It was the principal of the matter that killed me!

FAKE IT TILL YOU MAKE IT

I was a bridesmaid in Mexico two weeks later. I'd gained weight. I felt like a fat salmon in the orange dress I was to wear. My boobs looked like they were ready to breastfeed every starving child in need, but that too was an illusion. I was a million light-years from being able to breastfeed a child. I couldn't and wouldn't stop crying. *It must be the cyst*, I thought. It must have been spewing hormones of depression, of crying, as I couldn't stop. If tears release toxins, then why the hell was I not crying holy water by now? I needed to get it together and put on my happy face—"Fake it till you make it." My friend would despise me if I ruined her wedding photos with a sad face on what was to be the happiest day of her life. I reminded myself, *Some people actually do believe in love, and it actually does work for some.*

I took the flight to Cancun, Mexico, and thought as I sat there on the plane. I thought of this Spanish movie called *Amantes* that starred my favorite Spanish actress, Maribel Verdú. Maribel plays a sweet girl named Trini who works hard and has saved a nice nest egg. Sound familiar? She hopes to marry Paco, a guy who needs both a job and place to live after leaving the military (I don't know if he was living in a hotel or what). Sounds very familiar, huh? He then starts an affair with Luisa and, of course, is captivated by this bad girl who owes money to some bad guys! Trini, the innocent girl, does everything to get Paco to love her, even loses her virginity to him. The movie is set in the 1950s, so this loss of virginity is a big deal.

  Paco is temporarily into Trini during the post-virginity phase but goes back to Luisa, the experienced bad girl. The sweet virgin girls usually never win, no matter what era we shoot a movie in! The plan is to get the money from Trini, her hard-earned nest-egg money. Paco tells Trini that with the money, they could buy a bar (not a CrossFit gym) together. Luisa just wants Trini dead and wants Paco to put the poor girl out of their lives, put Trini out of her future misery of chasing someone she can't have. Instead, Paco takes the money straight out of Trini's purse and takes it to Luisa. Trini knows that this guy has fucked her over, that he's in love with Luisa, that there will be no bar, and that she'd rather be dead, and she knows that Paco wants her dead, too. So she begs Paco to kill her, to stab her, right there on a park bench by a fabulous Catholic church. And the motherfucker does! I remember loving this movie when it came out in the early 1990s. I could relate to this poor woman, and I was now feeling Trini's pain from Paco's betrayal.

  There was a reason I connected to this movie and remembered it years later. I wondered if Jacob would try to kill me off. I figured he wouldn't, as it would take so much energy and detailed planning, characteristics that were not in his nature. And I was no longer trying to please or to have Jacob. In addition, like hell would I allow him to literally kill me. Figuratively, he was doing a pretty good job. The moment after learning of Jacob and Oksana's baby together, I vowed never to look again at any internet site or Facebook page that could further cause me harm. And I haven't since. Jacob must be the most toxic thing I've ever allowed into my life. I think it would have been healthier to smoke a pack of Marlboros daily and tan in a tanning booth for twenty-five years than to have had him in my life for one year. He was a human vial of toxins that I allowed into my life. We need a vaccine against people, male or female, like him.

Lesson Number Two: Rid yourself of toxins. The blood knows to rid itself of any waste, any toxin, collected along the way before heading back to the head and heart.

I took a shuttle to Playa del Carmen and checked in. I reminded myself to *be happy*. I met Liliana in her room the next morning. We walked back to my room, and I weakened and told her what happened with Jacob.

"Let's go get massages so you can relax!" she said.

"Great idea!"

I'd been in Mexico less than twenty-four hours; I was going to do my best to enjoy this time. I was going to let it all go. I lay on the massage table so that my masseuse, Mauricio, could massage my back. The moment he laid his hands on my lower back, I felt it: a release, a warm release. I'd started my period *again*! Ten days early. I was a reproductive nightmare. I was *always* on time, every twenty-eight days exactly, at 8:00 a.m. or 10:00 p.m.—yes, at 8:00 a.m. or 10:00 p.m. on the nose. Now, I was having crazy, misbehaving cysts and early cycles. I dug my face deep into the face cradle and silently cried. I was such a pro at crying silently. I should have been an actress in a daytime soap opera. I prayed that I didn't stain the towels on Mauricio's massage table. When you have been having periods for twenty-seven years, you learn how to maneuver yourself not to make a mess. I tensed the areas that needed tensing to make it through the massage without a problem.

"I started my period ten days early," I told Liliana upon exiting.

"Oh, Julie! You're releasing all the buildup. He's not worth holding on to."

"I know. I need to buy tampons."

We went to the drugstore at the resort, and I paid eighteen US dollars for a box of tampons that would have cost four dollars in the United States. What did it matter? I'd already been financially fucked over by Jacob. I hated tampons and had been using the Instead Cup or Softcup for at least ten years; I knew I'd struggle with these damn tampons. Like with Joe, I knew that this wasn't war, not death, not torture…but I found pity for myself in everything.

I got myself together and mingled with Liliana's guests. I did shots. I sipped fruity drinks. I ran to meet the incoming ocean wave and wished it would take me away. My desire to skip this entire portion of my life was greater than my fear of drowning. I took wedding photos, smiling, laughing, throwing flowers up in the air, looking at the bride and groom, looking like I believed in love and marriage. I only fucked up one photo. It was the photo where the photographer had the entire wedding party line up on the beach. We all faced the ocean, and I guess at one point he told everyone to turn around and look at him. I never heard him give this order, and he should have noticed I was still looking at the ocean. In the photo, I'm the only one who still has her back turned to the photographer, staring at the ocean.

After the photos, I continued the charade. I drank, and drank some more, I ran through the sand, I danced, I small-talked, I took photos of all the happy people, and I wished with all my might to go home, have a cyst-free ultrasound (I scheduled an appointment from my hotel room), get inseminated, and become pregnant. Was all that too much to ask for?

I guess so. The month of March proved to be yet another disappointing month, but now with multiple new cysts. This time my appointment was with Dr. Klausen. He did an ultrasound, pointing out every landmark within me. "See that pulsating?" he asked.

"Yes."

"That's your breakfast! Your stomach is moving it along."

"So now what about the cysts?" I didn't have time for a lesson in digestion; my ovaries and eggs were aging by the second.

"Well, that cyst that sent you the ER was equivalent to taking a man's testicles and twisting them and then holding them really tight," he said, taking his hand and making a fist in a twisting motion. I saw the fury and would have loved to do that to Jacob. But this wasn't about Jacob.

"Uh-huh," I said.

"Well, we can wait another month, see if these cysts go away. If they don't, we can start thinking of other options, like surgery."

"Surgery," I repeated.

"It's a simple procedure, really, laparoscopic, similar to what you see with your laparoscopic appendectomy patients. A few small holes...." He was an artist selling his craft.

"And the recovery?"

"Some people are back to work within a few days. I can give you a few weeks off if you need them."

"OK, let's see what happens next month."

Another month. It was no longer a question, but a statement. Every month, I thought I wouldn't have the patience to wait it out, but I did. I had no choice.

The seasons were passing; spring, the time of procreation and blooming, was coming. Would this be the month?

My doctor gelled the wand and started the search. I no longer got excited over egg count. I'd get excited over a zero cyst count, though. He measured something and gave the measurements to the assistant, who typed them into my chart.

"See here," he said, pointing to the black circle on the monitor.

"Yes." I knew what it was.

"You have a few cysts on the right ovary, a complex cyst," he said.

"Yep." *It's all complex, all right*, I thought.

He measured my uterine wall.

"Do you know if your mother has endometriosis?"

"I don't think so."

"Hmm. I think you may have endometriosis, but I can't confirm that without surgery."

"So you think we should surgically remove these cysts?"

"Well, you can wait another month, but they seem to be sticking around. This is the third month now. If you have surgery, we can get you on hormones and then start the insemination process. It depends on how aggressive you want to be."

"Then I want surgery. I'm tired of waiting," I said without missing a beat.

This is what every surgeon wants to hear. "Great, my secretary will call you with an appointment."

My appointment was scheduled for May 25. I prepared my paperwork and decided to put in for three weeks off. I could use the time to recover, to write (my method of processing my life), and to do whatever it took to begin with a new post-surgery attitude.

GIVE ME SOMETHING TO BELIEVE IN

And so there I was, trying to drag myself out of a depression as I waited for surgery day. I knew I had to exercise, but I didn't want to be cooped up in a gym. Every time I walked into Gold's Gym, the combination smell of perspiration, circulating air-conditioned air, and floor mats reminded me of Jacob. I was tired of the one-lane path behind my house. I vowed to start jogging, forcing myself to start with three miles a day. I ran the hard pavement, trying to cut some fat and boost my mental state. I was running in the streets while down the road was Jacob's gym, which wouldn't have come into existence if it hadn't been for me. I was alone, motivating myself, as he ran this gym, befriending his clients, raising a family, holding Russian grand openings for a gym I funded.

I was in the biggest funk of my life, and I couldn't swim, float, paddle, or run away. I meditated, I stopped meditating, I searched high and low, and I went to therapy and stopped. Yet nothing made me feel alive. I worked, and I slept, slept, slept.

After finding out about Jacob and the baby, all I wanted to do was sleep or cry. I hated every man. I hated my friends who abandoned me during what was the most difficult time. None of them had experienced infertility, so they couldn't relate or never realized what an impact this all had. I lost hope in everyday human beings. I was losing belief in myself. It was all very pathetic, but when the desire for a baby is raging, and depression is escalating, and cysts are flourishing, and God-knows-what's happening to your hormones, it's no wonder you're a hot reproductive mess.

My friend Zane said he was at a club one night and the bartender had a tattoo on her arm that said, "Love conquers all." He asked her if she truly believed in that. She said, "Yes, it's all I have." She said she was thirty-eight years old, never married, and if she didn't believe that love conquered all, then she'd have nothing to believe in. I wasn't a believer in the "Love conquers all" cliché. But I understood her; she had to believe in *something*. I, too, had to believe that there was *one* good man out there—even if he wasn't for me. I needed this belief for whatever reason, just for womankind!

I impatiently waited the month for my surgery. Maybe this surgeon would be the man to give me something to believe in.

IT'S JUST A TROLL

My surgery was to remove a cyst. It was to be simple, quick, easy, and laparoscopic. My pre-op nurse struggled with my veins while starting an IV and attempted small talk while doing it.

"So you and your husband are trying to have a baby," she said.

"I'm not married," I replied.

"Oh, so you and your partner?" she asked in an attempt to be open and nonchalant.

"I'm not a lesbian," I said.

"Oh, no, I wasn't meaning that. I was meaning like a boyfriend or something," she said. Something? People have babies with "something"? Yes, they do! My "something" was a vial of sperm from a stranger. Is that the "something" she was referring to?

"I'm doing this alone," I said. I wasn't in the mood to explain myself moments before surgery.

"Oh, wow, you're brave. That must be difficult," she said.

"No, not really," I said, not elaborating.

"I mean it's so hard financially and all. What do you do for work?" she asked inquisitively.

"I'm a nurse, like you. I work for this hospital, too," I said.

"Oh!" she said, as in *Oh, shit!*

I know it's human nature to be curious and to judge a single Mexican woman trying to impregnate herself. She probably thought I was yet another woman her taxes would support. I get it. But I wasn't Nadya Suleman, implanting myself with a dozen embryos while six other children ran around at home. Oh, you see, there I go, judging. I have no right. Yes, I was single. I was trying to have a baby. I was trying to make the most of my life in the way I dreamed it would be, like every other goal-driven dreamer.

After the surgery, as soon as I woke up, my mother told me what the surgeon had said: that it was "a mess in there."

"What do you mean?" I asked. *A hot mess? Or a let's-tidy-this-up mess?*

"He said you have severe endometriosis and that most likely you will have to do in vitro fertilization. He said he ran out of time in the operating room. It was that bad."

I went home to recuperate and patiently wait for my follow-up appointment. I didn't want to think of the "mess in there." And what kind of medical terminology is that? Give me a medical term, something that I can look up, investigate, analyze, or ask other doctors about. Don't give me "a mess."

I sat on my couch; the recovery was far more difficult than I'd imagined, mentally and physically. A lovely little finch couple had made a nest outside my living room window, high up on the electrical unit of the fan. I spent the days watching the male bird fetch food and bring it back to his bird-wife. When momma bird left the nest, on rare occasion, the male bird would stand on one of the fan's blades to keep a look out. They made a lovely team, a lovely couple, as they protectively and affectionately tended to their coming family. *It seems so easy and natural for them*, I thought. *Why can't I be a finch? Why is it one obstacle after the next?*

I went to my follow-up appointment with a positive attitude. Whatever the doctor said would only be a bump in the road, nothing that I couldn't handle.

"Well, I knew you had endometriosis, but I was surprised at how severe it is," he said as his opening statement.

"So now what?"

"Didn't you have any symptoms?" he asked. "When you had sex, didn't it hurt?"

"Well, yes, sometimes. But I thought…I ignored it most times," I said, trying to recollect my sexual encounters. Yes, there had been some very painful times, but not always.

"It's not supposed to hurt. That's one of the signs. However, some people have mild endometriosis and severe pain, while others have severe endometriosis and mild pain," he said in a soft, educating voice. "I literally ran out of operating time. I only booked the operating room for two hours, and I thought that would be plenty. I didn't expect this; it's such a mess around your uterus. I was really surprised. Your ovaries are embedded in endometrial tissue and attached to your uterus. I couldn't even find your ovaries at first. I tried to shave away what I could. And I wasn't sure how much I should do, as I didn't want to create more scarring along the way."

He stared at me. I stared back.

I breathed. Swallowed. "So will I be able to have a baby?"

"Well, it was such a mess in there, I called in Dr. Thao to take a look. We both agree that in vitro would be your best bet. After another surgery," he said.

"Another surgery?"

"Yes, it's what I'd recommend. You have a large fibroid sitting on top of your uterus. IVF is so expensive, you'd want to have no complications, and sometimes a fibroid can present complications. We'd remove the fibroid before IVF, and then you would have to have a cesarean section," he said, as if this were standard. And maybe it was.

"What about continuing artificial insemination? It seems like we're giving up so soon," I said, pleading my case.

"It's up to you," he said.

"Well, can I still get pregnant with artificial insemination?" I asked.

"Anything is possible. Definitely possible."

"Then I think we should try that before jumping to IVF," I suggested.

"Sure. We'll put you on Clomid and Menopur injections," he said.

"OK." Another fertility drug, Menopur, designed to help make eggs.

"We'll try that route and see what happens. I have seen it happen. We'll get you pregnant one way or the other," he reassured me.

Every visit had unexpected results, unexpected truths. He handed me a copy of his operative note that detailed the findings. It read as follows:

Preoperative diagnoses:

 1. Persistent ovarian cyst

 2. Rule out endometriosis

Postoperative diagnoses:

 1. Severe pelvic adhesions consistent with severe endometriosis

 2. Ovarian cyst, pathology pending

Operation:

 1. Right and left ovarian cystectomy

 2. Lysis of adhesions

The patient had severe pelvic adhesions. A gel-like coating over the uterus. This was felt to be fresh endometriosis, not menstrual blood in any way, as it was very tenacious. The patient also had multiple uterine fibroids that appeared to be serosal and maybe a few intramural, but more serosal and anterior. The patient had open tubes bilaterally and severe pelvic adhesions. The tubes and cul-de-sac were adherent to each other in the midline and above the cul-de-sac. The ovaries were somewhat cystic. The left side appeared to be more hemorrhagic/endometriotic. The cyst wall was able to be removed. The cyst wall on the right appeared to be very different and kind of a fluffy cyst. Pathology is pending on that. Neither Dr. Thao nor myself are positive what it was. The adhesions were very severe. We were able to free up the adhesions and free up the tubes. A considerable amount of denuded tissue was noted. Both tubes were noted to be open to dye. The liver was free of adhesions. The uterine cavity appeared to be normal in size. No polyps. No fibroids. No indentations. The ostia were able to be visualized on both sides. Approximately 200 cc of sterile water was used. The area was irrigated. There was a considerable amount of ooze from that gel material over the uterus, so this was cauterized to stop the ooze. Fibroids were not originally removed secondary to increasing adhesions, though now the tubes are quite adherent. In vitro fertilization is most likely the patient's best chance for pregnancy. With in vitro fertilization, consideration for myomectomy should be done.

The patient tolerated the procedure well and was taken to the recovery room in satisfactory condition.

My surgeon knew I was a nurse; he wanted me to take this printout home and read it objectively. In a nutshell, I'd interpreted and summarized everything down to:

Purple dye moved liked a beautiful river through my open tubes! My uterus was of normal size. I had a variety of cysts: some fluffy and artsy, some stubborn and sticky, and some bloody and wretched. But, they were able to remove them! I could get on Clomid and any other hormone now to have a baby! Most patients in this situation should *consider* having another operation and doing in vitro fertilization. I was in "satisfactory condition." And despite the hell I'd put myself through with Jacob, there was no notable toxic residue lingering! My liver looked fantastic, by the way. Wow, physiology is truly amazing.

"It's like you've waited too long," one friend said when I read her the report. "It's as if your uterus was like, 'Hey, you're not using me, so I'm going to self-destruct.'" This was her way of consoling me. But she was right. Old cars can't start up if their engines aren't turned on every now and then.

"Well, I don't see the *c*-word anywhere in here, so that's good," was my other friend's consolation. She was saying, "Hey, you should be happy you don't have *cancer*!" And I was.

But I still had that hope that I could *indeed* get pregnant. The first stage of grief is denial. I was holding on tight to that first stage. You hear stories all the time of So-and-so who couldn't get pregnant and, *voilà*, is now a mother of five! I wasn't trying to make a Fabergé egg, encrusted with gems and gold. But the gem I did have was this "Diamond in the Sky" plan to have a baby. I wanted to make what most women can make, a simple little egg, just the right size, to meet up with injected perfect sperm and implant in my normal-size uterus. That's all I was asking for. But all eggs, Fabergé or not, are considered a symbol of renewed life and of hope.

What came first, the chicken or the egg? The chicken, I say, as eggs are so difficult to make.

I was started on Clomid and Menopur the following month. I was elated, my mood elevated—must have been the hormones or knowing that I was a take-charge woman! A few co-workers shared the responsibility of giving me the final intramuscular shot of hCG to initiate my ovulation every month. This took place in my kitchen, my living room, or the medication room at work, wherever I happened to be at the designated hour.

Every two weeks after insemination, without fail, without fanfare, without welcome, my menstrual cycle would begin. And I'd pick up another round of hormones to start the attempt all over again. Every month, I thought it would be different, but every month resulted in the same outcome. I was losing hope. My vials of sperm were dwindling down.

In October, when I went for my ultrasound, cysts were noted on each ovary. "Too bad, because you've had such a great response to the hormones," the doctor said. "Let's see if this is a transitory cyst, and we'll check again next month."

In November, I saw Dr. Thao. He had a bad rap for having no bedside manner. I didn't care; I didn't need to be held and caressed. I needed to get pregnant! And that didn't require any bedside manner from a doctor, lover, or husband. Every visit to the doctor, I feared the discovery of something new.

I was waiting for him to place the speculum inside of me, open me up, struggle with my cervix, and then tip it at the perfect angle to find the culprit. I imagined the doctor would point that bright, shiny lamp toward my cervix, squint, and say, "Well, well, well, lookee here," as he lifted my cervix a little more to the left.

"What?" I'd ask.

"The culprit," he'd say, "is a *troll* living right here under your cervix! No wonder we've been encountering problems. It's a troll, of all things, making a cozy habitat here. A troll. My, my. Well, I'll be darned," he would say in amazement as he removed the nuisance of a critter while telling me the history of the troll. "The troll is Nordic in origin. How and why this one traversed land and sea to make a home in you, a Mexican, is baffling. But you see, trolls love hiding in the most remote of places, places rarely visited, under rocks and caves, where lightning can't hit them. Did you know that's how to kill a troll, by lightning? Trolls never, ever do anything beneficial for humans. No worries now that we have discovered him! I'll chop him to itty-bitty pieces for you and throw him into a biohazard bin for incineration!"

And this *bad* mythical creature, this curse, would be out of me, out of my life. And the conception of my baby would become a reality and not part of some Mexican or Nordic folklore.

Dr. Thao began the ultrasound search, and by now, I'd learned how to decipher a cyst, an egg, a hemorrhagic cyst, but on the screen appeared a rectangular black formation. Possibly the bridge the troll lived under? He stared at it for a long time before speaking. I didn't know what it was, but I knew it was bad before he even spoke. Something in the way he stopped and looked at me, lying there on my back, told me that this was the end of this fucked-up journey. I found this doctor to be exactly what I needed, incredibly direct.

"See this black area here?" he asked.

"Yes."

"Those are your fallopian tubes. They're lying horizontally across your uterus. They're blocked."

I nodded and stared at the screen. There it was, in black and white.

"But they weren't blocked when I had the surgery," I said.

"This is a possible complication of the surgery."

"What now?"

"I'd like to go over your medical file in detail and break it down for you," he said delicately and slowly; he didn't want me to miss a word. "Your chance of conceiving by artificial insemination is maybe one percent. Why Dr. Klausen hasn't told you this is beyond me. However, allowing you to keep doing what you're doing is false hope that's just torturing you. The fluid that's in the fallopian tubes is flowing into the cavity of your uterus. It's not toxic to you, but it would be to an embryo. So not only would it be nearly impossible for your eggs to travel down the tubes, but if one did implant, you would never be able to carry the baby to term."

False hope that's torturing me. False hope is torture. I'd learned that many moons ago with Joe, but I'd never expected it with Joaquin.

He went deeper with the ultrasound wand, into spaces I didn't know existed. I was numb and stared at him. *Please tell me he's looking for a loophole to this mess.* Instead, this doctor-archeologist discovered even more in my ruins.

"Your left ovary is attached to the back of your uterus," he said, "and your right ovary is midline, attached to the front of your uterus. Anatomically, the fallopian tubes and ovaries aren't even in the right place. If your left hand were attached to your spine, would you be able to use it?" he asked, placing his hand behind his back to impersonate my left ovary.

I shook my head no in response to his question. "Everything is a mess in there" had been the words of my surgeon. I heard Dr. Thao's following words, warped but decipherable, as if I were underwater, drowning. My worst fear.

"I'm sorry," he said.

I continued to stare at him. He was the first man ever to apologize to me and mean it.

"It's as if you're hearing this for the very first time," he said kindly. "I don't mean to be the bearer of bad news. Have you thought about in vitro fertilization?"

"Not really," I whispered in aching disappointment.

"Well, make an appointment to see me and the nurses next week. We can go over some information with you. You would still need to have your fallopian tubes removed prior to in vitro because, as I said, that fluid is toxic. We would have to harvest your eggs, if possible, and see how healthy they are. Considering your age, you may want to look into purchasing donor eggs. I know this is a lot to take in. I'm sorry. But you have a one percent chance of conceiving on your own and about a fifteen percent chance of carrying to term. So many factors to consider. You have a higher risk of having a child with Down's syndrome, something to think about. You know, I'm a father of a special-needs child, and even being a doctor, at first I only heard what I wanted to hear and not what was really being said…." He rambled. I knew it was his way of consoling me, and I appreciated it. "I'll have the receptionist make an appointment for next week. I can give you a further breakdown of your medical record and the chance I think you have of a successful IVF."

"Sure," I said.

The only thing I remember next was standing in the parking lot, having a complete breakdown. I was sobbing, sweating, shaking, dialing my mother. I could barely speak. She must have thought I'd been attacked, raped, or robbed. No need to call the police, but yes, my reproductive system was currently being attacked, my plan savagely raped, and I'd been robbed, mercilessly, of my chance of motherhood! I was the victim but would be the one serving this lifetime sentence without my own baby. Somehow, I managed the words, "He said I can never get pregnant."

She said she'd drive over.

I screamed, "*No!* I want to be left alone."

And I did. I didn't know what to do with myself. I don't know how I got from the clinic to my car. Everything around me swirled, as if I were in the eye of the storm, yet everything was in slow motion. I drove home, blurry-eyed and desperate. *My Joaquin, my Joaquin, my Joaquin* was all that repeated in my head. The moment I lay down, I fell asleep for four hours. I'd emotionally knocked myself out. I had to go to work later that night, and I did.

I prayed that I'd get the worst of the worst cancer patients so that I didn't feel sorry for myself. Instead, I was assigned a patient, whom I had before, that complained about everything; he had a rash coming on and carried on as if he were dying. I know it's all relative, but I wanted to scream, "I don't give a fuck about you or your fucking rash! You, who complains about every fucking thing, something as simple as a rash, and yet you were able to procreate? And I can't? I hate this job. I hate this life! I've worked the past five years preparing for this baby. I've changed careers to be able to afford this child! I don't care about your rash! I don't fucking care!"

But of course, I didn't. Instead I administered his scheduled dose of steroids and placed a fake, caring smile on my face as I nodded in agreement with everything he said.

I carried on at work and in front of my friends and family as best as I could. And I cried every day, every moment that I was alone.

I returned the following week to get my "percentage" quote on IVF. Dr. Thao once again reviewed all the reasons I couldn't get pregnant. I'd definitely need surgery to remove the fallopian tubes, the cysts, and the fibroid, as I'd be placed on heavy-duty hormones in order to produce as many eggs as possible. And my grand total, my grand chance of conceiving through IVF: 15–25 percent. At a grand cost of twenty thousand dollars. The high cost didn't bother me as much as the low probability of giving birth and the high probability of my heart shattering and never beating again.

"So you have to ask yourself if it's worth it," the doctor concluded.

"Adoption would cost as much," I said.

"Adoption isn't guaranteed, either," the nurse chimed in.

"You don't have to make decision right now. It's overwhelming. Think about it, and let us know when you're ready. But I wouldn't waste too much time, given your age," he said.

And so there it was, stated in plain, Asian-accented English: I, Julie Guardado, couldn't conceive, couldn't carry a baby. Ever. *Finito. Ya estuvo. Nunca.* The dream, the opportunity, the miracle, wouldn't happen for me. I remember my cousin Diana once wrote an essay about how we're all statistics of something or another. She was a statistic of teenage pregnancy. I was on the opposite end of the spectrum—I was a statistic of infertility. It felt like I was only millimeters away from becoming a statistic of insanity as well. Insanity, secondary to infertility, should become a certifiable diagnosis covered by all insurance. I should do a thesis on that.

It is said that having a child changes your life. I'd like to add that being told that you can never have a child of your own *also* changes your life. What those changes are, I'm still learning—as I'm still changing. It's early in the game. The change is instantaneous and continuous. I usually welcome change, but was this change or a dead end? Or is it that dead ends and change go hand in hand?

Anger. Pure anger. It swirled inside of me. I felt no compassion, no acceptance, just clinging. Clinging to anger, regret, memories of past sexual encounters where I should have tried to get knocked up but was too nice a girl to do that. Despite having had an affair, I guess I did draw the line somewhere, and that was bringing a child into the world that would change the life of the father. Worse yet, I was still clinging to the *feeling* that I *could* get pregnant, right here, right now. But my brain told me that I couldn't.

It is also said that "hell hath no fury like a woman scorned." So true. I wanted to create havoc, to see rage, but it took all the energy I had even to rise out of bed. There were days I slept nineteen hours. I was mentally and physically wiped out. All this rage and sadness lived solely in my brain, as my body, my mouth, and my actions remained silent and still for those first few days. I knew how to carry myself at work and cry once I was safely in my car driving home.

To be a woman. This is what we do, what we are created to do. *How can I not be able to do this?* That question repeated in my head. I'd see women with terrible diseases and declining health, pregnant and giving birth. I wasn't diabetic or overweight. I didn't suffer from peripheral vascular disease, I ate more vegetables than a rabbit—which procreates incessantly, by the way—and I'd never had the flu in all my life. Yet I couldn't conceive, couldn't carry a child. I didn't have any heart condition, unless you take broken-heart syndrome into consideration. Broken-heart syndrome is a real condition wherein someone thinks he or she is having a heart attack. But in reality, it's passing symptoms, such as chest pain and an irregular heartbeat that are brought on by an intense, emotionally, or physically stressful situation. Because of this, stress hormones go wild and cause symptoms that are like a heart attack. But it's not; it's just broken heart syndrome. Lesson Number One: *The brain and the heart are the most demanding organs. They expect and receive no less than what they demand—the very best that their environment can offer.*

To be a woman. Big fucking deal. Thank God I believe in reincarnation. I better not return in my next life as any female creature or female cell of any kind—not a queen bee, a nymph, a black widow, a cow, a doe, a she-wolf, a hen, a mare, a tigress, a vixen, or a bitch. I want to return as a male creature—a rooster, a buck, a stallion, a ram, a wolverine, a tiger, or a raging bull. Ah, a raging bull. I felt like such a failure as a woman.

I wanted a gun. No, a shotgun. Hold your thoughts; it's not what you're thinking. A string of break-ins were occurring in my city, across the street from where I lived. Two nurses I worked with had robbers come into their homes during daylight! They had guns, which they would have used on the criminals, and suggested I get one, too. They said the mere cocking sound of the shotgun scared the intruders away. I told Meena and Dahlia about it. Meena said, "Right now you'd shoot anybody, unless they were delivering a baby to your front door."

"That's damn right," I said. "They better have a Moses basket with a newborn in it or else I'm shooting their ass."

"Is that such a good idea right now, Julie?" Dahlia asked. I sensed her worry. She thought I'd get a gun and kill myself. But I wasn't that insane, yet. However, I did feel that if I got hit by a huge 7UP delivery truck, I probably wouldn't fight for my life. And placing a bullet through your head isn't a guaranteed death anyway. Believe me, I know. I've taken care of patients that attempted suicide by a gunshot to the head. Some would be fine and others brain damaged forever, becoming a burden to their families. I was learning that no matter how much you plan your life, absolutely nothing is guaranteed—not the creation of life nor the destruction of it.

And absolutely nothing, I believe, happens out of the blue

either. Cancer patients don't suddenly have cancer. Meteors don't suddenly flash across the sky. Everything, good or bad, is always working its way to revelation. We humans are too stupid to realize it. For years, inside my belly, cells were spewing over, landing willy-nilly wherever they could, creating endometrial confusion, a Tower of Babel, pulling in my ovaries to glue them against my uterus, to misplace my fallopian tubes and fill them with fluid. This retrograde fluid would have been perfect if I were trying to give birth to a salmon accustomed to toxic water.

    I envisioned how for years and years, as I earned a music degree, playing happy little Mozart tunes on my flute, as I worked as an international music publisher, as I laughed with friends, as I cried over worthless men, as I became a nurse—tiny, evil Oompa Loompas, wearing overalls, working night and day and holidays, too, had been diligently shutting down my reproductive system. And that, my friends, is life. Accept it.

    In my brief waking hours, I roamed around my home. I saw everything in a new light. I looked at things that I wouldn't need to padlock or place up high for the safety of a child. I looked at bottles of wine that I could drink to my heart's content, or misery. I looked at the spacious home that now felt so empty. I was still new to Facebook, I'd finally given in to it—I rummaged through useless posts from friends about their lives and troubles: "Baseball season is so far away!" "It's cold outside, brr." "I got done paying bills!" I wanted to comment, "Who gives a fuck?" but I didn't. Every person lives in his or her own bubble, and it was enough trying to survive in my own.

    And like every previous time I'd been low, I wanted Joe. I knew better than to call. I typed his name into a Google search—nothing. I typed his wife's name and his name into a Google search. A baby registry highlighted their names. She'd done it again. Conceived. They were having a baby girl, due in a few short weeks. Of course. Everybody had moved on with a baby. Jacob and Blondie. Joe and his "lady." Perhaps I would have tried this method of securing a man, too, if I had the ability to conceive. No use in wondering about the could-have-, would-have-, or might-have-beens. But he, Joe, did want this. He must have. It takes two. I calculated the months from his wife's discovery of me to their conception: only three months. I'm sure she felt stronger in their marriage by adding another child to it. She was holding a few ace cards now. And he felt he owed her *anything* she wanted. It didn't even matter. I'd once been overwhelmed with sadness at losing him, but now I'd lost so much more—the opportunity to have my own baby. I was over him.

    I was over Joe.

    Beautiful Joe.

    I was over Joe.

    I was really over Joe.

    Dante.

    Finally.

    Glory.

    Glory.

    Hallelujah, hallelujah, hallelujah.

At least I'd conquered one thing in my life.

Several months back, I'd had lunch with Jared. I had told him I thought I could be pregnant this time, and when I wasn't, I texted him that I wasn't. Several days—yes days—later, he texted me saying he was sorry to hear that and that he'd have to bang me soon so that "having sperm put into you will be fun again." This was what I had to look forward to. This was what I did look forward to. I eventually took him up on the offer. I dragged myself over to his house, with no makeup, wet hair, and my thick glasses on. And I was wearing my pajamas.

"You don't have to talk about it if you don't want," he said after we made out on his sky-blue casting couch.

"I know," I said. "I don't mind telling you. You're a doctor, and you understand what I'm saying. People keep saying, 'Well, do this and that.' They don't get it."

"Do you want to have sex?"

"Of course I do."

"What if you *did* get pregnant?"

"I'd be happy. I'd ask nothing of you, Jared. I'd have papers drawn up stating that. Well, I'd want your entire family's health history and for you to meet him or her at age eighteen if he or she had questions about you."

"I'd almost be sixty years old by then!" He couldn't envision himself that old.

"I'd be fifty-eight."

"OK," he said and led me upstairs to his room. And Jared

was true to his word; it was just banging, no connection and not even feelings for him on my part. Now I was truly "comfortably numb." I woke up early the next morning, dressed, and left him sleeping in his bed, the way he wanted. I was still in that first stage of grief, and I hoped to be pregnant.

No such luck. It's OK to lightly hope for something unexpected but not to be in complete denial. I was ready to bury the denial stage.

There are comments one should never make to a woman who can't bear children. Most times I'm truly unable to speak the words, "I can't have children," to others, simply because I don't want to deal with their stupid comments that are intended to make me feel better. I have come up with a list of things *not* to say to barren woman, listed in no particular order of annoyance:

Comment: "You can borrow my kids anytime. Then you won't want any."

My thought: Fuck off. You're right. Your children are hellions, but I don't want to borrow them. I want my own kids, hellions or not. *Borrowing* someone else's kids isn't remotely the same as having your own children. It's a stupid comment and should be banned.

Comment: "Consider yourself lucky; you won't have to deal with nine months of nausea and getting fat."

My thought: That's stupid. You're a fat ass, and you're dumb. You think I'd give up the opportunity of a child—*a child!*—simply because I might be nauseated and gain weight? If nausea and weight gain were that awful, then planet Earth wouldn't be approaching a population of seven billion. I roll my eyes at the absurdity of this comment.

Comment: "It'll happen when you least expect it!"

My thought: Really? Is spontaneous conception like spontaneous combustion? I mean, even the Virgin Mary was expecting it, as she was told in advance by the Angel Gabriel! Everyone knows I don't have a partner, aka an endless sperm supply, yet everyone has fallen back onto the cliché of getting all your dreams when you least expect it. It's an illogical comment and also should be banned.

Comment: "Forget what the doctors say; they aren't God! If God wants you to have a baby, you'll have a baby."

My thought: Oh, Lord! This is probably the comment I hate the most. Because if this is true, then God has proven he does *not* want me to have a baby, and that opens a whole other discussion of religion, faith, beliefs, miracles, and so forth. And these comments are rooted in the belief of the Old Testament. In Genesis, God promises Abraham that his old, barren wife will give birth to a son, despite her being way past childbearing age. And yes, in Genesis 21:2, Sarah becomes pregnant and gives one-hundred-year-old Abraham a son. Really? I don't believe it. Sarah was probably of childbearing age but *looked* old, and from there the fable developed that God gave this old lady a miracle baby. They named the son Isaac, which means "he laughs." In Genesis 21:6, Sarah declares that God has brought her laughter. And all those who hear of her having a baby at an old age will laugh with her. I agree. We'll laugh because it's a joke; it's not real. This entire section of the Bible should banned for giving false hope to women who believe it and then force those beliefs on a barren woman. Some people still need to learn the difference between beliefs of the church and reality!

Comment: "But did you see J. Lo, Halle Berry, and Kelly Preston? They're in their forties and had children."

My thought: Uh-huh. You're going to compare me to Jenny from the Block, Bond Girl, and John Travolta's wife, when we know nothing of their medical backgrounds or money-bought opportunities to have children? Perhaps they did have children naturally, but I have medical problems that they obviously don't have.

Comment: "It's probably a blessing in disguise. You were probably going to have a Down's syndrome baby, considering your age and all."

My thought: Go fuck yourself. Yes, I know the statistics show that women over forty years of age are at increased risk of having children with Down's syndrome. But this simply isn't consoling when you know you would love your baby unconditionally.

Comment: "Kids are expensive anyway."
My thought: Duh, and...? I don't even know what comment to make on that one besides asking, "As expensive as Jacob? He was like a child."

Comment: "It's not meant to be."
My thought: Shoot me! Really? Yet meth addicts, alcoholics, and teenagers with no future are having babies because *it's meant to be* for them? But, yes, I knew that some things are not meant to be. I didn't want to hear it.

Comment: "If it's a mommy that you want to be, well, there's an endless number of children who need good homes. You can still be a mommy."
My thought: Yes, I understand that. But I wanted to experience the conception, the carrying, the delivery, that instant moment of bonding when a woman's oxytocin spews over like a waterfall for her newborn. I wasn't *there* yet to adopt.

And if you happen to be a Fertile Myrtle and are friends with a woman going through infertility treatments, avoid calling her to talk about your abortion, of all things! No matter how close your friendship is, do not—I repeat, *don't ever*—call an infertile woman and explain (a) your carelessness in getting pregnant, (b) your not knowing how you could possibly be pregnant, and (c) the play-by-play, casually explaining in a nonchalant tone how you terminated it with a homemade concoction similar to the morning-after pill. At this point in time, a woman who is trying to but can't have a baby (a) has no sympathy for you or your situation and (b) will never relate to you, as she does not have the *luxury* of terminating a baby for *any* reason. I'm pro-choice, believe it or not, but at this juncture of my journey, I didn't have the frame of mind or the emotions to hear such stories. If I had, and my friend felt it necessary to terminate her pregnancy, I'd have driven her to the clinic myself and nursed her thereafter, like I did two years later when she had her second abortion. And don't, after your detailed mission-accomplished home abortion, then ask how my adoption plans are coming along! Don't be that shallow, inconsiderate, and insensitive to your infertile friend. True story.

And then there are comments that I appreciated hearing. Really! Some of those comments were:

"I'm sorry for your struggle. I admire your strength." Thank you, Olivia.

"You must take time to grieve this loss. You may never get over it, but you'll survive this. Don't rush your next move." Thank you, Mom.

"That plain sucks." Thank you, Helaina.

"I'm angry for you." Thank you, Deteldra.

"I don't know what to say." Thank you, Liliana.

"I'm here for you." Thank you, Dahlia.

"Life is unfair." Thank you, Diana. You'd think that this is something I wouldn't want to hear. But I did, as it confirmed what I was feeling and what's true, whether I had a baby or not. Life is unfair. We learn this at a young age and must constantly be reminded of it. It's something we should never forget. Otherwise, we get too comfortable and expect everything to go our way. This is life; you will not get everything that you want. You won't even get the things you think are guaranteed. Nothing is guaranteed. Period.

I thought that by January 2012, I would have memorized all the rules and regulations about adoption and I'd be well on my way to receiving that child. But it didn't happen that way.

The first few months I spent crying and making halfhearted attempts looking into adoption. Then I had an intense desire to live. I'd spent the last five years planning this baby and not really living. I wasn't ready to delve into the process of adoption. "You must not really want a baby," a friend said. That wasn't true. I didn't want to be disappointed again. I knew I wasn't mentally strong enough to have another grand disappointment, to go through something like that alone. I wanted to enjoy life, not destroy my life. And that's what would happen if I entered a failed adoption. Personally, emotionally, it was a risk I couldn't afford. The demise of my own life. Lesson Number One: *The head and heart are the most demanding of organs. To settle for less, or to allow some other physiological process to compensate, would place these organs, this precious life (my life), at a high risk for demise.* Some people couldn't understand that. I couldn't live through a failed adoption and I knew I wasn't going to attempt IVF. The landscape of my life had completely changed, and I wanted to make the most of it. Life is unfair, but it's how you respond to that unfairness that matters most.

I started working out again, at a CrossFit gym. I was leery of joining CrossFit 916, as I was afraid the trainers would demean me, the way Jacob had, or compare me to fabulous athletes. But no, not all CrossFit trainers are the same. The gym owner and trainers were welcoming. They were young and made working out fun. It was the first positive step I made that had nothing to do with Joaquin or Isis but was solely for me, Julie.

I then booked a meditation retreat for May, followed by a three-week vacation to Cambodia and Vietnam, alone. There's true healing in being alone with your thoughts, whether in meditation or in a country where you don't understand one word being spoken. I was going to get through this, one way or another. Slowly but surely, the crying episodes were further apart. They still occurred—and still occur—but the pathetic feeling that haunted me, too, slowly faded. I was lucky. Just as I can't stay mad at another person for a long time, I easily grow sick of being down about my little, downright stupid life dilemmas. I wasn't completely healed, but I was healthy and I was grateful.

The year that followed was what I refer to as a "transitional year." There wasn't one enlightening moment where I understood where I was in my life, or why. On occasion, I still did the only things

I knew how to do, like call Jared. Things like that were knee-jerk reactions, really, safeguards. I'd take five steps forward and three steps back. I know, I know! But it was better than calling Joe!

I found it easier to revert than to spring forward with men. It helps keep the tally of men down when you continue to sleep with an ex. It's sex recycling. Sexcycling, if you will. You get what you need and your total number of men slept with never increases. I needed a new approach, but for now, this worked for me. Not that I wanted to sleep with Jared, because at that point I didn't. But I needed male interaction, even just for conversation. Jared was going to go bike shopping with me. After looking at bikes, he needed to kill some time before his next rendezvous, so we went across the street to have a margarita.

Jared knew how to enjoy every moment of life, and he also consciously or subconsciously knew how to enhance his ego. He talked at length about how he knew that Lab Girl still had feelings for him. He asked my advice on how to "help her move on."

"Cut her off," was my direct response.

I explained how with women, regardless of what you say, if your actions can give them one inkling of hope, that's what they'll hold onto, as they think, *This time he'll see what I'm worth and want to be with me.* That's what Lab Girl was doing, and he provided countless interactions with her to support her belief. They went out, went skiing, went parachuting, still slept with each other, confided in each other, and picked out art together. And above all else, she boosted Jared's ego whenever needed. She wasn't his soul mate, she was his ego mate.

"She's fun to hang around with," he said, justifying his actions.

"Then be with her," I said.

"I can't. If we were together, we'd end up floating off into the ether."

"So what's wrong with that?" I pushed. Jared had mentioned this "ether" scenario many times before to me. Lab Girl would be happy to know that I was on her side, to either get him 100 percent or, although painful, to be cut off by him 100 percent so that she could find someone commitment-worthy.

"I can't go floating off into the ether. I have children!" Perhaps he wasn't as adventurous as he thought. He had limits, even though he considered himself a modern renaissance man. He once told me so. A renaissance man, of any kind, has no limits. I didn't point out that contradiction, but I relished in it.

He complained again about her and her childish ways. He explained how infuriated he was when he caught Lab Girl teaching his youngest child about how babies are conceived. Yet he wasn't going to cut her off. When she no longer served that purpose of ego elevation or whatever he got from their exchange, *then* he'd cut her off. Jared had practically become an advocate for divorce, as his divorce experience and life thereafter had benefited him to no end. He did what he wanted, and he didn't do what he didn't want to do. Therefore, if he truly wanted Lab Girl to be his one and only girlfriend, she would be. If he truly wanted her to move on, he'd have allowed her that freedom, as well. But he wasn't ready. He not only sucked the nectar out of everything; he, more importantly, knew how to find the nectar and didn't waste his time on anything that wasn't the nectar. No wonder he kept Lab Girl's honeysuckle-pheromone breasts around so much. He was a hummingbird, and to some small extent, I admired it. However, the years of youth he was stealing from Lab Girl, knowing full well he'd never commit to her, made me sick. My biggest regret has been the time and youth I wasted on men, as those are the things that I can never restore.

I ran into Jared a few weeks after our bike shop trip. He asked me what I'd decided. It was mid-July, and in my opinion, summer was nearly over and I hadn't decided anything! He said he had a motorbike race the next day (of course he did!). I, on the other hand, had an OB-GYN appointment. As soon as I drove off, I headed to the bike shop to buy my bike. What was I waiting for? Nobody was going to give me what I wanted. Playing a damsel in distress wasn't going to bring any man on a white horse. I'd remain Julie, a damsel in distress. I needed to go out, get it, and enjoy it. *Find the nectar and suck it!* In that moment, I saw what Jared's purpose in my life was: he was my catalyst. I needed to wow myself. I needed to stop waiting. I know that many people think I've done so much—traveled the world, had two major careers (publishing and nursing)—but to me, I haven't lived. My expectations are so much higher.

Jared attended a wedding with me. After the wedding, he drove us home at a-hundred-plus miles per hour in his convertible BMW. Did he think he was indestructible? We'd both been drinking, and this was completely irresponsible. Thankfully, we made it to my home safely, drank, and ate some more. He lifted, or perhaps I lifted, my dress, and we had sex on the couch. The more carelessly I behaved, the higher chance for pregnancy. Isn't that how it works? My friend Zane said sex for any women over forty was going to be terrific, simply because of hormones and finally feeling sexual liberation. I wanted to confirm whether Zane's theory was correct. I couldn't take his word for it. How would he know? He was a thirty-one-year-old gay guy that would never hit pre-menopause!

Zane was wrong. Jared and I didn't even kiss! It was pure, dry sex solely (in my head) for baby-making purposes. Was this the type of sex that the Bible says we're to be having? God forbid. There was no human connection, no caressing, no love or liking involved. As I said before, bedside manner isn't a requirement for conception. The sex was horrific. It was like eating dry garlic croutons with no water in sight! And it was over, for him, so fast.

Jared was currently obsessed with Ayn Rand's book *Atlas Shrugged*. He stated, "I *am* Francisco d'Anconia." He was referring to one of the characters of the book. This Francisco guy was a rich, smart businessman who had a mighty way with the ladies. The fact that Jared had to verbalize, "I *am* Francisco d'Anconia," the way he had said he was a renaissance man, proved that he was *not* Francisco d'Anconia. A true ladies' man doesn't have to say it; he just *is*! Jared said it with such conviction, I knew that he believed this about himself, and to prove that he embodied this character, he said, "I want you to introduce me to Meena's sister."

Jared had met my friend Meena earlier in the evening. We both agreed she was a beautiful girl, but Jared's observation was that she demanded too much attention from her husband, and he could never be with someone like that. I mentioned to Jared that she had a sister with whom I was also good friends and who was beautiful and sexy.

"Why do you want to meet her?" I asked.

"So that I can fuck her," he said unapologetically.

I couldn't believe this motherfucker. He was no Francisco d'Anconia. A true womanizer makes a woman feel like no other woman on earth exists, especially after sex. This was crossing the line. Although Jared and I shared stories, I didn't think it was OK to express wanting to fuck each other's friends, especially after having sex! But why should I be surprised by his lack of character? Throughout the years of knowing Jared, I could never decipher whether he was naïve, had no filter, or was a plain asshole. That comment confirmed it: he was a plain asshole. And I was over it, over him. Nothing about him appealed to me. Who the fuck did he think he was? Oh, yes, Francisco d'Anconia—that's who.

OK, so who did he think I was? He surrounded himself with women that allowed this behavior. I refused to be another of his female cronies. His remarks, his conversations, his character—I suddenly found myself disinterested in him on every level. Even the immediate spark of anger I felt toward his comment was soon blasé. I was unimpressed by the long-drawn-out banality of it all. Everything that came out of his mouth now sounded like white noise.

We went to bed, and he fell fast asleep as I lay there, a night-shift worker not ready for sleep. Please, let me be a man in my next life; the quality of sleep alone is a benefit! Had sex with Jared always been this way, and had we simply used the situation because it was available? Yes, because it was available, with no emotion or strings attached. The way it had always been. I thought of Lab Girl and how Jared would never "float off into the ether" with her. Even though my life hadn't worked out as planned, I suddenly comprehended that I was in an even better position than Jared. I could, if I wanted to, float off into the ether with whomever or whatever. It all came down to my future choices.

My past actions were not an indicator of my intelligence. I knew that. But it was time to start making decisions that *were* equal to my intelligence. The moment he stepped out my door, right there and then, I deleted Jared's number from my phone. That simple swipe on my smartphone was my first realization of how easy it was to wipe out toxins from my life.

MY LIVER THEORY

For quite some time, I'd been wondering why I took so long to grasp the lessons that were taught in utero: *The brain and heart are the most demanding organs. They expect and they receive no less than what they demand. Rid yourself of toxins.* And the lesson at the moment of birth: *Learn to breathe.*

Perhaps I'd had it wrong all along. It's not the heart or head that one should rely on to make decisions; it's the liver! Let me tell you a little about the liver and my theory:

High in the right upper quadrant of every human being's abdominal cavity sits the liver, a triangular vital organ. The liver is unassuming. It does not beat. It does not inflate. It does not shed a tear. It does not feel butterflies swarming about. In essence, the liver does nothing to give you any rush, any sensation of feeling alive. However, the fundamental nature of the liver is to do everything in its power to keep you alive.

In the simplest and narrowest of explanations, the liver breaks down yucky bacteria and old, worn-out red blood cells. It excretes toxins. It's a built-in purification system. It excretes toxins. It's oh-so-cathartic. It excretes toxins. Yes, I'm repeating myself. It excretes toxins, without your having to make any emotional decisions to do so.

Bile, a dark-green fluid, is produced by the liver. When a meal is consumed, bile is released into the intestines via the gallbladder, a bile storage unit, so to speak. The bile salts break down the fatty acids contained in that meal. Without this breakdown, lipids and fat-soluble vitamins, like vitamins A, D, and K, couldn't be properly absorbed. The liver has a clever, built-in recycling and manufacturing capability. During the breakdown of fat, bile salts are sent back to the liver and rereleased several times over the same meal. Talk about regurgitation. A small amount of bile salt is lost along the way, but the liver just makes some more out of the cholesterol it extracts from the blood.

Now, the bile has broken down your heavy meal, and as a bonus point, has removed some cholesterol out of your system, which will be flushed away with your next poop. At the best of its ability, your body will shit out the crap you put into it in the first place and don't need!

And if all that isn't enough to impress you, the liver is the only organ that can regenerate itself. Up to 75 percent of the original liver can be cut off, rejected, and tossed into a biohazard bag, while the remaining 25 percent will begin to regenerate and make itself whole again. The new liver won't have the appearance of the original but will be able to carry out all the above-mentioned functions to help keep you alive and well.

All medical terminology set aside, you want a healthy liver, even for vanity's sake. When you have a failing liver, it's noticeable. The toxins make you itch, and your skin turns yellow. You look like a walking corndog dipped in mustard. It's truly an external manifestation, a cry for help.

So here was my thought: what if I could behave like my liver and give no thought to my head or heart? I'd break everything down the way bile salts do and look for the toxic crap to get rid of. And if I didn't, I'd turn yellow. That would definitely be an incentive not to deal with anyone toxic. But then I realized this theory wasn't practical or realistic. It didn't fit my personality, and it seemed to focus only on the negative, and nothing positive, by trying to find toxins to say, "Gotcha! Now get lost." And the theory focused only on Lesson Number Two and didn't provide the overall care that I deserved and demanded I give myself.

If I had lived my life like a liver, I wouldn't have had Joe, Jared, or Jacob in my life. Perhaps I subconsciously brought my J-series of men into my life, including the attempt to have Joaquin, specifically to teach me Lessons One, Two, and Three. And like the liver, I felt as if 75 percent of me had been cut off, rejected, and tossed into a biohazard bag. And the remainder of me had regenerated and was making itself whole again! And like a newly regenerated liver, I didn't appear to be the same person anymore, because I wasn't. I had changed. Again, like the liver, I was doing everything in my power, in my fundamental *human* nature, to keep myself alive and well.

I still thought about Joe and wondered how his family life turned out. I finally went on that long-desired medical mission trip to Senegal, Africa. The one about which Joe had said, "Nobody's gonna wait around for you to do all that stuff." And he was right. I was happy—yes, happy—that "nobody" was "waiting around" for me when I returned. I wouldn't want anyone to wait for me. I'd want them to join me or move on. Life's too short to wait.

I rarely see Jared anymore. He has become an acquaintance. If I hadn't slept with him, he'd simply be a face I vaguely recognized. I know him enough to have no desire to learn more about him. And if someone doesn't make time for you, it's because that person doesn't want to. The person doesn't see a role for you in his or her life, and that's OK. I'm completely at peace with not being his friend, his honeysuckle, or his definition of *wow*. I'm learning to wow myself, and that's a much better feeling.

And then there's Jacob, my biggest challenge. He'd been making regular payments of 250 dollars per month. Then he'd a miss a payment here and there. I wanted to completely close this chapter of my life. I sent him a letter requesting that he find a way to pay me in full. He blocked my text messages and sent me an e-mail stating I was harassing him and he'd now block my e-mails. I was to contact him *only* by snail mail, which I did. He stopped paying completely. I sent him reminders that payment was due. He threatened to get a restraining order against me if I sent him any further payment reminders. My girlfriend Dahlia, who knew every detail of this dragged-out ordeal, told me it wasn't worth the time and frustration. I knew that, but I held on to, "It's the principle of the matter!"

Then in mid-February, as I drove to CrossFit 916, I passed his place of business, which I'd foolishly funded, as I did every time I went to the gym. The window signs were down; inside it looked empty. In the parking lot in front of his gym was a flatbed truck, stacked with the padded flooring he'd initially purchased with the loan. There was something very symbolic about that flatbed truck slowly pulling away. First, I couldn't believe my timing. I knew I was meant to see this.

I was near the point of resignation, thinking and accepting that he'd never pay me. But then I came across an article on a new CrossFit gym opening fifteen miles from my home. Lo and behold, he'd done it again. The article stated that Jacob was the manager of this new CrossFit gym, and his soon-to-be wife wasn't only the owner but also a nurse! Imagine that! Jacob was easily meeting new nurses and hooking up with them, and he didn't even have health insurance. How is it that a man with no insurance can meet so many nurses that will pay his way? Not only pay his way but marry him and have his child? Yep, Oksana and baby were gone. Perhaps that baby wasn't his; he had dumped me for a pregnant woman. He was a real family man now, with a future wife nearly twenty years his junior. Her future poor credit, her poor life, her poor soul—if she only knew. He'd locked her in. He'd found the winning lottery ticket again. It's definitely a refined skill that he has. I was so ecstatic that it hadn't been me!

Despite being free of him, I knew I couldn't and wouldn't let it go. A man with this repetitive behavior of homing in on women and their hard-earned money must be stopped. There's a huge difference between helping someone along the way and being completely taken advantage of.

In some respect, I didn't blame Jacob for doing this. He was accustomed to this type of hustle. I completely blamed myself for allowing it. I asked my friend George if he could recommend a lawyer. He could. I told him my situation, and he said, "You deserve to be made whole again." Those words sang like a sweet melody in my heart. I contacted the lawyer and provided him with every envelope, receipt, letter, and e-mail exchange between Jacob and me. He said I had a good case against Jacob, despite not having a written contract. I said, "Let's do this." I was ready to sue.

It had taken me so long to get the courage to stand up to Jacob. I was no longer afraid of him. I wasn't going to waver, not just to stop him—because his future behavior can't be predicted or controlled—but to prove something to myself. And the proof was that I wasn't going to be his stepping-stone or doormat, that I had the strength to do this, and that I learned my lesson.

I knew that suing Jacob was the only way I could apologize to myself for my stupidity.

The lawyer filed the paperwork, which Jacob failed to respond to. I won a judgment against him for the full amount plus court costs. My lawyer followed up with a letter stating he best take this judgment seriously, as we were prepared to garnish his wages, take him to collections, or get a court order for him to appear before the court to list his assets. If he failed to do that, too, then a warrant for his arrest would be issued.

We waited patiently for his response. And two days before his deadline, he sent a letter to my lawyer, admitting he owed me the money but couldn't afford the full amount and was willing to make minimum monthly payments. The gleam of victory was within my heart, knowing he had to sit down and finally acknowledge all of this. We're currently in negotiation to determine what he can pay. If he fails to comply, we've filed the paperwork to garnish his wages. Honestly, I'd like the full amount up front so that I wouldn't need to utter his name ever again. If he makes payments, that could mean years of having to deal with him. His payments could last longer than his new gym or marriage. Whether or not I collect a cent of what he owes, I have prevailed on many levels: I'm not the one stuck with Jacob, I've stood up to him, and I've legally and rightfully won. Like my friend Zane said, "You can die knowing you fought." Well, yes, but I know for a fact that on my deathbed, I won't be thinking of Jacob or this lawsuit.

And finally, the *J* that taught me the most, Joaquin. The little baby boy that I'd never give birth to, who would have had the name Joaquin. I was certain it would have been a boy. I never dreamed that it would be neither a boy nor a girl, that it would be a nothing, that I would be childless. The death of that grandiose dream, of this little boy who lived in my demanding heart and head and whose name was Joaquin, is what truly taught me to get my ass up, to wake up to reality—as it felt that I had been sleepwalking the first forty years of my life—to get over personal devastation, and finally, to live.

I still ruminate over this baby I call Joaquin. At times I feel like I failed him, failed to bring Joaquin into existence. I failed myself, and I permit myself to cry over that, ever so briefly and every so often. I'll never experience that immediate post-delivery moment, wondering if all the holes in his heart are closing properly and if his blood is learning the new route. And as a protective mother, I'd naturally wish that in his life, he never experience a sense of drowning. Gosh, he seemed so real, within reach, but remained beyond my grasp.

If you look up the meaning of the name Joaquin, you get a variety of definitions: lifted by God, God will establish, God will exalt, God gives strength. I prefer the word *Universe* in place of *God*. The name Joaquin holds true: the Universe did establish what would or wouldn't be. And through my despair over Joaquin, the Universe or the experience of trying to have Joaquin, is what eventually gave me strength. Despite not getting to experience the one thing I always wanted, a baby, a *Joaquin*, life is still incredibly good. Or rather, I'm making it good.

It hasn't come easy, but at least I finally know how to assemble it. Joaquin is, and probably will always be, a very tender, fragile subject in my heart. And I'm OK with that, because paradoxically, it's the fragile and tender subjects that make us strong and resolute in the other aspects of our lives that require those firm qualities. With my permission, he'll reside in a small cove, nestled somewhere in a chamber of my still-beating heart. And if I breathe just right, just deeply enough, just slowly enough, all within the same translucent inhale and exhale, *Joaquin*, I can still feel him close to me while I gently let him go.

During a guided meditation, I heard Deepak Chopra explain

how we need to build matrices for ourselves. He was speaking about a matrix for healthy eating habits and choices that could be readily available. But that's when it hit me: my matrix of all these *J*s that I'd created was an unhealthy system to turn to, much less rely on.

In utero, it's easy to demand the best for our heads and hearts because the fetus is already in a perfect environment, unless its mom is a crackhead. And it's easy to see and wash away toxins when our surroundings are pristine. When the fetus leaves the uterus, it needs to rebuild that nourishing environment. Instead of a cozy uterus, build a matrix. And I really like the word *matrix* as it's finally taking me away from all the reproductive lingo.

I picture my matrix as an industrial-built, iron-strong, crisscrossing railroad track. Each track, placed on solid ground, represents an aspect of the precious cargo it'll sustain and carry: me.

This matrix is now being constructed with supportive family members, a handful of trustworthy friends, and a "work hard and travel far" slogan. It's nonobligatory charity donations to organizations that fight for human rights or save iguanas and turtles or mentor inspiring actors. It's meditation retreats in my house, or wherever I may be. It's medical mission trips anywhere from Sacramento, California, to the Appalachian Mountains, to Massawa, Eritrea, to hear Italian spoken on the continent of Africa. It's being open, being creative, and being encouraging. It's spending time with nature, protesting inertia, and divorcing myself from negativity in all forms. It's picking in-season veggies from the local farmer and having friends over to try new recipes. It's going to bed with a good book and waking up ready to be present and flexible for whatever situation comes my way. It's focusing wide, not just deep. It's finding a way to contribute to the world and the life that's unfolding and passing before me. My matrix is many things that I haven't even thought of yet, because I don't know what I don't know. But I'm unrelenting in my quest to discover as much as I can and to continue to reach beyond the ordinary.

When the great matrix is established, but ever evolving, then it's easy to give yourself the very best of your environment. You finally have a healthy environment to pull from. No matter what freight train you decide to jump on, chances are it's gonna be a fabulous ride. It's then far easier to see waste approaching, whether it's with time or people, or both, and to easily avoid its tactics.

Is all well that ends well? Well, I know these are the tools—my tools—and like everyone else, I'm doing my best. I no longer question incessantly why things happen or don't happen. I'm learning not to waste time beating myself up for mistakes made, as I love and embrace everything they've taught me. And like everyone else, I have down episodes for specific reasons or no reason at all, but they no longer conquer my day, my week, or my year. Knowing they'll pass, I let them be.

I let me be.

And when I do that, it's like a new birth I give to myself, after a self-induced, hard-labored, buttocks-first delivery. It's like a greater force is pulling me out, but this time, I don't resist. It takes a confidence that is known and unknown to give birth to myself. It's like the cutting of my own umbilical cord. My heart beats. It is whole. My lungs expand. There is no sense of drowning.

    And I breathe.

ACKNOWLEDGMENTS

Haydee Vicedo, the words *thank you* don't even begin to encompass my extreme gratitude for your existence, friendship, guidance, and patience! I thank you for encouraging me to write from the moment I mentioned this project to you. It wouldn't have come to fruition without your unyielding support. Thank you for editing my heart (my words) and yet never once judging it. That alone is a human quality precious beyond measure.

Gaurav Dhanoya, I'm so grateful for how strongly you believed in this book and in me. Thank you for being *you* (even when you drive me nuts) and for wanting the best for me. I'll always remember our nights drinking wine, having dinner, discussing the book and scary movies. You were always the break I needed from writing to clear my brain and start again. You were my reset button throughout this process.

Amanda Hearon-Steckler, Julie Chen-Burton, Kimberly Juarez, Lisa Limbaugh-Guardado, Megan Cosby, Nicole Renfroe, and Olivia Perez, thank you for being my cheerleading team this past year. You always provided listening ears and encouraging words.

Contact Info

E-mail: julie@julieguardado.com

www.julieguardado.com

Instagram: @julguardado

FB: @authorjulieguardado

Twitter: @JulGuardado

Made in the USA
Coppell, TX
28 August 2021